SUPERHEROES, MOVIES, AND THE STATE

SUPERHEROES, MOVIES, AND THE STATE

HOW THE US GOVERNMENT SHAPES CINEMATIC UNIVERSES

TRICIA JENKINS AND
TOM SECKER

UNIVERSITY PRESS OF KANSAS

Published by the University Press of Kansas (Lawrence, Kansas 66045), which was organized by the Kansas Board of Regents and is operated and funded by Emporia State University, Fort Hays State University, Kansas State University, Pittsburg State University, the University of Kansas, and Wichita State University.

Library of Congress Cataloging-in-Publication Data

Names: Jenkins, Tricia, author. | Secker, Tom, author.
Title: Superheroes, movies, and the state : how the US government shapes cinematic universes / Tricia Jenkins and Tom Secker.
Description: Lawrence : University Press of Kansas, 2021. | Includes bibliographical references and index.
Identifiers: LCCN 2021012548 (print) | LCCN 2021012549 (ebook)
ISBN 9780700632763 (cloth)
ISBN 9780700632770 (ebook)
Subjects: LCSH: Superhero films—United States—History and criticism. | Motion pictures—Political aspects—United States—History—20th century. | Motion pictures—Political aspects—United States—History—21st century.
Classification: LCC PN1995.9.S76 J46 2021 (print) | LCC PN1995.9.S76 (ebook) | DDC 791.43/652—dc23
LC record available at https://lccn.loc.gov/2021012548.
LC ebook record available at https://lccn.loc.gov/2021012549.

British Library Cataloguing-in-Publication Data is available.

Printed in the United States of America

10 9 8 7 6 5 4 3 2 1

The paper used in this publication is acid free and meets the minimum requirements of the American National Standard for Permanence of Paper for Printed Library Materials Z39.48–1992.

CONTENTS

LIST OF FIGURES

ACKNOWLEDGMENTS

Iron Man and the Hulk are our favorite superheroes, and like them, we often work best in a team, especially when we can draw on the strengths and specialties of those around us. Indeed, this book is the product of a team of "super" individuals, who each contributed their experience and expertise to its completion. Jeremy Latcham, producer and executive producer of several Marvel movies, was incredibly generous with his time, detailing his relationship with various government agencies over the years. We are only sorry that we could not find a place to include his "naked Thor" story because it was awesome. Gratitude is also due to screenwriter James Schamus and NASA's multimedia liaison, Bert Ulrich, who were also gracious enough to answer a multitude of questions about the government-entertainment complex. Likewise, several scientific technical consultants were key to helping us understand how the Science and Entertainment Exchange works and how scientists contribute to superhero movies, specifically. Daniel Bodony, Sean Carroll, Jim Ferguson, Steven Kutcher, and Clifford Johnson: we sincerely appreciate your willingness to help this project.

Tricia would also like to thank David Bonnet, Ben Martinez, Shannon Bontrager, Penelope Ingram, and Michael Bonnet for their feedback on various sections of this book and for their friendship over the years. Matthew Alford and Tanner Mirrlees, thank you too for your valuable insights and reader reports that helped make the final version of this book much stronger. And finally, to Nathanael O'Reilly and Celeste Jenkins-O'Reilly: you are last here, but never least. Tricia says, thank you for watching all of the superhero movies with me and for loving me all of these years. I am sure it takes some glorious superpowers, at times, to accomplish this feat.

Tom would like to thank all the hardworking entertainment liaison officers for their dedication and service to the cause of propagandizing several generations of citizens all over the world. Without their labor and craft, especially in answering his FOIA requests in such a lackadaisical manner, this book could not exist. He would also like to thank his mother, who shall remain nameless as a final gesture toward the dying concept of personal privacy, for all her affection and support, as well as for watching as many superhero films as her patience could tolerate so that they could discuss them. Finally, he would like to thank everyone who reads this book and tells others about it. You are the real heroes.

SUPERHEROES, MOVIES, AND THE STATE

INTRODUCTION. HOLY BOX OFFICE, BATMAN

UNDERSTANDING THE RISE OF THE SUPERHERO GENRE AND ITS TIES TO THE GOVERNMENT-ENTERTAINMENT COMPLEX

The Rise of the Superhero Film: The Industrial and Cultural Factors

Although it has only existed since 2008, the Marvel Cinematic Universe (MCU) is now the most profitable film franchise in history, surpassing even the Star Wars, James Bond, and Harry Potter brands. As of January 2021, the MCU—which refers to a string of interconnected movies featuring Marvel characters in the same narrative universe—has released twenty-three titles and earned $22.55 billion in global box-office sales. *The Avengers: Endgame* (2019) ranked as the highest-grossing film of all time, before recently being overtaken by *Avatar*, and, according to Box Office Mojo, nine of the thirty top-grossing films worldwide belong to Marvel Studios (including each of the *Avengers* movies, *Black Panther* [2018], *Captain Marvel* [2019], *Captain America: Civil War* [2016], *Spider-Man: Far from Home* [2019], and *Iron Man 3* [2013]). Superhero films starring DC characters have enjoyed remarkable success too. At the time of this writing, Box Office Mojo ranks *Aquaman* (2018) as the twenty-third highest grossing film ever; *The Dark Knight Rises* (2012) is currently secure in the thirty-first slot; and *Joker* (2019) stands as the top-grossing R-rated film and the first to reach the billion-dollar mark.[1]

While some industry executives have worried about audiences' "superhero fatigue," the DC and Marvel franchises show few signs of slowing down, outside of COVID-19 delays in production. In 2020, DC released *Birds of Prey* and the second *Wonder Woman* film on Christmas Day. In 2021, Marvel plans to release four more titles: *Black Widow*, *The Eternals*, *Shang-Chi and the Legend of the Ten Rings*, and a currently untitled *Spider-Man: Far from Home* sequel. In 2022, four more titles are set to be produced, including *Thor: Love and Thunder*, *Doctor Strange in the Multiverse of Madness*, a second *Black Panther* film, and a second *Captain Marvel* installment. On the DC side, James Gunn is planning for his *Suicide*

Squad's release in 2021, the same year that *The Batman* and *Black Adam* are also set to debut, while in 2022, Warner Bros. plans to premiere its second *Shazam!* title, as well as *The Flash* and *Aquaman 2*.

Since 2000, nearly one hundred superhero films have been released, both saturating and dominating the global film industry and leaving film scholars to ask: why superheroes and why now? Part of the answer is technological, as recent advances in computer-generated imagery (CGI) have made these stories more feasible, prompting Yvonne Tasker to claim that digital imagery is so central to the genre that it can be considered both dependent on the technology and to have facilitated its advancements.[2] Undoubtedly, CGI has allowed for the cinematic realization of fantastical, comic-book settings, including *Black Panther*'s Wakanda and the numerous intergalactic worlds of *The Guardians of the Galaxy* (2014), *Captain Marvel*, *The Fantastic Four* (2015), and *Doctor Strange* (2016). Digital imagery has also made it possible for superhero characters to perform physically impossible feats with greater realism, enhancing the visual spectacle of Spider-Man, the Hulk, Iron Man, Superman, and Wonder Woman's derring-do.

Another explanation for the growth of superhero films involves the financial position in which Marvel found itself in the late 1990s. In that decade, revenues from comics and trading cards began to collapse, and a "series of bursting financial bubbles and questionable business deals" saw Marvel's stock plummet from $35.75 a share in 1993 to a mere $2.375 just three years later.[3] Facing considerable debt, Marvel more aggressively turned its attention to the cinematic licensing of its characters, finding some initial success with *Blade* (1998) and the *Spider-Man* and *X-Men* movies. Yet the returns on these box-office hits were slim. Marvel only earned $25,000 for the adaptation rights for *Blade* even though the film grossed nearly $70 million at the box office; the company had only negotiated a small flat fee from Fox for *X-Men* (2000), which also ended up being a hit, and even though the first two *Spider-Man* movies raked in $3 billion through box-office, DVD, and broadcast sales, Marvel saw only $62 million, or 2 percent, of the revenue. Avi Arad, head of Marvel Films at the time, lamented that "we were giving away the best part of our business."[4]

Licensing its characters to other studios also meant that Marvel had little to no control over the quality associated with its brand—something that had plagued the company since the 1980s. While Captain America had graced American movie screens in 1944, it would take until 1986's *Howard the Duck* for another major movie to feature a Marvel property. Although George Lucas produced that film on a budget of $35 million, and it enjoyed heavy promotion, the film was a box-office flop, bringing in only $16 million in ticket sales. Other ill-fated attempts included *The Punisher* (1989) and *Man-Thing* (1995), and most famously, when Roger Corman was licensed to produce *The Fantastic Four* in 1994, Arad bought back the rights and reportedly "destroyed every print of the film" because he deemed it too embarrassing to the Marvel brand to ever be released to the public.[5]

In order to maximize its profits and have tighter quality control, then, Marvel, which had filed for bankruptcy in 1996 to restructure its holdings, took out a loan of $525 million to open its own film studio in 2005 and named Kevin Feige as its president just two years later. The development of Marvel Studios was considered risky since Fox already owned the adaptation rights to *X-Men*, and Sony possessed the rights to *Spider-Man*—the company's two major franchises at the time.[6] It was not clear, in other words, if Marvel Studios would be able to find financial success with cinematic versions of its lesser-known properties, such as Thor, Iron Man, Doctor Strange, Ant-Man, and others. In retrospect, these concerns are amusing, given the profits that its movie slate has generated and the fact that just one year after launching the MCU, the Walt Disney Company purchased Marvel Entertainment for a whopping $4 billion, signaling a remarkable turnaround for a company that had filed for Chapter 11 just twelve years earlier. Thus, Marvel's attempts to recover from the comic book industry's financial crisis of the 1990s through movies partly explains why the genre has proliferated in the 2000s. Today, by leveraging the resources of Disney and its holdings, Marvel has gone on to create a powerful and prolific transmedia franchise that spans far beyond its comics, as evidenced by its television series *Agents of S.H.I.E.L.D.* (2013–2016), *Agent Carter* (2015–2017), *Daredevil* (2015–2018), *Jessica Jones* (2015–2018), *Luke Cage* (2016–2018), and *Iron Fist* (2017–2019), as well as its DVD one-shots and video games released primarily for PlayStation through Marvel Games.

While Warner and DC Comics have been aligned under the same parent company since 1967, the New York City publisher and Burbank's Warner Bros. Studios have largely operated independently of one another. As a result, several DC properties, including *Wonder Woman* and *The Flash*, "languished in development at Warner Bros. for years," and its adaptations of other brands have been met with mixed success.[7] *The Dark Knight* (2008) was the first superhero film to generate $1 billion in worldwide ticket sales, while *Smallville* (2001–2011), a series about a young Superman, ran for ten successful seasons on the CW. However, *Watchmen* (2009) was a box-office disappointment, bringing in just $185 million worldwide, even though it cost roughly $135 million to make.[8] Likewise, the revenue from *Superman Returns* (2006) failed to warrant another sequel, and *Catwoman* (2004)—an embarrassing flop starring Halle Barry—earned just 82 percent of its production costs back at the global box office.

In order to compete with the newfound success of the MCU, Warner Bros. began to concentrate more fully on its DC properties in 2009, hiring Diane Nelson, who had overseen the company's Harry Potter franchise, to head its new DC Entertainment Unit "with a mandate to better exploit its properties across the studio's movie, television, interactive, digital and consumer products businesses."[9] Part of Nelson's strategy was for DC to create its own extended universe to rival that of Marvel's. Today the DCEU refers to a string of films tied together by narrative continuity that began with 2013's *Man of Steel* and was later followed by *Batman v. Superman: Dawn of Justice* (2016), *Suicide Squad* (2016), and *Wonder Woman* (2017), before finally bringing each together in a true team setting in 2017's *Justice League*. *Aquaman*, *Shazam!*, and *Birds of Prey* are also deemed part of Warner's extended universe, although these later films are not as narratively intertwined with the others, functioning more as stand-alone titles.

The third answer (and the most important to this book) as to why superhero films have dominated movie theaters in the last two decades is cultural. In his excellent work, *Avengers Assemble: Critical*

Perspectives on the Marvel Cinematic Universe, Terence McSweeney argues that superhero films provide strong wish-fulfillment fantasies on both personal and national levels. These films offer up "powerful individual fantasies about who we *could be*: stronger, faster, more virile and more attractive," but they also provide "fantasies of empowerment on the global stage"—something Americans needed from their movies after the attacks of 9/11.[10] Much in the same way that the James Bond franchise projected images of British dominance in the era of its empire's collapse, superhero stories offer what Lawrence and Jewett call "a mythic massage," which works to assuage cultural anxieties by providing us with national heroes who act when our institutions and elected leaders fail.[11]

While American superhero films rarely mention 9/11 or the War on Terror by name, McSweeney writes that "they self-consciously evoke them almost obsessively," both in their thematic motifs and in their "detailed recreations of its mise-en-scène." In these films, which span from Christopher Nolan's Batman trilogy to the more recent releases of the MCU, the War on Terror is essentially "restaged and refought in allegory."[12] Or, as Philip Smith and Michael Goodrum write: "By telling a story with a different location, happening to different people and with different outcomes," these stories allow the horrors of 9/11 to be stripped of their immediacy "whilst maintaining a certain kernel of truth." Such reenactments, which cannot help but explore the emotional and traumatic toll of September 11, thus facilitate "a healing process" that cannot be accomplished in documentaries or docudramas about the same topic.[13] This concept echoes Mikhail Bakhtin's ideas about genre memory, when he posits that genres function as "'organs of memory' for particular cultures, providing crystallized forms of social and cultural perception that embody the world views of the period in which they originated, while carrying with them 'the layered record of their changing use.'"[14]

As part of their healing function, post-9/11 superhero films project a very specific vision of America's responses to global threats that reinforces the idea of American exceptionalism and righteousness. In the aftermath of 9/11, the master narrative promulgated by the Bush administration was one where America functioned as a reluctant superpower, legitimately used military force for good around the globe, and served as a morally superior nation.[15] This narrative evolved precisely because the attacks of 9/11 called into question the mythology of American innocence. As Donald Pease explains in *The New American Exceptionalism*, when George W. Bush pointed out that the United States had not been subject to foreign invasion outside of Pearl Harbor until 9/11, "he linked the public's belief in the myth of Virgin Land with the historical record."[16] However, he also failed to articulate that the myth of the Virgin Land had an underlying "moral rationale: Virgin Land was inviolate because the American people were innocent. In describing the surprise attack as a 'wound to our country,' Bush Jr. interpreted this violation on mythological as well as historical registers. The wound was directed against the Virgin Land as well as the U.S. people's myth of themselves as radically innocent," despite the obvious and glaring omission that its European settlers had destroyed and exploited the Native American communities that preceded them. Nonetheless, the national and cultural responses to the 9/11 attacks, Pease argues, needed to restore the mythical order of things—a need that would be amplified even further, suggests Anthony Spanakos, in the ensuing War on Terror, as legislation such as the Patriot Act; policies such as rendition, drone strikes, and indefinite detention; and the dubious rationale for the war in Iraq continued to challenge the concept of America's moral righteousness and ushered in an age where civil liberties are/were often discarded in the name of national security.[17]

As part of their national, mythological restoration, modern superheroes function only in a reactionary capacity; or, mirroring the ways that the US "positions its own militarism as wholly defensive," superheroes, writes Peter Bruno, never wage "pre-emptive offensive interventions, but instead, violence always originates with the enemy" to which the hero simply responds.[18] None of the films in the MCU, however, challenges the idea that "righteous violence is the path to redemption," and these films continue to promote notions of American exceptionalism by placing the United States at the center of the world, "both as its global leader and also as the world's primary victim of acts of violence." This can be seen in the fact that the vast majority of the world's superheroes, such as Steve Rogers, Bruce Banner, Tony Stark, Hawkeye, Captain Marvel, the Falcon, Batman, and Superman, are American, and "those who are not have been largely Americanized or convinced of its superiority." For example, Black Widow, a former Russian secret agent, leaves the KGB to "go straight" and join S.H.I.E.L.D. in the MCU, while the Sokovian twins, Pietro and Wanda Maximoff, begin *The Avengers: Age of Ultron* wanting to punish Tony Stark for his role in their parents' death but end up joining the Avengers, and by extension the United States, in the third act.[19] This function of cinema is not new. In *From Russia with Love* (1963), Tatiana Romanova begins as an agent of the KGB, trying to solicit secrets from James Bond, only to end up defecting to England after being seduced by 007 and the British, capitalist democracy he represents. As James Chapman and other scholars have illustrated, these stories speak to the continued power of art to assuage cultural anxieties about a nation's prowess that permeate it after a traumatic event—whether it be the collapse of the British empire or the attacks on 9/11.[20]

Of course, superhero movies do not just circulate in the United States. *Iron Man* alone premiered in eighty countries in the spring of 2008, and most superhero films generate more than half of their box-office revenue in international markets. As Tim Gruenewald writes, "The popular appeal and commercial success of these films is global, spanning Europe; the Asia Pacific; North, Central, and South America; and Africa," with the top ten international markets for *The Avengers*, in descending order, being "China, the European Union, South Korea, Mexico, Brazil, Russia, Australia, Japan, Venezuela, and Taiwan."[21] These films' popularity overseas suggests that superhero films are polysemic and resonate with different cultures for reasons other than their post-9/11 healing powers. For example, *Variety* and CGTN—China's English-language broadcaster—suggest that the MCU has been immensely popular in China because many of its fans were millennials born into one-child families, who spent their "formative years" reading the only-recently-available Marvel comic books and admiring its superheroes "who suited their increasingly individualistic mindset."[22] Robert Downey Jr., because of his character's do-what-I-want attitude, "acquired the status of a spiritual guru," they suggest, and thus viewing Marvel films, in costumed throngs, became a type of coming-of-age ritual for many young Chinese moviegoers.

The Government-Entertainment Complex and the Production of Superhero Films

Because of the global popularity of superhero films, Tanner Mirrlees argues that they accomplish three important feats for the United States on the world stage. The first is that these films bolster US economic power, as they generate billions of dollars for American media conglomerates and their merchandising partners annually. Second, they promote American cultural power by serving as a conduit for US imperial ideologies. *Iron Man*, for example, gave ideological support to the US occupation of Afghanistan following 9/11, as the film depicts the region as "full of fanatical terrorists" who wish to kill Americans and Afghan citizens. The film's early sequences also pit "dumb" Arab-Muslim terrorists against Stark's genius to highlight the notion of American exceptionalism, and Stark's decision to eradicate the Ten Rings terrorist organization to save Afghan lives gave "popular credence to the post-9/11 liberal imperialist idea" that the United States has an obligation to use its military might to liberate the citizens of the world suffering under oppression.[23] Third, superhero films are profound champions of US military power, as many of these films are collaborations between the Department of Defense (DOD) and Hollywood resulting in internationally distributed "militainment." However, outside of Mirrlees's work, which only addresses *Iron Man* in detail, the ways that the DOD works with Hollywood to produce superhero militainment is mostly overlooked in scholarship on the genre.

Several books have outlined the important role that the Pentagon plays in American cinematic production, including Matthew Alford's *Reel Power*, David Robb's *Operation Hollywood: How the Pentagon Shapes and Censors the Movies*, Tom Secker and Matthew Alford's *National Security*

Cinema, Roger Stahl's *Militainment, Inc.: War, Media and Popular Culture*, Laurence Suid's *Guts and Glory*, and Mirrlees's *Hearts and Mines: The US Empire's Culture Industry*. These books collectively show how the Pentagon has long worked in the preproduction and production stages of Hollywood filmmaking, leveraging access to its facilities, personnel, and hardware to secure positive self-imagery in popular cinema. While the formal nature of this relationship is explored in the first chapter of this book, the military-entertainment relationship is a mutually beneficial one. It offers filmmakers access to expensive hardware and unique filming locations at nominal costs, thereby increasing their profit margins. Leveraging access to this hardware, however, also allows the DOD to pursue "an extensive, highly politicized policy of self-promotion and revisionism through popular cinema."[24] As the DOD's former entertainment liaison, Phil Strub, admitted, when evaluating which scripts the DOD will support, "There's no question: I will plead guilty to bias in favor of the military. I wouldn't be able to look myself in the mirror and go to work every day if I didn't believe the military is a force for good." He added that if any script depicts the Armed Forces as a "malign" entity, the DOD "won't provide support."[25]

Because superhero stories often have military themes and heavily rely on action-based sequences that require helicopters, fighter jets, tanks, aircraft carriers, unique filming locations, and technical advice to help situate their narratives in a more realistic context, many films in the genre have relied on the military's production assistance, including Ang Lee's *Hulk* (2003), the first two films in the *Iron Man* trilogy, the first two *Captain America* films, *The Avengers*, *Captain Marvel*, *Man of Steel*, and *Suicide Squad*. The reliance of superhero filmmakers on this assistance is a particular boon to the armed forces, as the genre is one of the best PR and propaganda vehicles available. In addition to these films' extraordinary popularity both domestically and abroad, almost all superhero movie plots feature a world (or universe) threatened with violence by an outside force, necessitating that the heroes vanquish the bad guys with violence of their own, often while fighting alongside the real US military or other NATO forces. While the superhero genre has produced military-related villains, it has more consistently foregrounded current and former military members as positive and heroic characters, often associating military service with being a superhero him or herself. Steve Austin, Frank Castle, Steve Rogers, Nick Fury, Carol Danvers, Wade Wilson, James Rhodes, Maria Hill, Logan, Sam Wilson, and others are all military veterans of one stripe or another. By associating themselves with fictional superheroes, then, the DOD is able to encourage movie audiences to see servicemen and women as the world's real-life superheroes, with all of the corresponding recruitment and propaganda benefits that idea implies. Furthermore, superheroes are almost always exceptional individuals with powers beyond what any ordinary person can manifest or experience, and thus these protagonists function as individual metaphors not just for the DOD but for US exceptionalism more broadly. In these narratives, superheroes have not only the responsibility but also the right to visit large-scale, lethal violence on their opponents because someone special has to police a world that is full of threats, which is often how the DOD aims to position itself in global affairs.

The formal connections between superheroes and military service that have been forged by the military-entertainment complex can be seen as early as the 1970s, when different branches of the armed forces assisted the television series *Wonder Woman* (1975–1979), the *Six Million Dollar Man* (1973–1978), and the *Bionic Woman* (1976–1978)—the latter two of which were science fiction characters made "super" by government-developed cybernetics. In the *Wonder Woman* episode "Flight to Oblivion," the Pentagon's entertainment liaison Donald Baruch approved air force production assistance at Van Nuys because it would be "of value" to have Wonder Woman featured in an air force uniform, presumably because such an image blended the heroism and popularity of the character with that of military service in children's minds.[26] In the *Bionic Woman* episode "Angel of Mercy," the air force also gave approval for the crew to feature Jaime Sommers taking off and landing from its planes, as it linked the branch to Jaime's efforts to rescue endangered diplomats and demonstrated that, despite her bionic powers, she still needed help from the military to accomplish her work.[27] Likewise, the producers of the *Six Million Dollar Man* episode "An Eye for an Eye" successfully requested to shoot the entire episode at Edwards AFB.[28] Eventually renamed "The Deadly Test," the episode features Steve Austin temporarily assuming command of a test pilot training school to serve his required two weeks of reserve duty, again linking superheroes with military service, but in the course of duty, Austin also prevents an international assassination attempt on an Arab prince and thereby helps to preserve Arab-Israeli peace.[29]

By leveraging their assets for script changes, the military was also able to diminish potentially negative messages in individual episodes. In *Wonder Woman*'s "Trouble in Paradise," Richard Vane, the show's location manager, sought naval support to bring its cast and crew of roughly sixty people to film on the bridge of a destroyer.[30] The navy and the Pentagon agreed to support the project, so long as a joke about naval personnel drinking on the job was eliminated, that references to the country's "new neutron bomb" be changed to a "nuclear bomb," and that a line about the navy creating a cover story to hide a "neutron breeder test station" from the public be omitted as well.[31] Likewise, when the producers from ABC launched *The Bionic Woman*, they approached the air force about supporting its series, since Jaime was to be a schoolteacher on a base. The air force agreed to cooperate but successfully secured several changes to the pilot script, written by Kenneth Johnson in 1975. Originally, Jaime was meant to be a new teacher in a classroom full of problem children. The script noted that "if Atilla the Hun ever had kids, they'd be in that class" and that Jaime had been given the "dirty dozen."[32] These kids, the dialogue explains, "chewed up four teachers in three months" and are not only "army brats" but have individual adjustment and discipline problems. The air force requested that her classroom be composed of normal rather than problem children, and that the "totally derogatory remarks about Air Force dependents" be removed.[33] In the episode that aired, the students are sympathetically described to Jaime as struggling with tough, authoritative parents and constant relocation, and although a few troublemakers are in the class, Jaime is able to quickly get them under control through use of her bionic powers.

As these examples illustrate, the relationship between the DOD and superhero texts goes back many decades and proves beneficial for the military's image and producers' bottom lines. However, this relationship is not without its complications. Often, superpowered protagonists are depicted as more powerful than the Pentagon, rendering them as secondary units or even useless. Some films such as *Man of Steel* and *Captain Marvel* have managed this potential conflict well, either by showing the hero fighting shoulder to shoulder with the military or by incorporating a military backstory that attributes the protagonist's exceptionalism to their military training and experience. Other films in the genre have been more problematic, most notably *The Avengers*, where the Pentagon could not find a way to incorporate the newly formed superhero team into their command structure and had major objections to S.H.I.E.L.D. taking the unilateral decision to nuke New York City to try to repel an alien invasion. As we discuss in chapter 2, this conflict ultimately led to the DOD withdrawing from the movie mid-production, and to Strub giving multiple interviews explaining the issues that led to the falling out. Indeed, the tension regarding who is the best protective force—superheroes or the military-backed state—is a central theme of numerous films in the genre, including those in the *X-Men*, *Captain America*, and *Avengers* installments. In these films, the state either tries to register superpowered individuals in order to control them, or the state tries to subject superheroes to a global governing body that possesses the right to detain and imprison those who act against their wishes.

Because many superhero films employ DOD production assistance, and because many of the genre's tropes are intertwined with issues of weapons development, super-soldier programs, veterans, and questions regarding state sovereignty, government jurisdictions, and the right to use lethal technologies, these movies are ripe for an exploration of the strengths, limitations, and cultural ramifications of the military-entertainment complex. However, the Department of Defense is not the only government entity that plays a role in cinematic production. As Tricia Jenkins's *The CIA in Hollywood: How the Agency Shapes Film and Television*, Simon Willmett's *In Secrecy's Shadow: The*

OSS and CIA in Hollywood Cinema, 1941–1979, and Richard Powers's *G-Men: Hoover's FBI in American Popular Culture* all demonstrate, other government agencies, including the Central Intelligence Agency and the Federal Bureau of Investigation, have also played a role in shaping the narratives of radio, film, and television productions for decades. And today, the number of government and quasi-government agencies with formal entertainment liaison offices extends well past the arms of the security branches to include the National Aeronautics and Space Administration, the Department of Health and Human Services, the Centers for Disease Control and Prevention, and the National Academy of Sciences. These entities are not as powerful as the Department of Defense in securing script changes, but they are nonetheless important influencers in film and television production.

Indeed, these nonmilitary organizations have had a hand in shaping the superhero genre and its reception. For example, FBI agent Dale Shelton consulted on *Man of Steel*, while the CIA's Office of Public Affairs provided unofficial promotional support to *Black Panther*. NASA, a prolific player in Hollywood production, has provided either production assistance, space-related imagery, or promotional outreach on *Iron Man* (2008) and *Iron Man 2* (2010), *The Avengers*, *Avengers: Age of Ultron*, *The Justice League*, films in the *Thor* series, *The Dark Knight Rises*, *Ant-Man* (2015), *Aquaman*, *Guardians of the Galaxy*, *Man of Steel*, *The Winter Soldier* (2014), *Wonder Woman*, and HBO's *Watchmen* (2019). Meanwhile, the Science and Entertainment Exchange—the entertainment liaison office of the quasi-governmental National Academy of Sciences—has connected superhero filmmakers with scientific and technical consultants on the Iron Man, Thor, Ant-Man, and Avengers films, as well as on *Man of Steel*, *The Winter Soldier*, *Doctor Strange*, *Captain Marvel*, *Spider-Man: Homecoming* (2017), *Green Lantern* (2011), and *Black Panther*. The exchange has also provided assistance to the TV shows *Agent Carter*, *Agents of S.H.I.E.L.D.*, and *Luke Cage*. While the government-entertainment complex is primarily a US phenomenon, we should also note that it sometimes extends beyond America's borders. The British Ministry of Defense (MOD) helped provide filming locations to *The Avengers*, *Wonder Woman*, and *Black Widow* (2021), but only after conducting PR assessments to judge whether supporting these products would benefit the MOD's media objectives.

Perhaps more than any other popular genre in Hollywood, then, superhero films have enjoyed production and promotional support from a wide variety of government agencies. War films are often supported by the DOD and spy films by the CIA or FBI, but few of these same films ever engage with NASA. Likewise, while many science fiction filmmakers work with NASA or the Science and Entertainment Exchange, there is usually little or no support on these same products from the various arms of the security state. Thus, an analysis of the superhero genre presents a unique opportunity not only to compare and contrast the operating procedures, aims, and impacts of different governmental offices but to see what happens when those entities' aims conflict on projects where multiple offices have provided assistance, such as on *The Avengers*. In other words, an examination of this genre helps reveal how NASA operates its entertainment office differently from the Pentagon, who, in turn, operates its office very differently from the National Academy of Sciences and how each entity's operations, leverage, and aims influence (or fail to influence) the messages moviegoers receive at the box office. In short, by looking at these offices' efforts in a single genre, this study helps widen scholars' understanding of not just the *military-entertainment* complex but the *government-entertainment* complex as a whole.

The Aims of Government Entertainment Offices

Before we cover the scope and methodology of this book, we want to outline the seven basic agendas that motivate various government agencies to engage in the entertainment complex, because they help reveal what is at stake for the state, its citizens, and even international viewers of these movies. The first and most obvious is recruitment. Paul Barry, the CIA's former entertainment liaison officer, stated that when he and his predecessor, Chase Brandon, reviewed scripts to decide which projects the agency would support, they always looked for films that would help the agency "recruit, develop and retain individuals" from a needed and diverse talent pool.[34] Thus, the agency heavily supported *The Recruit* (2003), which featured Colin Farrell undergoing an intense but glamorous training process at the Farm and dialogue that suggested the agency needed applicants who could speak Farsi. In the DOD's Instruction on Support to Entertainment Media, recruitment is also stated as an explicit goal. While the DOD engages in a wide variety of recruitment techniques, few, if any, provide access to such a diverse and large audience as Hollywood movies, and few, if any, have the potential to generate the same type of results. For example, when *Top Gun* opened in May 1986, military recruiters manned tables outside of theaters to field questions from new, wannabe flyboys. These efforts, alongside the movie's glamorous depiction of Top Gun pilots and dramatic dogfights, resulted in a 500 percent increase in applications by those seeking to become naval aviators.[35] For anyone who is concerned about their own relatives, friends, and loved ones potentially risking their lives by joining a branch of the security state engaged in violent operations, this means of recruitment is a legitimate concern. More broadly, anyone who is concerned about where the brightest minds are deployed in our societies, and to what ends, should consider the widespread and long-term impact of the government stationing resources in Hollywood to try to get the pick of the litter.

The second reason why the government attempts to influence popular media is that it affords the state with huge public relations benefits. As demonstrated by Michelle Pautz's study of audience responses to the CIA-supported films *Argo* (2012) and *Zero Dark Thirty* (2012), cinema can have a vast impact on public, political opinions. Pautz polled audiences before and after watching these two films and found that, for 25 percent of viewers, their opinions of government agencies shifted in a more positive direction after viewing. The study also examined more general questions such as whether America was headed in the right direction and found that 22 percent of viewers demonstrated an improved view of the country's trajectory after watching one of these movies. Perceptions of government trustworthiness and faith in government agencies such as the CIA and the military, as well as top officials such as the president, also improved post-viewing, with the percentage of people whose opinions changed for the better ranging from 22 percent to 33 percent.[36] For those who are skeptical of or opposed to the US government's domestic, economic, or foreign policies, government-supported entertainment is a significant obstacle to overcome in persuading wide public opinion to ally itself with that opposition.

On a similar but far more controversial note, entertainment liaison offices also work with Hollywood to dilute, normalize, or cover up the various scandals, crimes, and corruption that occur in government agencies, particularly within the security state. While it is a local rather than federal government agency, the Los Angeles Police Department's entertainment contracts forbid any film or television producer from portraying its officers as performing "any unlawful, immoral, racist, or reckless act," including "unlawful battery, assault, beating or shooting, planting of evidence, racist comments, hate crimes and reckless driving."[37] These rules work to sanitize its officers' histories while simultaneously negating the LAPD's long history of police brutality and racial targeting, which ignited unrest in Watts in the 1960s, led to the Rodney King riots of the 1990s, and in 2020 prompted the city's mayor to announce a $150 million budget cut to its police force in response to the Black Lives Matter protests, where the police were again criticized for using excessive force against the city's protesters.[38] Likewise, Jeff Cohen reminds us how the series *The FBI* (1965–1974), which he calls one of the "great feats in propaganda history," painted a "largely distorted portrait of a supremely ethical, non-politicized institution" for nine years on American television. The bureau partnered with ABC on the series, which lent the network access to its case files, locations, and its official logo in exchange for control over scripts and story lines. J. Edgar Hoover supported the series because it allowed him "to polish the bureau's image in the mass media as a means toward more power and more funding," but it also masked the fact that during the show's long run, the bureau "was systematically abusing the First Amendment rights of countless civil rights and peace advocates, from grass-roots activists to John Lennon and Martin Luther King Jr."[39]

A fourth motive for government agencies to work with Hollywood is to maintain or enhance their social and political relevance in society. Following the Cold War, both Congress and the public questioned if the CIA should continue to exist, given that its ostensible purpose of fighting the communists had been surpassed by world events. In the 1990s, Sen. Daniel Patrick Moynihan introduced bills to abolish the CIA and have its functions subsumed by the State Department. To combat the idea that the agency was no longer relevant, the CIA set up its own entertainment liaison office in 1996 to convince the public and Congress that the agency was still necessary through movies and television shows. In one of its first Hollywood collaborations, *In the Company of Spies* (1999), the film features a mentally unstable North Korean leader buying ICBMs from the Russians in order to acquire launch capabilities for its nuclear technology. The ICBMs would allow the North Koreans to strike the US West Coast, not to mention its troops in the demilitarized zone, and this intelligence is discovered by Langley. In sum, the film helped highlight the agency's real concerns that many of the USSR's arsenals were left unguarded after its collapse and were now being sold to unpredictable regimes, and the movie helped drive home the idea that the United States still faced significant foreign threats. This messaging, combined with the 9/11 attacks and later CIA-supported texts that further emphasized the threat from terrorists, helped the agency thwart any subsequent discussion of its own abolition. While the disbanding of NASA was not on the congressional agenda in the early 2010s, Bert Ulrich, NASA's chief media officer, admitted to us in an interview that his agency had somewhat dropped out of public view once the space shuttle program ended in 2011. "People were still asking me if I had a job," he quipped.[40] However, as chapter 3 reveals, NASA's recent use of social media, the Curiosity rover's landing on Mars, and the agency's work on roughly 150 space-related movies per year has proven vital in reestablishing the agency's reputation as an important and forward-thinking institution in the minds of the American public. In fact, Ulrich cited *The Avengers*, *First Man* (2018), *Hidden Figures* (2016), and *The Martian* (2015) as having a particularly strong impact on bringing NASA back into (positive) public consciousness.

On a similar note, budgets also explain why the government works with Hollywood, especially as competition between different agencies for limited public resources becomes more fraught due to various world events. For instance, Carl Sagan was often worried that funding for the controversial SETI (Search for Extraterrestrial Intelligence) Institute would be pulled, and thus to increase the perceived value of the institute, he supported the movie adaptation of his novel, *Contact*, which, in 1997, featured SETI actually discovering a radio signal sent by an alien culture.[41] Major David Georgi, a consultant assigned by the army to several films, also recognized the funding aspect of Hollywood collaborations, stating, "We want to show Congress what we can do. Obviously, a movie is not always 100 percent factual, so when we get Congress to watch it, they see [us] in a favorable light, and down the road, this [helps] with funding."[42] The prevailing idea seems to be that congresspeople watch movies and TV shows too, and they are more inclined to accept and/or continue to vote through large or increased budgets for those parts of the government that regularly appear in heroic fashion in their popular media or are shown making valuable contributions to society. And indeed, the Pentagon, which has the most robust entertainment program in the US government, continues to dominate congressional budget allocations year after year, while programs such as public education and health care are frequently cut.

Sometimes offices have far more benign agendas too, such as educating viewers about important topics. Rick Loverd explains that the Science and Entertainment Exchange (SEEX) is primarily dedicated to better depictions "of science—and science characters—in fictional, mainstream media projects." He states that while the exchange does not "advocate for science in an overt way," it hopes to provide Hollywood with an alternative to simply "making things up," by providing writers and directors with ideas that are sourced from relevant science.[43] Likewise, both the CDC and USC's Hollywood, Health and Society program provide the entertainment industry with information regarding health-related story lines, including those dealing with COVID-19, toxic mold, smallpox, cancer, autism, motor vehicle crashes, obesity, and more. These offices aim to help writers provide accurate information about disease transmission, treatments, and precautionary behaviors to help viewers facing health-related issues.

Finally, entertainment liaison offices work in Hollywood because films offer a unique opportunity to reach and affect the beliefs and attitudes of foreign audiences, not just the US public. For example, Chase Brandon argued in the early 2000s that because "terrorists watch TV too," the CIA was interested in having shows, such as CBS's *The Agency* (2001–2003), feature far more advanced technology than what the CIA actually possessed in order to convince would-be criminals that, should they try to carry out an attack on US soil, they would almost certainly be caught by the agency at the airport.[44] This concept was again played out in the new CIA-supported *Jack Ryan* TV series (2018–present), where some genuinely clever terrorists who stage a multiphase attack in DC are thwarted due to the dedication and ingenuity of the agency.

These seven categories highlight the main reasons that government agencies work with Hollywood productions and thus how difficult it can be for viewers to learn about, question, or effectively evaluate their own government agencies given how awash their popular culture is in state influence. But Hollywood studios are also deeply invested in this relationship. In the late 1990s, the Clinton administration considered abolishing the military's Hollywood offices as part of the DOD's cost-cutting measures, but this only provoked a wave of entertainment industry executives demanding that the office be maintained and that Strub and others keep their jobs. The president of the Motion Picture Association of America, Jack Valenti, personally wrote to Secretary of Defense William Cohen and spearheaded an effort whereby "dozens of top Hollywood film executives also wrote letters on Strub's behalf," keeping the DOD's Hollywood office in business.[45] As Jonathan Turley observes, "For people like Valenti, the issue is not censorship or propaganda, it is the bottom line. . . . The major studios tend to produce the type of portrayals of the military that Strub prefers: uncritical and intensely patriotic,"[46] while the military, in turn, makes it significantly cheaper to produce any film requiring military hardware. Because of this mutually beneficial nature, it is unlikely that the military-entertainment complex, let alone the entire government-entertainment complex, will ever be disbanded.

The Structure, Scope, and Methodology Employed by This Book

Given the widespread goals, the important cultural stakes, and the number of agencies involved in Hollywood, *Superheroes, Movies, and the State* works to more fully explicate the government-entertainment complex by focusing on its influence in the world's most profitable movie genre. The first two chapters of this book focus on the DOD's relationship to superhero movies. The first illustrates how the Pentagon's entertainment liaison offices have historically worked with film and television producers before detailing how its recent involvement in the genre has resulted in narrative tropes and characters that promote, rather than challenge, the authority of the military. Using archival materials that pertain to the DOD's work on *Hulk*, *Iron Man*, and *Iron Man 2*, this chapter illustrates how DOD-assisted films project sanitized images of war and present themselves as a benevolent and righteous force. They also reinforce the concept of the military-state's sovereignty, especially when faced with the threat that superpowered beings present, and they reveal how the military often scapegoats its private contractors for any corruption, greed, war-mongering, or ethics violations that exist within the military-industrial complex. Chapter 2 then takes a reverse approach, demonstrating how superhero movies that do not receive production assistance from the DOD often adopt a more subversive approach toward the military and government officials, representing superheroes as necessary challenges to or replacements for government authorities that have grown corrupt, unethical, and/or inept. Case studies for this chapter include *The Incredible Hulk*, *The Avengers*, *Iron Man 3*, *Captain America: Civil War*, and *Captain America: The Winter Soldier*.

Moving beyond the military-entertainment complex, chapters 3 and 4 explore the role of space and science within the superhero genre.

Chapter 3 examines America's renewed interest in space exploration, as well as NASA's emergence as a Marvel Studios partner. We interview Bert Ulrich, NASA's chief media liaison officer, to understand how NASA views its role in Hollywood, how its methods and goals differ from those of the DOD, and how NASA has worked to reestablish its significance in the minds of the public through film. Using *The Avengers* as a case study, we also show how this film's narrative and public reception worked to celebrate science and peaceful space exploration, before comparing its messages to the ones in the DOD-assisted *Man of Steel* and the USAF-assisted *Captain Marvel*, whose release coincided with the development of the US Space Force—the newly created sixth branch of the US military. These three films showcase how NASA and the Pentagon vie for control of public perceptions of space—presenting it either as a realm for crucial scientific discovery or as "the ultimate high ground" for the next stage of military combat. Examining the underappreciated role that the Science and Entertainment Exchange (SEEX) plays in the development of film narratives, chapter 4 then outlines the role of the science advisor and the SEEX's growing influence in Hollywood film production. Using the Thor and Ant-Man movies, as well as *Black Panther*, this chapter examines the role advanced technologies play in the superhero genre and how the SEEX is trying to positively alter our conceptions of the role of both science and scientists through these works.

Our final chapter begins by addressing the relationship between identity politics and the protagonists in superhero movies, analyzing how and why the conventional white male leads that have traditionally fronted the genre have been supplemented by female characters and characters of color. Using *Wonder Woman* and *Black Panther* as our primary examples, we explore whether these films represent an important new direction for the genre; are simply conventional, militaristic narratives with unconventional leads; or are progressive and conservative texts simultaneously. We also present close readings of these texts, focusing on the representation of the CIA in *Black Panther* and of the Central and Allied powers in *Wonder Woman* to show how both films employ historical revisionism to benefit established powers, despite being heralded as unconventional, or even radical, texts because of their diverse leads.

The book then concludes by reiterating some of the book's main themes before casting an eye to possible new directions in the genre. Focusing on Amazon's popular and highly acclaimed TV series *The Boys* (2019–present), the conclusion contrasts the thematic trends in post-2000 superhero films with those in the recent series, which subverts and satirizes many of Marvel and DC's tropes. We ask whether the genre's messages of American exceptionalism and reliance on singular saviors pose problems for twenty-first-century audiences, and how *The Boys* might help the genre explore other solutions and characters as correctives.

Limitations

Like all books, *Superheroes, Movies, and the State* is limited in regard to its scope. For one, it is focused only on contemporary superhero films. It does not significantly address the rich history of Marvel or DC Comics, their television series, video games, or older films. Part of this decision had to do with limiting the scope of what are incredibly, if not overwhelmingly, prolific transmedia empires. However, we also believe that the films of the MCU and DCEU remain at the core of those franchises and thus deserve the most attention. As Liam Burke writes, "Although transmedia franchises are marked by a horizontal distribution of content, they tend to rely on a 'driving platform . . . the medium that will reach the greatest audience and furnish the core storyline.'" These key texts are often described as the "mother ship" that then generates "flow tags" that "direct consumers to other narrative units." Burke points to the case of Phil Coulson to demonstrate how the MCU's films are indeed the franchise's mother ship. Played by actor Clark Gregg in the movies, Coulson was first introduced as a S.H.I.E.L.D. agent in *Iron Man*, but his popularity as a character earned him appearances in subsequent MCU movies, some DVD one-shots, and, eventually, a leading role on the *Agents of* S.H.I.E.L.D. television series. It was not until *after* Coulson had debuted in *Iron Man* that his literary "counterpart was introduced to the original comic book continuity (designated Earth-616), making Coulson 'canon' in both the comic book and cinematic universes." Similarly, the Guardians of the Galaxy were not given a dedicated monthly comic book until 2013 to build interest in their upcoming film. When that film proved to be a box-office hit, the lesser-known heroes witnessed a rapid expansion of their own comics, "including *Guardians 3000*, *Guardians Team-Up*, and *Marvel Universe Guardians of the Galaxy*, while *The Legendary Star-Lord*, *Rocket Raccoon*, and *Groot* all received solo titles." As Burke summarizes, when one factors "in the prequel comics that accompany most theatrical releases as well as the video games that often fill in the gaps in big screen narratives, Marvel Studios is the first production company to fully realize the potential hinted at in earlier transmedia" franchises, such as the Matrix, with the films resting at its very core.[47]

Additionally, this book privileges the MCU over the DCEU largely because the MCU has had far more financial success, a greater number of titles released, and more critical and fan acclaim than its rival. According to Rotten Tomato scores, of the first five DCEU films, the only one "certified fresh"—meaning that the majority of critical and fan reviews are positive—is *Wonder Woman* at 93 percent, while the rest are denoted as "rotten." The last three films in the franchise have fared better, with *Shazam!* pulling a 90 percent fresh rating on the site. In comparison, Marvel does not have a single movie that gets classified as "rotten," even though they have significantly more titles to rate (twenty-three compared to DC's ten at the time of this writing). Marvel's lowest-rated movie, *Thor: The Dark World*, only gets as low as 66 percent (compared to DC having two films at 27 percent), and *Black Panther* ranks at an astounding 97 percent fresh.[48] The second reason that we privilege the MCU over the DCEU is that there are simply more documents available for MCU films than for those involving DC characters, at least as it pertains to the government influence exerted over these productions. Despite the DOD's best attempts at obfuscation, we have collected fairly extensive records on MCU films, especially those in Phase One of the shared universe, whereas the only

DCEU movie where FOIA requests have borne significant fruit is *Man of Steel*.

Methodology

As the above paragraph implies, this book is largely steeped in archival research, as we mined the primary documents exchanged between government entertainment offices and Hollywood producers and writers working in the superhero genre. This type of work is not easy. In his own research, Alford found that "since 2002, the DOD seems to have stopped keeping detailed records about the script changes it requests or the textual negotiations it engages in, or, at least, when researchers make use of Freedom of Information Act (FOIA) to request such material, they are rejected."[49] These same woes have plagued the research of this book. Beginning in 2014, Secker filed hundreds of FOIA requests to try to address the scarcity of primary source material regarding the government's contemporary influence in Hollywood, especially as it pertains to the DOD. While his effort resulted in thousands of pages of documents (which are available for free on his website),[50] the bulk are diary-like reports from the entertainment liaison offices, which contain little information on script input or revisions, although they do provide an abundance of illuminating data on other aspects of the military-entertainment complex, such as details on the type of support provided, the timelines of these projects, and whether and why the DOD considered them PR successes. But even obtaining these reports has not been without complication and difficulty. For example, a 2016 request to the US Navy for liaison office reports, script notes, and production assistance agreements took two years to get an initial response. The navy claimed they had no copies of any script notes or production assistance agreements and announced that they would be withholding eight hundred pages of office reports in their entirety.[51] After a lengthy appeals process where Secker pointed out that the navy had previously released script notes and production assistance agreements, the navy acquiesced to a degree, releasing both the office reports and nearly one hundred production assistance agreements. However, they maintained that they could not reveal the details of their script input and claimed they could only find one set of script notes, which were for an unmade film and almost entirely redacted. In the appeals process, the navy also admitted that it possesses over 240,000 pages of annotated scripts for hundreds of TV episodes and more than a dozen films, and these are just from the last few years of working with Hollywood. They refused to release any of them, however, citing commercial confidentiality as justification.

Despite these issues, this book is still able to employ numerous documents obtained from government entertainment liaison offices that inform our critical readings of the genre and the government-entertainment complex more broadly. In some cases the documents do outline requests for script changes and even ideas that the military pitched to filmmakers for inclusion in the final product. These documents shed light on the military's concerns and aims, but they only tell part of the story. By closely analyzing the films themselves, we can also see which military ideas or revisions made it into the final cut and which ones were rejected by the filmmakers. We can also use a close textual analysis of the films to decode the ideological messages they promote. To further complete the picture, we also interviewed numerous players in the government-entertainment complex, including MCU producer Jeremy Latcham, roughly a dozen science advisors working on behalf of the SEEX, screenwriter James Schamus, and Bert Ulrich, the entertainment liaison officer from NASA, to further understand how and why government agencies invest in the production of superhero films and how their support (or lack thereof) influences those film's final narratives. We also look at governmental, critical, and public responses to these films to assess the impact of these narratives from a variety of perspectives.

Overall, this book is important. The superhero genre is ripe for an exploration of the government-entertainment complex—not just the military-entertainment complex—as it showcases its wide-ranging and sometimes profound impact on entertainment products, which influence the dominant political, social, and economic trends of our age. The work that these agencies engage in is undoubtedly propaganda. While that term has developed a negative connotation in the last several decades, as David Welch defines it, propaganda is simply "the dissemination of ideas intended to convince people to think and act in a particular way and for a particular persuasive purpose."[52] He notes that it varies from information and education in that propaganda seeks to narrow our perspectives, whereas the former seeks to extend them. David Culbert offers yet another definition, arguing that propaganda is simply "the controlled dissemination of deliberately distorted notions in an effort to induce actions favorable to predetermined ends or special interest groups."[53]

And yet we recognize that government entertainment agencies do not represent traditional forms of state-sponsored propaganda because, as Turley writes, the government does not directly generate these popular films and "does not compel others to produce" them. Rather, the US government works to achieve its results through indirect influence, leveraging its resources in order to secure positive images and messaging. "Unlike crude regimes, like North Korea, which try to control all information in a society," Turley writes, "the US military cannot (and culturally would not) attempt such authoritarian objectives." (Turley was writing in a pre-Trump era.) Indeed, government entertainment liaison officers often "recoil" at the suggestion that they are engaged in propaganda because it is viewed as un-American. "Instead these officials view their heavy-handed editing and threats in purely business terms—supplying things of value in the form of military resources in exchange for benefits in kind."[54] Precisely because this relationship does not look from the outside to be traditional government propaganda, it is all the more powerful. As propagandists have long understood, manipulative strategies work best when people don't realize they are being subjected to them, making blockbuster films excellent vehicles for propaganda due to their ability to appear to outsiders as inconsequential forms of popcorn entertainment. Thus, one of the primary ways to combat the effects of US propaganda is to expose how the government-entertainment complex operates. We believe that the wildly popular superhero genre, which reaches many millions, if not billions, of viewers around the globe, and whose messages have often been influenced by one or more arms of the American state, is an excellent case study for this line of inquiry.

"IF YOU GET KILLED, WALK IT OFF"

HOW THE DOD PROMOTES CLEAN WARS AND US BENEVOLENCE

I

As early as D. W. Griffith's *Birth of a Nation* (1915), the Pentagon has actively engaged with the film industry, providing producers access to unique locations and expensive war equipment in exchange for favorable military or political images.[1] This symbiotic relationship has grown significantly over the last century because, as David Robb summarizes, "The Pentagon has what Hollywood wants—access to billions of dollars' worth of sophisticated military hardware to put into movies; and Hollywood has what the Pentagon wants—access to the eyeballs of millions of viewers and potential recruits."[2] Indeed, since the turn of the twentieth century, the military has supported close to a thousand major movies and well over a thousand TV episodes, with a notable increase in activity since the arrival of digital and on-demand platforms and the change in the Department of Defense's regulations, which now allow them to support reality television programs.[3]

The military's entertainment program offers either full cooperation to producers seeking locations, personnel, and hardware (such as helicopters, planes, tanks, and ships) at minimal cost, or limited cooperation for those only seeking technical advice, stock footage, and installation visits. In order to receive full cooperation from the DOD, producers must submit a script and an outline of the types of support they are seeking, as well as proof that cinematic distribution has been secured. Producers seeking full cooperation must also meet four main criteria before their application will be approved. The work must depict a "feasible interpretation of military life, operations, and policies," and it must also be "considered to be in the best interest of public understanding of the U.S. Armed Forces and the Department of Defense." The script "may" also enhance recruiting and retention programs, and, finally, it must not contain material that "appears to condone or endorse activities by private citizens that are contrary to U.S. Government policy."[4] These guidelines suggest that if a script meets these criteria then full cooperation will be granted, but usually the approval process involves significant negotiations between the Pentagon and the film's producers, with the military leveraging or withholding its assets in order to secure either minor and/or major script rewrites to make it appear more favorable on screen. In its production assistance agreements, the DOD also secures final review and approval rights for those scenes with which it has assisted before a film can be released to the public.

As Alford writes, filmmakers dealing with combat story lines regularly cooperate with the DOD to achieve their cinematic goals with reduced overhead, and thus routinely promote "the dubious notion that the United States is a benevolent force in world affairs and that unleashing its military strength overseas has positive results for humanity."[5] Likewise, Roger Stahl argues in *Militainment, Inc.* that because of this production system, the notion of "clean war"—a term that refers to the manner of presenting war in a way "that maximizes viewer alienation from the fact of death in order to maximize [a] war's capacity to be consumed"—has grown increasingly prevalent in DOD-assisted films. The concept of clean war, he argues, was a direct reaction to the Vietnam era, when "conventional wisdom among policy elites held that unsupervised roving reporters" and nightly displays of the increasing American body count "had corrupted the will of the body politic and lost the war." As such, the military has since worked in multiple entertainment and news mediums to render soldiers' deaths, and even their serious injuries, invisible. This is partly evidenced by President George H. W. Bush's 1991 policy to disallow press access at

Dover and Andrews Air Force Bases: "the entry points for returning caskets."[6] Other common issues that the DOD seeks to either mitigate or eradicate from scripts include the depiction of service members committing war crimes and sexual assaults, current troops and veterans suffering from mental illness or committing suicide as a result of their service, the military's use of chemical or nuclear weapons, and military personnel's use of alcohol and drugs.[7] Films that depict any of these subjects are likely to be denied Pentagon cooperation or to be the object of heavy rewrites spearheaded by the military's entertainment liaison offices. As stated in Tanner Mirrlees's *Hearts and Mines*, the geopolitical goals of the US military and the state do not always "march in lock-step" with the profit-maximization goals of the US entertainment industry, but because the DOD often helps moviemakers lower their overhead expenses, "the US Empire's cultural industry points to a more collusive relationship than is often recognized," resulting in the Pentagon's ability to manage public awareness and opinion on a variety of issues.[8]

The specific results of the Pentagon's negotiations with any particular filmmaker are not always clear because script development is a closed rather than public process, and because the documentation generated and released by the DOD regarding its work in Hollywood is often sparse or nonexistent. However, a significant amount of documentation about the Pentagon's work on Universal Studio's *Hulk* is available to scholars, and this film, especially when contrasted with the Marvel Cinematic Universe's *The Incredible Hulk*—explored in chapter 2—provides an excellent case study of how DOD-assisted films vastly differ in their ideologies from those that do not rely on the military for production assistance. A cultural and textual analysis of *Hulk* also reveals how the Pentagon's assistance helps it offer fictional arguments or images that counter the news media's more factual and damaging ones. This chapter begins, then, by examining the Pentagon's influence on *Hulk*, but several other superhero films have likewise sought and obtained the military's full cooperation over the years, including *Fantastic Four: The Rise of the Silver Surfer* (2007), *Iron Man*, *Iron Man 2*, *Captain America: The First Avenger* (2011), *The Avengers*, *Man of*

Steel, *Suicide Squad*, and *Captain Marvel*. In general, these films support scholars' assertions that DOD-assisted films circulate the concept of "clean wars" and promote images of a righteous and benevolent armed force, but as we illustrate, they also helped build consensus for US foreign policy and/or worked to reinforce the concept of the military-state's sovereignty, especially when faced with the threat that superheroes present to their power. As chapter 2 reveals, superhero films that do not receive military production assistance are far more apt to explore the dangers of centralized military power, especially when it is left unchecked by an equally powerful entity, like a superhero. While this chapter does not have the space to analyze every DOD-assisted superhero movie, we have chosen to explore *Hulk*, *Iron Man*, and *Iron Man 2* in detail to illuminate how the Pentagon's influence helped circulate several favorable cultural ideologies about the US state, especially during the early stages of the War on Terror.

Hulk (2003)

Ang Lee's *Hulk* opens in the 1960s with David Banner, a military contractor, secretly working to create an American super-soldier by infusing various animals' DNA with the human genome. When the military's General Ross forbids such experimentation because it is dangerous and unethical, Banner surreptitiously conducts the experiments on himself, inadvertently passing his modified DNA to Bruce, his newborn son. Years later, Bruce is shown working as a geneticist with his former girlfriend, Betty Ross (also the daughter of General Ross), using radiation to cure human diseases. When a gamma ray machine misfires in their lab, Bruce throws himself in front of a colleague to absorb the radiation himself. Because of his mutated DNA, Banner survives the blast, but it also causes him to grow into a giant green monster when stressed or provoked, and the Hulk's anger and destruction are beyond the bounds of Bruce's self-control. The military is then tasked with containing the national security threat that the Hulk now poses, while the character of Talbot (Josh Lucas), who works for a modern-day defense contractor, Atheon, attempts to thwart those efforts in order to study the Hulk and profit off of the super-soldier science that Bruce embodies.

Lee's *Hulk* received full cooperation from the Pentagon after the film's coproducer, Larry Franco, approached it for numerous pieces of military hardware, including a variety of weapons, bases, Comanche helicopters, and F-22s that appear in the film's final cut. The film's screenwriter and producer, James Schamus, recalls that he and Lee also toured Holloman AFB because Lee was interested in learning more about how certain weapons worked and might be employed in the movie.[9] After reading the initial script, however, the DOD's head entertainment liaison officer, Phil Strub, had several reservations. He offered up five pages of notes, telling Franco that "in the past, we've usually been able to offer suggestions within the context of existing plot and characters. These, however, are pretty radical. I hope they don't have the effect of aggravating everyone, because we certainly aren't trying to intrude on the creative process. It's just that I see no other practical, straightforward way of communicating our concerns."[10] Based on these notes, it is clear that Strub was concerned about how the military attempted to neutralize the Hulk throughout the film, arguing that the Pentagon appeared too aggressive in its treatment of the character, and that, at times, the military seemed too cowardly as well. He also wished to distance the DOD from the private contractors that were working on the super-soldier experiments, ensuring that the military would not be seen as dabbling in unethical, human genetic manipulation.

Undoubtedly, Strub had better luck shaping the image of the military's performance and benevolence than he did distancing the outfit from the contractors. While General Ross's character explicitly states in the movie that manipulating human DNA is off limits and orders Banner Sr.'s experiments shut down, Strub also requested that the desert base used by Banner be clearly marked as a *former* military base now in civilian hands and that all military uniforms present at the base be eliminated. He also wanted Ross removed as head of the lab and replaced with a civilian contractor, noting that he does not want the audience to think "that the military was responsible for what later . . . happened to Banner senior and junior."[11] None of these changes were actually made in the final cut, which almost always shows Ross in military uniform and in charge of the bases used by its contractors, although one line was inserted near the start of the film stating that the president's national science advisor had final control of the base used by Banner Sr. One reason why Strub may have been unsuccessful in securing these changes is that Schamus saw the film, from "the very first draft," as a criticism of the entire military-industry complex (MIC). "I was quite interested," he said, "in how the military is in many ways a gigantic grift—a revolving door of generals-lobbyists-contractors—producing their own 'blow back' to generate more demand for their endlessly proliferating production of destruction." "The imbrication of for-profit 'civilians' in every aspect of military life," he stated, "is . . . not in my book a positive." Schamus believes *Hulk* is far more critical of the MIC than the DOD understood, but because the contractors and not the military are the film's villains, the Pentagon seems to have taken little umbrage with these plot elements.

As to the depiction of the military's competence, benevolence, and bravery, Strub was much more successful in improving its image. For instance, when the Hulk is destroying the Atheon lab in the original script, Strub wanted it made clear that Ross has a tactical plan to mitigate the Hulk's damage. "He doesn't think they can stop him, but maybe they can slow him down and tire him out. Then when the military engages the Hulk, they're . . . luring him from one place to another, hoping to exhaust him. So when his team retreats, it's part of the plan, not a panicked 'run for your lives' scenario as originally written."[12] In the same sequence, Strub also objected to Talbot grabbing "a super-huge kick-ass automatic weapon" to destroy the Hulk, only to have the bullets bounce back at him, riddling Talbot to the ground. Either Strub or Matt Morgan, Strub's equivalent at the Marine Corps' Los Angeles public affairs office, circled the very next line on the script in protest: "The troops: witnessing it all, turn tail and run for it."[13] In the film's final cut, the military performs more positively. Ross tactically leads the Hulk out of the Atheon lab so that the military can more effectively pursue him in the desert, and the scenes of retreat (and potentially, cowardice) are revised. When Talbot is about to unleash a grenade launcher at the Hulk, the military personnel run *before and as* the blast occurs. They run not out of fear but out of foresight of Talbot's stupidity, as the blast bounces off the Hulk and destroys Talbot instead. Their choice, in other words, is depicted as smart, not cowardly.

In his most interesting to notes to Franco, Strub also requested that the writers dramatically temper the direct action taken against the Hulk and that outside of the deadly military strike at the end to obliterate the Absorbing Man (formerly Banner Sr.), all other military operations should focus on "nonlethal" means. One scene in the original script, for instance, featured the Hulk running through the Sierra Nevada mountains with the military in hot pursuit. When the Hulk is shown jeopardizing the life of a rock climber, Strub recommended revising the scene from one where his helicopters fire on the "Angry Man" with a civilian in the area to one where the military merely distracts the green giant while the climber makes it to safety. Instead of launching a B-52 strike at the Hulk in another part of the sequence, Strub further suggested that the military drop "cave bunker busters to knock down rock formations," simply trapping the Hulk, rather than trying to kill him. And in yet another sequence, Strub offered his own idea that the Hulk climb atop one of the F-22s trying to prevent him from destroying San Francisco, whose pilot would then decide to climb into the atmosphere to get the Hulk to pass out due to the altitude and fall back to Earth.[14] In total, Strub's concern was that the military was seen as taking too many lethal actions to kill the Hulk rather than contain him—attempts that distanced the military from its preferred image of a benevolent, if powerful, force.

Indeed, the image of a more benevolent military is central to building viewers' sympathy toward the state in *Hulk*. In Lee's version, the baby-faced actor Eric Bana plays one of the kindest and most tender versions of Bruce Banner ever to appear on screen (he is often shown sobbing, naked, and longing for Betty's love), and the military's efforts to kill rather than capture the Hulk suggest that it sees him only as a monster, forgetting that underneath all of the Hulk's rage, there is still a kind human who has been victimized by his father and science run amok. In a rarer scene when the military is actually trying to kill the Hulk after nonlethal methods have failed to contain him and he is approaching a highly populated area, Betty reminds her father that each military agitation only increases the Hulk's rage and fuels his strength. Instead, she proposes that she go to meet the Hulk in order to calm him down by appealing to Bruce's human and tender side, thus returning him to Banner. In a touching moment, Ross acquiesces and calls off the attack, allowing the Hulk to find Betty, whose plan is successful. This emphasis on the military's recognition of its enemy's humanity and its successful attempts at diplomacy depict it as open to at least some nonviolent conflict resolution, but scenes like this also helped combat many of the real-life issues that were plaguing the DOD when the film was released.

More specifically, *Hulk* was released in June 2003, roughly one and a half years after the United States invaded Afghanistan as part of its initial phase of the War on Terror and just a few months after the Bush administration invaded Iraq on the unsubstantiated claim that the country possessed weapons of mass destruction. Given that Lee cast look-alike actors for both Bush and Condoleezza Rice in the film, Lee was obviously cognizant of his political climate, yet the film's emphasis on the military's benevolence and Ross's repeatedly stated concerns about protecting civilian populations from the Hulk represented a stark contrast to the situation on the ground. Indeed, the US military operations in Iraq felt anything but benevolent to those involved. In addition to invading the country based on circumspection, the nature of the conflict, which often took place in heavily populated areas such as Baghdad, resulted in numerous civilian deaths. The Project on Defense Alternatives at the Commonwealth Institute in Cambridge, Massachusetts, for example, estimated in 2003 that approximately 11,000 to 15,000 Iraqis had died in the first month of the war's initial combat phase, including 3,200 to 4,300 civilian noncombatants.[15] In 2005, using updated numbers, the Iraq Body Count Project increased the number of civilian casualties during that same initial combat phase to nearly 6,900, many of whom were parents who left behind orphans. The project also reported that at least 17,425 civilian injuries had been inflicted between March and April 2003 alone, and that both the civilian deaths and the injuries had been primarily caused by US air and ground operations using explosive force. As the conflict continued, the IBC Project reveals that at least 24,865 noncombatant civilians had died due to the conflict by March 2005.[16]

Additionally, the military's own policies governing the new War on Terror were growing more ethically questionable. In what are now known as the 2002 Torture Memos, the US attorney general, Arthur Gonzalez, argued that international humanitarian laws, like the Geneva Conventions, did not apply in the War on Terror, stating that "none of the provisions of Geneva apply to our conflict with al Qaeda in Afghanistan or elsewhere through the world because, among other reasons, al Qaeda" is not a nation-state, or "a High Contracting Party to Geneva."[17] This policy, approved by President George W. Bush, was never introduced to Congress nor revealed to the public at the time, but it allowed for the Department of Justice (DOJ) to authorize the use of a variety of enhanced interrogation techniques (i.e., torture), leading to a heightened culture of abuse of foreigners held in US detention centers abroad. This abusive culture would be made most infamous by the Abu Ghraib prison scandal, which involved members of the US Army and the CIA torturing and humiliating Iraqi detainees in March 2003. While the Bush administration tried to spin Abu Ghraib as an isolated incident, scholars such as Alette Smeulers and Sander van Niekirk argue that the prison was just "further proof of a widespread pattern" of abuse in US detention centers and that "the only thing that was particular about the Abu Ghraib case was that pictures of the abuse were brought to the attention of the media," devastating America's image, especially in the Muslim world.[18]

These reports stood in stark opposition to the military's depiction in *Hulk*, where it is highly concerned with avoiding civilian casualties (albeit American ones) and as operating within appropriate ethical boundaries. These images were often secured by the DOD itself, as the film's writers largely agreed to many of Strub's demands. These included incorporating Strub's "nonlethal" ideas, such as the sequence where pilots cause the Hulk to pass out due to altitude while riding atop an F-22 to save San Francisco, and the sequence where the military is shown dropping bunker busters to trap, rather than kill, the giant in the desert (although the rock climber was eliminated from the final script). According to Schamus, he did not object to these changes, not because he wanted to polish the military's image but because "personally I always wanted the film to be a soft PG-13; I have never much liked a lot of violence in family films, and my big thing at the time was working with Ang to try to recreate the childhood feeling of reading comics—hence the design elements of the film with multiple panels etc., which I still love." Schamus continued, "While I always wanted a certain kind of classic Universal horror intensity, I really didn't care if there was much in the way of bloodletting, so my guess is I took little or no umbrage at the non-lethal" requests made by the DOD.

On a similar note, the scene in which the military's manned helicopters crash while trying to contain the Hulk feature the pilots explicitly reporting that they are unharmed so as to deemphasize the danger of combat missions. This was another result of the DOD's influence on the script, as Strub asked for this scene to be rewritten so that the crew emerge from the helicopter to show they are OK after the Hulk leaves them in the desert (see figure 1.1). This revision exemplifies the DOD's frequent insistence on cinematic clean wars, as they "work to televisually hide" the dead and injured bodies common to war and thus "successfully erase all trace of that which anchors war to the moorings of the real."[19] Indeed, Hollywood movies featuring combat missions too often feature helicopter crashes where service members are unharmed and battle scenes where thousands of bullets are dispatched but where felled American soldiers or even permanently injured combatants are rarely featured. Such narratives work to support military recruitment efforts by downplaying the physical and emotional effects of war and help limit viewers' sensitivities to the cost of military operations abroad. The reality of combat, of course, is quite different. According to the Wounded Warrior Project, more than 52,000 US service members had been psychically wounded in the War on Terror by 2015, and as many as four hundred thousand service members now live with the "invisible wounds" of that war, including combat stress, traumatic brain injury, depression, and post-traumatic stress disorder.[20] As the US military had to actively employ stop-loss measures to ensure it had enough soldiers to fight in Iraq and Afghanistan during the time of *Hulk*'s release, one can see how important these cinematic depictions became for their recruitment efforts.

In the end, then, the Pentagon's influence on *Hulk* helped downplay the negative repercussions of combat and secure an image of the military as a brave, benevolent, and ethical force, highly concerned with protecting civilian lives from the Hulk's rampage. Although the movie was shot before the US invasion of Iraq, the DOD's manipulation of the script also helped *Hulk* serve as an important counterpoint to the state's actual performance and policies in the region, as the war in Iraq coincided closely with the film's release. Schamus, however, believes that despite the film's DOD support, the military missed a lot of the more subversive elements of the film. "I remember saying to Ang when our [DOD] trip was approved that they must not have read the script too closely," as he felt the entire story revolved around the MIC's "incompetence and obfuscation," and he considered the Hulk "as the very embodiment of 'blow back.'" Additionally, he points out that the film included a scene where the Hulk is shown throwing American tanks around in the desert while Egyptian-British musician Natasha Atlas sings an Arabic piece on the soundtrack. It is not clear if Lee included this scene to appeal to Middle Eastern audiences. The film was released in the region and may have thus included this scene to help those viewers identify with the Hulk as a victim of American military aggression. However, Schamus argues that "no one at the time seemed to make the connection between the plot and our ongoing imperial misadventures—not that we can claim any courageous or brave political chest-beating. Still, funny."

Despite these ideological subversions, however, the military was overall pleased with its final depiction in the film, as it successfully contains the threat the Hulk presents and ultimately reinforces the legitimacy of the militarized state. As Jeffrey Ewing writes, superhero narratives are always ripe with themes regarding the power and legitimacy of the state.

(b)(6) I'm very apprehensive about sending these notes to you. For one thing, they're incomplete, (b)(6) won't have (b)(6) input until later, perhaps as early as today (Monday). But the main reason for my hesitancy is that in the past we've usually been able to offer suggestions within the context of existing plot and characters. These, however, are pretty radical. I hope they don't have the effect of aggravating everyone, because we certainly aren't trying to intrude on the creative process. It's just that I see no other practical, straightforward way of communicating our concerns.

(b)(6)

DoD "Hulk" Notes of Sunday, Feb 3.

Overall: The primary purpose of these notes is civilianize the desert lab and the direct action against the Hulk, leaving only one actual deadly military strike, against the Absorbing Man at the end. All the other military operations would be nonlethal and other unconventional attempts to contain, distract, or subdue the Hulk, or to provide reconnaissance information regarding him. There are also some technical suggestions.

Pg 71, Sc 134, MAIN HALLWAY SEQUENCE: At the start of this sequence, the leader of the first unit tells Ross that the Hulk is coming right at them. Ross's comments should indicate that he has a tactical plan - obviously something caused the Hulk to emerge - what was it? He doesn't think they can stop him, but maybe they can slow him down and tire him out. Then when the military engages the Hulk, they're operating as coordinated teams, luring the Hulk from one place to another, hoping to exhaust him. So when his teams retreat, it's part of the plan, not a panicked "run for your lives!"

An alternative to helicopters attacking the Hulk would be that they spot the climber and fear that the Hulk will harm him. They fly around him to distract him and try to lure him away in another direction. He falls for it and while the climber scrambles to safety, the Hulk grabs the propellers, and the scene continues as written, except that the crew climbs from the helicopter after the Hulk leaves it lying in the sand.

An alternative to the B-52 strike is that the bomber is dropping cave bunker busters, knocking down rock formations to trap the Hulk in a box canyon, but he realizes what's happening and narrowly escapes.

Figure 1.1: Three excerpts from the DOD's script notes on *The Hulk* sent to its producers on February 3, 2002. On file with the authors.

> In short, modern states definitionally require the sovereign centralization of control over the legitimate use of violence (among other features), and the totality of these features grant advantages to states over other historical forms of political organization. The absence of monopolized control over such legitimate use of violence is a strong challenge to state sovereignty, both in political theory and in terms of the legal framework that governs states and their interrelations in the wide system of states.

Superheroes, like the Hulk, thus pose a major threat to nation-states because they force countries "to contend with heroes that cannot be effectively countered" and render their power meaningless. If heroes (or villains) exist whose power states cannot check, the state can only "maintain the illusion of sovereignty at the whim of said superpowered beings."[21] As such, the military has a vested interest in being seen as an effective challenge to the Hulk because its very legitimation (at least in the world of cinema) depends on it. Thus, it is key in *Hulk* that the military be shown containing Banner and the security threat he represents.

Finally, the film clearly lays the blame for the development of the Hulk at the feet of private military contractors, rather than at those of the military itself. After all, it is the elder Banner's experiments, against the military's wishes, that create the monstrous DNA, and it is Talbot's experiments on the Hulk that unleash his rage, thereby putting civilian populations in grave danger. This neat dichotomy between the military and its contractors, however, belies the modern nature of the American military. As Stacy Takacs writes, the military has largely courted the work of privatized military and security firms who now "provide the bulk of the logistics, training, security and support services required to stage war" because these contractors are often cheaper but, more importantly, not subject to the same types of regulation and oversight as the actual military, thus offering "an expedient way to bypass the legal and political restrictions on the use of force to achieve policy goals." Because private military contractors stand to make a lot of money from providing these services and goods, there is little incentive for them "to pursue diplomatic means to resolve security crises, and war becomes a self-perpetuating profit machine," run by both the military and its private contractors.[22] Schamus, based on our interview, clearly agrees.

Interestingly, while the military was pleased with its depiction in the final film, audiences rated *Hulk* poorly, highlighting the fact that military-added production values and positive military imagery do not always translate into box-office sales. Film critic A. O. Scott of the *New York Times* called the film "incredibly long, incredibly tedious, [and] incredibly turgid," citing the film's inconsistent acting, incoherent story line, ridiculous premise, and a CGI Hulk that mostly looks like a "Gumby on steroids" as the picture's major flaws.[23] Likewise, the film's Metacritic score averages just 54 percent, while fans on Rotten Tomatoes give it only a 29 percent approval rating, based on nearly 429,000 votes. As a result of its poor reception, Universal failed to make a second installment before 2006, even though the film's ending was clearly a setup for a sequel. This allowed the property's production (although not distribution) rights to revert back to Marvel, which then released its own version of the film, *The Incredible Hulk*, in 2008, as part of its new cinematic universe. As chapter 2 will explain, *The Incredible Hulk* did not seek US military assistance and thus the image of the armed forces is strikingly different from that depicted in Lee's version. All was not lost for the DOD within the context of the MCU, however; the 2008 release of *Iron Man* helped the military build support for both itself and its policies in the War on Terror from the very outset of the franchise, as the next section reveals.

Iron Man (2008)

When *Iron Man* launched the MCU, it established many of the stylistic and tonal elements that audiences would come to expect from Marvel films. The combination of high-octane action, quippy dialogue, and fantasy wish-fulfillment proved enormously successful and eventually turned the film franchise into the world's most lucrative. The story opens with the protagonist—billionaire playboy and military-industrialist Tony Stark—touring Afghanistan and showing off Stark Industries' latest generation of the Jericho missile. During the trip, his group is ambushed by Afghan rebels, and Tony is seriously wounded when the rebels fire Stark-produced shrapnel bombs at them. His chest is riddled with tiny pieces of metal, and he passes out. Stark then awakens to find himself kidnapped by a group of militants called the Ten Rings, who are holding him captive until he builds a Jericho missile for their use against local villagers. Meanwhile, his fellow captive, Yinsen, builds an electromagnetic device that is surgically grafted into Stark's chest to prevent the shrapnel from reaching his heart. Stark and Yinsen develop a miniature arc reactor to power the device before building a prototype of a flying suit of armor that Tony intends to help them escape the Afghani cave network where they are being held.

While Yinsen dies during the battle, Stark escapes and is rescued and returned to the United States by the air force. At an impromptu press conference, he announces that he is shutting down the weapons manufacturing wing of Stark Industries before disappearing from public view to refine his design for the Iron Man suit. Meanwhile, it emerges that Stark's number two, Obadiah Stane, has been secretly selling weapons to the militants and even hired them to kidnap Stark as part of his plot to take over the company. Stark completes work on his Iron Man exosuit and uses it to take revenge on the Afghan insurgents and to liberate a town they have taken over. Stane then builds his own version of the Iron Man suit, which is much larger and cruder than Stark's design, leading to a showdown between the two. Stark prevails, and at the end of the film, he announces to the world: "I am Iron Man."

Like *Hulk*, *Iron Man* was heavily supported by the Pentagon, and especially by the US Air Force, which provided "script research, wardrobe and dialogue assistance, on-location filming at Edwards AFB, and filming access to F-22, C-17 aircraft, and HH-60 helicopters."[24] They also provided on-set technical advice through the Combined Air Operations Center, 150 extras "to play military members from various services and Afghan nationals during days of filming," and the deployment of an F-22 Raptor "for directed photography."[25] In exchange for this support, the producers allowed the DOD to revise and approve the final script and agreed to "mutually beneficial marketing initiatives" after the movie's release to encourage military recruitment.[26] While it is unclear what these initiatives were, the agreement left air force captain Christian Hodge, who also served as the film's project officer, lauding the film's recruitment value because it "makes us look like rock stars," while Master Sgt. Larry Belen said he hoped that people would "walk away from this movie with a really good impression of the Air Force, like they got about the Navy seeing Top Gun."[27]

While documentation on the exact script changes requested by the DOD is not available for *Iron Man* as it is for *Hulk*, the relationship between the film and the US military was undoubtedly a complimentary one. For example, *Iron Man* champions the US invasion of Afghanistan after the events of 9/11 "by depicting it as a space of threat to America," as full of villainous terrorists, and as "a space that must be contained and controlled with military might."[28] The film, like the Bush administration, also contended that the "proper response" to a terrorist threat is militarized "violence, not diplomacy," giving further credence to the US invasion of the region. Indeed, director Jon Favreau said that when the Ten Rings are brutalizing nearby villagers, he consciously emphasized the terrorists' capacity to employ high-grade weapons. The film had to "make it so that everyone can root for [our superhero]," he stated. "If you just had Iron Man flying into some place full of a bunch of terrorists with low-tech weapons, and he's a high-tech American hero in that part of the world, it's tough to get behind that the same way you get behind Spider-Man saving a woman being mugged in Central Park."[29] While it is unclear if the Pentagon had a hand in shaping the depiction of the Ten Rings, Favreau's admission echoes script concerns the DOD had on *Clear and Present Danger* (1994), which portrays a highly trained team of elite US soldiers dropping into Colombia to take on a powerful drug cartel. The Pentagon insisted the filmmakers make changes so that "the scripted enemies [are] more than the undisciplined, semi-trained campesinos that are slaughtered by US Army personnel" and to "alleviate the depiction of US forces defeating 'innocent' or 'inculpable' guard personnel."[30] In order to make US violence seem justified, in other words, the enemy has to be seen as a deadly, culpable, and capable threat.

Iron Man also helped the DOD garner public support for its cyborg soldier research and development projects.[31] A military-funded project carried out by MIT and the University of California at Berkeley, for example, spent tens of millions of dollars developing the Future Force Warrior—a new development in combat gear featuring a headgear subsystem that provided maps, routes, wireless communications, and "integrated small arms protection." It also offered an "on-board physiological and medical sensor suite" that provided data on the wearer's body temperature, heart rate, blood pressure, hydration, stress levels, and sleep status.[32] While the suits were meant to roll out in 2010, the final product never materialized, a fate that also befell the US Special Operations Command's attempts to create their own TALOS (Tactical Assault Light Operator Suit) technology, which, like the Iron Man suit, was also meant to equip soldiers with flexible, bulletproof exoskeletons, a visual augmentation system, and communications technology. These suits, which cost taxpayers tens of millions of dollars, could ultimately not perform in close combat situations, and by 2019, both projects had been officially scrapped.[33] By linking these projects in press releases to the popularity of the Iron Man movies, however, the DOD was able to build consensus for their costs for almost a decade and mentally prepared the public for a new type of cyborg warfare. In fact, Jon Favreau revealed that the military even asked if it could use some of the *Iron Man* scenes to drum up support for its development projects. Favreau noted that the armed forces wanted to use his footage "as a demonstration of what their stuff [might do] because it can't do it yet."[34]

Deradicalizing Iron Man: Diluting Criticism of the War on Terror and the Military-Industrial Complex

Despite the Pentagon's support of *Iron Man*, the film is not a wholly positive depiction of the US military, the War on Terror, or the MIC. Stark's character arc sees him starting out as a shallow, glib, cynical billionaire who makes ironic references to "peace" and "freedom," while profiteering from the war in Afghanistan. Following his escape from the insurgents, he then renounces the weapons manufacturing industry, saying, "I realized I have more to offer the world than making things that blow up," and for much of the rest of the film, he risks his own life to save and protect others, abandoning many—but not all—of his self-centered playboy attitudes. This arc was praised by critics both for elevating the superhero genre and for its political messaging, which was seen as satirizing the ongoing War on Terror. The film was variously described as having "a sprinkle of anti-war and redemption themes," as being a "pacifist statement" and "militantly anti-war profiteer," with reviewers describing Iron Man as a "pacifist superhero" and as someone who "shuns arms manufacturing . . . [to] save Mankind."[35] What all these reviews overlook, however, is that Stark, having announced that he has more to offer the world than blowing things up, spends the second and third acts of the film developing a high-tech means of blowing things up. In effect, the Iron Man suit is still a symbol and manifestation of the military-industrial complex. The only crucial difference is that Stark alone is in control of it.

This development could be seen as an implicit criticism of the US military, as Stark, an individual of exceptional wealth and technical brilliance, does what the Pentagon cannot do. He takes down the terrorists menacing Galmira and, as he suggests in *Iron Man 2*, privatizes world peace. This is also emphasized when Rhodey calls up Tony after his assault on Galmira to ask if he has "any tech in the area," and Tony responds, "Sounds like someone stepped in and did your job for you." But while *Iron Man* addresses anxieties that the MIC "is controlled by greedy CEOs, who, motivated by profit, make and sell weapons to whoever will buy them," the film largely fails to critique that same complex because it reduces the system to just two individuals—a good war profiteer (Stark) and a bad one (Stane)—obscuring how the system itself relies on "near permanent war to sustain itself," instead implying that there are just a few bad apples that need to be removed from the system for it to work reliably and righteously.[36]

This lack of true criticism of the MIC in *Iron Man* is further highlighted by looking at the earlier 2004 version of the script, which was revised by David Hayter from the original script written by Miles Millar and Alfred Gough. This story is considerably more antiwar and critical of the weapons industry than the finished film, further demonstrating how weak the final film's critique of the MIC really is. In the 2004 draft, Tony's father, Howard Stark, is still alive, running Stark Industries, the massive weapons manufacturing business, which Tony opposes while working on developing advanced technologies for peaceful ends. When others suggest that Tony adapt his inventions into weapons, he repeatedly rejects this idea, reiterating, "No military contracts."[37] Tony discovers that Howard and fellow military industrialist Justin Hammer have been stealing his designs nonetheless, in order to weaponize and sell them under the table to North Korea and other "rogue states." He thus creates the Iron Man suit as a means of fighting back against his father and the MIC, whereas in the finished film, Stark's suit actually supplements the system.

The climax of the 2004 story sees Hammer and Howard Stark try to assassinate the US president so that his more hawkish vice president will take over. Hammer also tries to kill Tony by dropping him out of a Sikorsky helicopter. Hammer, who clearly represents the worst of US imperialism, rails at Tony before dropping him, asking, "Do you realize that the United States has bases strategically placed around the world? America is the last remaining superpower. Why do we negotiate with antagonistic countries, when we should be conquering them? With just one Presidential order, we could secure the entire world in just days."[38] When their presidential assassination attempt fails, however, Hammer and Howard employ four massive Stark Industries warships disguised as oil tankers to attack the US Naval Academy in Annapolis, obliterating navy and coast guard ships, in an attempt to usurp the conventional military with their new drone army and execute a coup d'état. Stark Industries' drones also attack Annapolis and repel counterattacks by the US military, leading to Tony joining the fight and helping defeat the drone army, not unlike what happens at the end of *Iron Man 2*. While Tony ends up fighting on the same side as the US military, as in the finished *Iron Man*, he only does so because they are under attack by the more dangerous force that is his father's drone army.

As such, the original script not only criticized the moral corruption of the arms industry but characterized the industry as seeking to rule the globe through violence. It also presented a much more explicit image of US military inadequacy and thus the need for superheroes to intervene and resolve the conflicts of the post-9/11 world. All of these elements, however, were diluted in the 2007 version or jettisoned entirely. Howard Stark and Justin Hammer were watered down from military industrial megalomaniacs into the Obadiah Stane character, who merely sells weapons to terrorists to increase profits and help him take over the company. Tony Stark briefly flirts with antiwar sentiments instead of being committed to them throughout, and he creates the Iron Man suit to take revenge on his insurgent captors, not on the arms industry itself. His sidekick James Rhodes was also changed from chief of security at Stark Industries in the 2004 version to the US Air Force liaison with weapons manufacturers in the film's final version, further solidifying Stark's complimentary partnership with the American military.

Likewise, at the end of the finished film, when Stane dons a bigger and more powerful armored suit to fight Tony, it is one of the few scenes that survived from the 2004 screenplay, except in that script, it is Howard who fights Tony. In the 2004 story, the suit that Howard uses is called War Machine, an obvious reference to the military's industries and the way they encourage perpetual war to remain profitable. The name War Machine does not appear in the 2008 film but was recycled for the sequel when Rhodes steals an armored suit and hands it over to the Pentagon so they can have their own in-house Iron Man. In the 2004 story, War Machine is a villainous overlord, but in the finished *Iron Man* films, he is our hero's best friend and sidekick.

Perhaps the crucial element that distinguishes the 2004 story from the eventual film, however, is who owns and controls the Iron Man weapon. In the 2004 script, Tony tells Hammer, "Better weaponry isn't going to restore order anywhere."[39] This is a total rejection of the military-industrial way of life and of the Pentagon's actions around the world. In the finished film, this message is inverted, most notably in the sequence when Stark develops the Mk II suit. He tells his AI assistant, J.A.R.V.I.S., to keep all the designs on his private server, because "I don't want [the Iron Man suit] ending up in the wrong hands. Maybe in mine, it can do some good." While this is an evolution from Stark's initial attitude in the film that "peace means having a bigger stick than the other guy," it is a significant departure from Stark's views in the 2004 script altogether.

This process of deradicalization continued during the production of the 2007 script. In a scene during Stark's captivity, Raza, the head of the Ten Rings insurgent cell, shows off his vast collection of weapons, including Stark Industries hardware. Stark asks him where they got these weapons, but Raza's reply is in a foreign language, without subtitles. Favreau revealed that the original dialogue had Raza saying, "Carter, Reagan, Bush, Clinton, Bush" before another insurgent adds, "They are all gifts," which Favreau said was a reference to how "weapons have been pouring into this part of the world for decades, under the administrations of both parties." Favreau explained that these lines were changed in the final story because they were "very sensitive" and "didn't sit well in the movie,"[40] presumably because it laid blame for Middle Eastern terrorism at the foot of the American MIC at the very time the United States was occupying that region in retribution for the 9/11 attacks.

In the end, the finished *Iron Man* film depicts Tony Stark operating outside of the military's chain of command and contains some limited criticisms of the arms industry. However, the movie still functions as a soft power promotion for the US military's expansionist approach in the world and contains several memorable sequences that are positive images of the Pentagon. One comes just after Tony has broken out of captivity and is wandering the deserts of Afghanistan (actually Lone Pine, California) when all of a sudden, a pair of air force Pave Hawk helicopters swoop in to rescue him, emphasizing the military's noncombat/rescue roles in a heroic light.[41] Shortly following this rescue, Tony is returned to the United States in the back of an Air Force C-130, and his arrival at Edwards AFB, complete with swelling music and tearful friends waiting for him, is a proud and poignant moment. Given that it has been established that Tony flew out to Afghanistan on his own private plane, the only reason to have him return via Edwards AFB is to make the military look good.

The Pentagon's negotiations probably also helped remove a scene from the 2007 script, where the air force actually shoots down Iron Man. In the final film, after Stark builds the Mk II suit, he sees a news item about terrorists attacking Galmira, Yinsen's hometown. A journalist shows him photographs revealing that Stark Industries–produced weapons are being used in the attacks, so Tony flies to Afghanistan to fight back. Using the Mk II armor, he defeats the terrorists, destroys their weapons, and hands their leader over to the local villagers so they can engage in frontier justice. As Tony flies off, he is detected on radar by the US Air Force, who sends two F-22 Raptors to intercept him, not knowing who or what they are dealing with but believing him to be a hostile aircraft in a no-fly zone. During their *Top Gun*–esque midair duel, Iron Man crashes through the wing of one of the F-22s, causing the pilot to punch out. In the 2007 script, the air force continues its pursuit of Iron Man as he hurtles toward Earth to try to release the parachute of the falling pilot, and at the end of the scene, the remaining F-22 fires on Iron Man, shooting him out of the sky. This was changed in the final cut so that after he successfully rescues the pilot and the parachute opens (which also reinforces the concept of clean war), Iron Man flies off, and Rhodey covers up for the incident by saying it was a training exercise. As Favreau revealed in an unofficial commentary for the *Iron Man* DVD, when Rhodey asks Stark, "Now what am I supposed to tell to the press?" about the incident, Stark's reply, "Training exercise. Isn't that the usual BS?" was improvised by Robert Downey Jr., and they ran with it.[42] While this cover-up moment could be seen as critical of the DOD,[43] it is a substantial improvement on the original scene. From the DOD's point of view, it is better for Rhodey to be shown in a comical moment covering up for Iron Man than for the air force to be shown blasting a beloved superhero out of the atmosphere.

Finally, in the script's press conference scene, Tony expresses doubt about not just his own company's role in the war in Afghanistan but the entire mission, saying, "I thought we were doing good here . . . I can't say that anymore. The system is broken, there's no accountability whatsoever."[44] During on-set improvisation, this line became, "I saw young Americans killed by the very weapons I created to defend them and protect them." As a result, this scene, which could have cast doubt on the entire war, became a one-sided reminder of the need to protect Americans and American interests. In fact, the only scene in the entire film that depicts the pain of ordinary Afghan people shows them suffering at the hands of the Ten Rings, the militant cell that had kidnapped Stark, not at the hands of the US military. Aside from one weapons test and an ambush, the only depiction of the US military in Afghanistan is when they rescue Stark in the desert. Like in *Hulk*, this omission belies the reality on the ground. In 2008, the year *Iron Man* debuted, the United Nations reported that roughly 2,100 Afghan civilians were killed as a result of the armed conflict in that year alone, a 40 percent increase in the death toll over the previous year and the highest since the US invasion began in 2001.[45] Additionally, over the course of the entire war, 111,000 Afghans, including civilians, soldiers, and militants, are estimated to have been killed, in addition to the 2,372 US service members and the roughly twenty thousand more US service members wounded as well.[46]

Iron Man 2 (2010)

Jon Favreau returned to direct *Iron Man 2*, which premiered as the third installment of the MCU's Phase One series after *The Incredible Hulk* was released in 2008. The sequel essentially revolves around three concerns that further conceptualize the relationship of private industry to the MIC and reinforce the righteousness of US military–backed violence. The first is Tony Stark's struggle to prevent the US government from appropriating the rights to his Iron Man suit, while the second involves Tony trying to handle his own existential crisis, as the arc reactor in his chest has started to poison his body. The film's third main plotline involves Russian engineer Ivan Vanko (Mickey Rourke), who is seeking to ruin Tony as he feels the Stark family never gave his own father, who worked on the original arc reactor technology, the proper credit or payment his labor deserved. As such, Vanko teams up with Justin Hammer, Stark's rival in the military contractor business, to help him develop a competing version of the suit, which Vanko then launches against the civilians attending Stark's In Defense of Peace Expo. A final climactic battle ensues with Iron Man and Lt. Col. James Rhodes defeating Vanko and his army of competitor drones.

Like *Iron Man* and *Hulk*, *Iron Man 2* enjoyed significant production assistance from the DOD. According to its Motion Picture and Television Production Assistance Agreement, it allowed the producers to again shoot at Edwards AFB for three days, granting them access to numerous locations, including the US Marine Corps' HMM-764 hangar, the Shadow Maintenance hangar, the air traffic control tower, and the Gun Butt weapons test structure and flightline. The filmmakers were also allowed to film a plethora of static aircraft, including the 0-17, 8-1, 8-2, F-22, F-35, F16, and CH-46, which were used in the film as background pieces, and the DOD agreed to provide roughly 125 extras to play military members on set, all of whom conformed "to individual Military Service regulations governing age, height, weight, uniform, grooming, appearance, and conduct standards."[47] An entry located in the DOD's Hollywood database also reveals that the military "provided unclassified technological specs" to the filmmakers, "set up research trips to Air Force bases, and gave the visual effects department access so they could meticulously and accurately reflect realistic aircraft markings on the War Machine character."[48] The air force also assisted in the designing of War Machine and provided additional extras for the film, including twenty-six airmen who participated in the closing ceremony sequence at the end of the film. The Marine Corps also provided Reserve Squadron personnel at Edwards AFB and was on set for review of "the drone scene," where Rhodey lands at Edwards in the War Machine exosuit.[49]

Alongside the introduction of the Black Widow character, the scenes shot at Edwards AFB are among the standout elements in *Iron Man 2*. For example, after stealing one of Tony's suits to stop his rowdy behavior at a birthday party, Rhodey returns to the base, where he does a *Top Gun*–style flyby of the tower, complete with an extreme-sports, GoPro-styled shot from inside the suit, as he makes his final approach to land outside of the hangar. The dynamic cinematography coupled with a dramatic score and the airpower featured in the background helps Rhodes's arrival feel powerful, patriotic, and triumphant (see figures 1.2, 1.3, 1.4, and 1.5). The fact that he is wearing a Stark suit also helps symbolically represent American troops as superheroes themselves.

The film's producer, Jeremy Latcham, told us that this sequence probably contains the largest amount of military assets ever featured in a movie, explaining that because Rhodes is a military man, the DOD was very eager to support the film. They even "organized a training exercise that coincided with our shoot, where they reworked their schedule to

Figure 1.2: Still of Lt. Col. James Rhodes landing at Edwards AFB in *Iron Man 2*.

Figure 1.3: POV shot of Edwards AFB from Rhodes's suit in *Iron Man 2*.

fly all of those planes out to California to allow for six billion dollars' worth of assets to be on the base that day." While Latcham admits that such efforts make it "dicey" when trying to determine whether or not such exercises are responsible uses of taxpayers' money, he states that from a producer's perspective, it was "great," because "we had access to all of this really cool stuff, which made the film look fantastic. It

Figure 1.4: Director's indirect-subjective shot while Rhodes makes his landing.

Figure 1.5: Rhodes in a Stark suit near the hangars on Edwards AFB.

was truly mind-boggling how many planes are in our wide shot when Rhodey lands."[50]

The character of Rhodey, Latcham argued, was also one of the main benefits that the DOD reaped from the film, as the air force "was able to portray a really talented actor as a high-ranking African American military officer" who made that position "look really cool and glamorous." Indeed, by featuring Cheadle in the role of a funny, competent, patriotic officer, and as a good friend to Stark, the air force was able to promote a public image of an integrated service that rewards, through advancement, Black airmen. But again this image somewhat belies reality. In 2016, the *Air Force Times* reported that after examining six years of statistics on promotions and selection rates, the figures indicate "that if you're a minority, your odds of being tapped for promotion—especially to the most senior officer and enlisted ranks—are not as good as they are for white airmen." Indeed, the group found that in 2015, 73.2 percent of eligible white officers were selected for promotion to the lieutenant colonel ranking, which is the one Rhodes possesses, "which is far higher than the 63.8 percent selection rate for [eligible] black majors, the 67.5 percent selection rate for officers of Asian descent, and the 47.6 percent selection rate for multi-racial officers."[51] Furthermore, the air force has been under increasing fire for its "inability to fix long-standing racial differences in its military justice system," which advocacy groups argue lead "to black airmen being punished disproportionately more" within the service for a variety of infractions. Protect Our Defenders president Don Christensen, a retired colonel and the air force's former chief prosecutor, argued in 2020 that the air force has long tried to "cover up data showing racial disparities in punishments by repeatedly concealing records" and "embellishing" its accomplishments, leading him to conclude that the air force "has done nothing in the last four years to solve the problem" whatsoever.[52]

Despite, or precisely because of, these factors, the air force was pleased with its depiction in *Iron Man 2*, and they promoted their work on the film in short videos and articles on both the air force's official website and on Military.com.[53] But despite this public affirmation, the film's depiction of the US Armed Forces is not without nuance or complication, although, as in the original *Iron Man*, these complications eventually resolve in the military's favor. More specifically, at the start of *Iron Man 2*, Tony opens the Stark Expo, where he boasts that "Uncle Sam can rest" because the Iron Man suit cannot be beaten by any foreign power. The Senate Armed Forces Committee takes a different view. Because the Iron Man suit is essentially a high-tech weapon, Senator Stern (Garry Shandling) claims that the government should have ownership of it, especially since Stark, a playboy still prone to drunken, reckless behavior, is not a trustworthy steward of the technology. Furthermore, when Rhodes is called to testify at the hearing, he notes that "because Tony Stark does not operate within any branch of the government, he represents a national security risk," even though he also assesses that Tony's assets outweigh his liabilities. When the Senate argues that Tony should be incorporated into the governmental structure, or at the least hand over the Iron Man technology, Tony quips that he is "not a joiner," and when Stern argues that the government needs access to his technology because other countries are already trying to replicate it, Tony shows the committee videos of those failed attempts, arguing that no one else is even close to replicating the suit in the next five to twenty years.

The questions about Tony's stewardship of the Iron Man armor are central to the film and amplified by the fact that Tony's arc reactor is slowly killing him. Facing the reality of his impending death, Tony begins acting erratically, giving his entire modern art collection to the Boy Scouts of America and turning over control of Stark Industries to his love interest and PA, Pepper Potts. The media personalities in the film amplify the concern over Tony's behavior, with CNN asking, "Can he still protect us?" and Bill O'Reilly questioning Tony's transfer of his CEO position, asking what Potts's qualifications are and claiming that "Tony Stark is not looking out for us and is done." During what Tony thinks is his last birthday party, he further fuels these concerns, as he gets wildly drunk while wearing the Iron Man suit, begins irresponsibly shooting watermelons as a party trick, puts lives at risk, and causes serious property damage.

As Daniel Malloy writes in "TM and © Stark Industries: Iron Man and Property Right," the fact that the Iron Man suit and the technology that powers it are owned by Stark Industries "raises some complex philosophical questions about property and responsibility." Because Tony's suit is capable of enormous destruction, he has a greater responsibility about how he uses the suit and who, if anyone, he lends the suit to. "In allowing someone to use the armor," Malloy writes, "Stark Industries has the responsibility of gauging what type of person this is. . . . If there is a reasonable expectation that person will use the armor for the wrong reasons, then Stark Industries is [morally] responsible for the consequences."[54] In *Iron Man 2*, the American military and the public are asking these same questions of Tony, especially since his flippant attitude toward authority, party boy lifestyle, and increasingly erratic behavior are fueling, rather than quelling, fears that he is not a suitable steward of the weapon.

Given this backdrop, it is significant that as Tony grows more reckless at his birthday party, Rhodes decides to forcefully end Tony's shenanigans by stealing another Stark suit to force his friend into submission. While Rhodes's move is championed by viewers because Stark clearly presents a physical danger to his party guests and because it saves Iron Man from further embarrassing himself (he has already peed in his suit as a party trick), the fact that Rhodes steals a secondary suit and returns with it to Edwards AFB for study provides the film with a complex set of legal and philosophical questions. Because Stark invented the Iron Man suit and has always refused to give his technology to the military, Potts correctly argues that Stark Industries has proprietary claim on both the suit and its operating platform and that Rhodes's actions constitute the military's theft of that property. Interestingly, in the Marvel Comic Universe, a similar story line unfolds when Stark Industries is contracted as a military supplier, providing them with all of the weapons they desire, *except* for the Iron Man suit, which Stark wishes to keep for himself. All of their contracts stipulate that the government has no rights to the Iron Man technology and that only Tony's fictitious bodyguard can wear the suit. The instant Stark reveals that he is really Iron Man in the comic series, however, his military contracts are voided, and the government immediately begins to develop weapons based on the technology, leaving Stark with no legal recourse to object.[55]

The film, however, presents a far more nebulous story line because here the military has no legal right to appropriate Tony's technology; Rhodes simply steals it and gives it to the air force without Tony's permission. Malloy writes that leaving the legal issues aside, from a moral-philosophical standpoint, the government may be justified in this appropriation because it will "allow it to better defend its citizens from superpowered threats," and this may be why the film, as described in the Edwards AFB scenes above, makes Rhodey's arrival seem patriotic and triumphant. In other words, by taking some of the most "advanced weaponry ever designed," the government, the film suggests, is now able to perform its protective functions "all the more effectively," and the scene visually links service members with the very power and glamour of superheroes. However, Malloy notes that the military's actions are also morally disturbing, as Rhodey's actions clearly represent the theft of Tony's intellectual and physical property and because "there is no way to guarantee that Stark's technology will only be used for protection and defense" by the military, as opposed to aggression, greed, and occupation.[56]

But while it first appears that the military—via Rhodey and those at Edwards AFB—are a thieving enterprise, in traditional Hollywood fashion the American military's benevolence and trustworthiness is challenged only temporarily, and the rest of the film works to justify the military's moves. Most importantly, when Tony is testifying before the Senate, he states that no one needs to worry about his sole ownership of the Iron Man suit because every other country is at least a decade behind its technology. What he doesn't realize is that Ivan Vanko fully understands how to make a functioning competitor product and, in partnership with Hammer, is capable of creating a whole army of them. Tony's arrogance thus proves dangerous and misguided, suggesting that the military was correct to worry that Iron Man alone is not enough to protect humanity and that he must work primarily as a supplement to American military power. Furthermore, the film never punishes the military for taking Stark's property; while Tony verbally jabs Rhodey for taking his suit without authorization, in the end he allows him to keep it and to even use it to fight alongside him in the film's final scenes against Vanko. The message is clear that Tony trusts the film's main military representative to handle the suit responsibly, believing that he will use it only for good, rather than for ill purposes. The scene's climactic battle, which features Rhodes and Tony outfitted in their suits, also suggests that the best way for the United States to defeat foreign threats is for tech geniuses like Stark to partner with military specialists like Rhodes who know how to strategically win battles. In both *Iron Man 2* and *Iron Man 3*, Rhodes must give Tony mini-lessons on combat strategy, including the roles of high ground vs. low ground, in order to defeat the films' main villains. The films suggest that the two are stronger together than they are apart. Thus it is no surprise that in the end, Tony doesn't sue or prevent the military from keeping Rhodes's suit even though he still refuses to be subsumed into any governmental chain of command. In fact, in *Iron Man 3*, Rhodes not only gets to keep Tony's suit, but he also gets to rebrand himself as a new superhero called Iron Patriot, after the name War Machine tests as too aggressive with focus groups in the film's narrative—an ironic commentary on the importance of the military's branding of itself as a benevolent rather than hostile force on the world stage.

Conclusion

The DOD's involvement with *Hulk* and the Iron Man movies are just some examples of the collaboration it has offered to recent superhero films. For *Captain America: The First Avenger* (2011), Camp Edwards also allowed Marvel's crews to film at its World War II barracks, justifying the decision because of the film's blockbuster status and because Captain America is a former soldier who possesses "the values of today's American soldier."[57] Chris Evans, the actor who plays Captain America, and Scarlett Johansson, the actress who plays Black Widow, also partnered with the United Service Organizations in 2016 to visit thousands of service members in Afghanistan, Turkey, Qatar, and Germany to boost morale by hosting variety shows and Q and A's. The DOD, as discussed at the start of this chapter, also assisted *Captain Marvel*, *Man of Steel*, *Fantastic Four: The Rise of the Silver Surfer*, *Suicide Squad*, and the comic book adaptation *GI Joe: Rise of Cobra* (2009). While it is difficult to know exactly how the Pentagon was able to influence each of these films at the scene level, it is clear that the military has worked for nearly two decades to positively portray its branches and legitimize its power through contemporary superhero films, and that these films, in turn, have worked to sanitize war, legitimize military authority, build support for US foreign policy, encourage costly research and development projects, and promote American military benevolence and righteousness in the public's mind. The films highlighted in this chapter also reveal how the military is invested in presenting itself as wholly separate from its private weapons contractors and security providers, with DOD-assisted texts regularly laying the blame for any corruption, greed, warmongering, or ethics violations at the feet of those contractors. This is not unique to the superhero genre, however; as Takacs writes, television media also scapegoats private contractors to "disavow responsibility" for questionable and aggressive foreign policies, "displacing the bad outcomes onto irresponsible private operators, whose symbolic sacrifice" often works to "redeem the mission and its 'official' operatives (that is soldiers, sailors, airmen and marines)."[58]

Of course, none of this means that superhero films have been unable to explore criticisms of the military itself. Film producers remain free to make movies outside of the Pentagon's full support program; they just cost more. And as Marvel Studios began to emerge from their bankruptcy woes, it gained the financial power to do just that. In fact, as Emily Todd VanDerWerff argues, while the Phase One movies of the MCU began as cultural responses to 9/11, featuring vulnerable but exceptional individuals who find the strength to overcome tragedy, Phase Two morphed into "stories about beings and organizations with nearly infinite power that would do whatever necessary to keep the homeland safe." The MCU's Phase Three movies then grapple "with the costs of the retribution they've doled out and the security systems they've built."[59] In other words, the MCU has grown increasingly critical of military and state authority, and thus, several of its films question the strength, "cleanliness," and benevolence of American military power, as evidenced by the next chapter.

"I TOLD YOU, I DON'T WANT TO JOIN YOUR SUPER-SECRET BOY BAND"

SUPERHEROES AND THE ANTI-ESTABLISHMENT NARRATIVE

2

In *War, Politics, and Superheroes*, Marc Di Paolo writes that politically themed superhero stories generally fall into one of three categories. The first—the colonial category—is almost extinct, having flourished during the Victorian gothic era. It features a superhero who travels overseas to an "untouched, uncivilized country to civilize it and plunder its natural resources, often before a third power stakes claim to the land first." Far more common in the contemporary era are the establishment and anti-establishment narratives. The former features superheroes who act "to preserve the social status quo" and/or to protect "the government and the populace from invading foreign hordes, enemy saboteurs, and homegrown criminals and terrorists." In anti-establishment narratives, "the superhero stands in opposition to an evil governmental, corporate or aristocratic villain," and consumers are encouraged to recognize themselves as victims of either an oppressive or incompetent system.[1]

While they are not without nuance, the DOD-assisted films discussed in chapter 1 are best categorized as establishment narratives, as they feature themes that reinforce the status quo. They support US foreign policy, lay villainy at the feet of private contractors rather than the government, and promote the legitimization of state violence through the image of a benevolent and righteous military. For the most part, the superheroes in the MCU's Phase One films—such as Iron Man, Captain America, Thor, and the Avengers—also work with, rather than against, the government, as evidenced by their partnerships with military officers, like Rhodey, or the agents of S.H.I.E.L.D. That does not mean, however, that superhero movies—even ones produced within the same cinematic universe—fail to generate anti-establishment narratives that challenge those very same concepts. Oppositional narratives are in fact vital to the serialized storytelling of cinematic universes, because, as MCU directors Joe and Anthony Russo explain, if your heroes and villains fail to evolve, face new types of threats, or adopt new perspectives, viewers are left with a mere "sequelization" effect that grows tiresome and unsustainable over the years.[2]

Scholars have also suggested that anti-establishment narratives were inevitable in the current resurgence of superhero films due to the prolonged nature of the War on Terror. As Peter Bruno writes, pre-9/11 and early post-9/11 superhero films reflected "a certain moral clarity in regards to its heroes," but later post-9/11 films operate "under the state of exception. That is, post 9/11 superheroes live in the world of the Patriot Act and Guantanamo Bay, where rights and laws can be suspended indefinitely in service of security against any threat deemed too dangerous." Such realities have spawned the creation of morally complex heroes, such as Batman in the *Dark Knight* trilogy, who uses surveillance technology to spy on every Gotham resident and tortures the Joker in order to keep others safe.[3] The post-9/11 environment has also led some contemporary stories, but especially those in the later phases of the MCU, to feature American institutions as a primary source of villainy. Indeed, Allan Austin explains that while DC-based films have long favored villains like the Joker, who are "external and 'other,' exotic, irrational, [and] incomprehensible," Marvel has "instead examined the internal American system as the source of its villains, who act in rational, albeit self-interested, ways." While the protagonists in both franchises occasionally take the law into their own hands, DC's "Superman and Batman spend little time considering, let alone critiquing, the system's problems and shortcomings" because evil, exotic villains make such considerations "superfluous."[4]

As the early Iron Man movies demonstrate, the MCU has always included greedy military contractors in its exploration of villainy, but the franchise's anti-establishment themes become far more prominent in its Phase Two and Three narratives when the value of the entire security state is called into question (although these themes are also featured as early as *The Incredible Hulk*). Most of these anti-establishment narratives did not receive Department of Defense production support because, by definition, they depict the military and other governmental structures as a dangerous threat to civilians/society, or because they challenge the common mythologies the DOD wishes to propagate in American culture. While several anti-establishment narratives exist within the MCU (and DCEU), this chapter explores the narratives of just five—*The Incredible Hulk*, *The Avengers*, *Iron Man 3*, *Captain America: Civil War*, and *Captain America: The Winter Soldier*. These films help contrast the nature of DOD-assisted and establishment narratives with unassisted, anti-establishment narratives, and to explore their cultural importance as popular and political texts.

The Incredible Hulk (2008)

As explained in the first chapter, Universal's *Hulk* mostly reads as an establishment narrative and received robust assistance from the DOD, but due to its poor reception, the studio failed to make a sequel before 2006, allowing the property's production rights to revert back to Marvel, who created its own version in 2008. Released just seven weeks after *Iron Man*, *The Incredible Hulk* is often considered the odd man out of the MCU. Not only is it the only fully anti-establishment narrative in Phase One, it also starred Edward Norton as the green giant, who was then replaced by Mark Ruffalo in all future installments. It is also the only Phase One film not to feature Nick Fury, and "conventions such as mid- or post-credits scenes had not yet been solidified, making this the only MCU film to completely end when the credits roll."[5] While *The Incredible Hulk* is also the lowest grossing of all MCU films to date, its director, Louis Leterrier, successfully worked to correct much of what failed in Ang Lee's version in regard to characterization. As Michael Curley writes, Lee's version forgot what made Bruce Banner/the Hulk a hero. In the comics,

> most of the time, Bruce Banner is a hero because he is all that stands between the world and this destructive monster. Keeping himself in control and trying to cure himself are his main objectives, as well as keeping himself out of the hands of people who would try to exploit the Hulk. Even so, Banner sometimes sees situations where people need help, and he helps them even though it may risk unleashing the Hulk. Other times, he finds a situation where he can direct the Hulk at a villain for the greater good.[6]

The Incredible Hulk works to restore these qualities, as it features a more heroic Bruce Banner, who at the film's end agrees to put himself in harm's way by transforming into the Hulk in order to save New York City from Abomination—an equal, if not bigger-sized giant, created from the same gamma-based materials. In this way, it is Banner/Hulk that functions as the film's main hero, stepping in when the military fails, whereas in Lee's version, the military plays the heroic role as it works to subdue the threat the Hulk poses to society.

In order to reposition the Hulk as the hero, the writers of *The Incredible Hulk* made over the military's representation in the anti-establishment tradition in order to villainize them. For example, in *The Incredible Hulk*'s origin story, there are no evil scientists or third-party defense contractors to function as evildoers. Instead, General Ross and Emil Blonsky (a captain in the British Royal Marines on loan to the US Special Operations Command) serve this role. General Ross tells Blonsky that he lied to Banner about the experiments the two were working on for the military, telling Banner that the projects were trying to alleviate human diseases. Banner believed in this good cause so much that when the program couldn't get human trial approval, he injected the material into his own body, but because of the deception, he became the Hulk instead of curing the human race. In reality, Ross knew that the experiments were aimed at developing a new super-soldier program (a concept taken directly from Marvel's Ultimate Comics in the early 2000s) to make the American military unbeatable—a narrative element that helped the franchise connect to *Captain America* in the universe building for which the studio is now so renowned.

As in Lee's movie, General Ross is shown using nonlethal methods to contain the Hulk when he is unleashed, but in Leterrier's movie the motive is different. Ross does not want to protect Bruce Banner, the human, or the civilian population from the Hulk. Rather, he wants to save the Hulk so he can protect his prototype and engineer more super-soldiers for his army—a move that seems reckless given his inability to contain the one creature that has been engineered thus far. Indeed, throughout the film, the military only wants to weaponize the Hulk and the science that produced him, despite the clear risks in doing so. Furthermore, when Ross realizes that Banner is incapable of controlling his rage or destruction, he seeks to capture him, but as military weapons appear ineffective for the task, he injects a smaller dose of the gamma serum into Blonsky. Throughout the film, Blonsky is tasked with fighting the Hulk, but because he does not have the same amount of power, he proves ineffectual. As a result, Blonsky threatens Mr. Blue, a university science professor studying the Hulk in order to cure him, and Blue, under duress, injects him with Banner's blood, thereby turning him into a raging Hulk-like lizard named Abomination. The military did not learn its lesson from Bruce, and now it has helped create two destructive monsters who pose a national security threat that the military cannot contain.

Leterrier's *The Incredible Hulk* is truer in spirit to the original comic book series, which debuted in 1962, than is Ang Lee's version. As Lori Maguire writes, one of the "oddest" things about the Hulk series was that his consistent nemesis was not a supervillain but instead the US military, and that throughout the series, General Ross and the DOD are depicted in a consistently negative light. Likewise, the original comic is often read as a critique of the military-industrial complex, as Banner, a scientist who works on military-grade weaponry, is "punished for developing potentially devastating inventions by being changed into a monster" by those very creations.[7] As Robert Genter writes, Stan Lee's *The Incredible Hulk* was designed as "an explicit warning about the dangers of scientific and technological developments" during the Cold War "and was one of many pieces of popular culture that used monstrous images to issue warnings about nuclear holocaust."[8] In the 2008 version, fears about genetic modification, especially when used for military purposes, supplant the fears of nuclear war, but both versions warn about the dangers of military experiments to dominate or even to profit in combat situations.

While Leterrier may have wished to return to the more pointed critique of the military embraced by the comics, the difference between his and Lee's Hulk versions also highlight the effectiveness that the DOD's entertainment liaison program can possess. By leveraging their military hardware during production on Lee's *Hulk*, the DOD was able to secure favorable images of itself in order to boost its depiction as a benevolent force and to offer counterarguments, through fiction, to the negative stories that had surfaced about its conduct in the early War on Terror. Because it played no role in *The Incredible Hulk*, the DOD was unable to soften that film's portrayal of the military as a power-obsessed, unethical, and even maniacal outfit, or to shift that role to its independent contractors. Instead, producer Avi Arad relied on the Canadian military for the hardware used in the film. The US Air Force bases featured in the movie were actually filmed at Canadian Forces Base (CFB) Trenton, and the Hercules aircraft featured in the movie was a Canadian Air Force plane, stationed at 8 Wing Trenton, flown by Canadian military pilots, and painted to look like a US Air Force plane. These production choices allowed the filmmakers to sidestep Phil Strub and his demands for favorable military portrayals, and thus *The Incredible Hulk* had full liberty to depict the US military however it chose. While *The Incredible Hulk*'s depiction of the armed forces is exaggerated and even cartoonish, it nonetheless reveals what is at stake for the military when it comes to its work in film production. As Ewing writes, the very definition of the modern state rests on "its claim to supreme authority within a territory," and that authority is often achieved by having "a relative monopoly on the means of violence" within that region, often through military force.[9] In *The Incredible Hulk*, however, the movie asks viewers to champion Banner, who represents a heroic and necessary challenge to the state's power, because the military is presented as dangerous to society, and thus the demise of the military and its research and development programs is championed in the film. The egregious actions of the military, in other words, encourage viewers to withdraw their support for it as an institution—a concept that the actual military spends millions of dollars every year trying to challenge or avoid.

The Avengers (2012)

Outside of *The Incredible Hulk*, the MCU's Phase One movies involving Earth-based heroes—*Iron Man*, *Iron Man 2*, and *Captain America: The First Avenger*—are best characterized as establishment narratives, but this trend began to weaken with the phase's culmination in *The Avengers*—a hugely successful, tentpole blockbuster that sees Iron Man, Black Widow, Hulk, and Thor team up to repel an alien invasion led by Thor's brother, Loki. Nick Fury, a senior S.H.I.E.L.D. officer who was fully introduced in *Iron Man 2*, discovers Loki's plot and with Black Widow's help recruits the others to form the Avengers, a world-class team of superheroes, to defend and protect the Earth. As with most prior entries in the MCU, the producers of *The Avengers* approached the Pentagon for assistance, first meeting with the army's entertainment liaison office in November 2010. Their report specifically notes that "the discussions focused on Army support and opportunities for connecting one of the film's superhero protagonists, Captain America, with his U.S. Army roots. The producers were very receptive to the input," and the army felt that the film would "broaden understanding" about the branch and advocated for cooperation.[10]

The original draft for *The Avengers* was scripted by Zak Penn, who had previously written the screenplay for *The Incredible Hulk*. In early 2010, however, Marvel approached Joss Whedon about rewriting and directing the movie. After Whedon read the original script, he told the studio, "I don't think you have anything. You need to pretend this draft never happened." Whedon then embarked on a total rewrite, and while Marvel gave him nearly free rein to reshape the script, they did give him some stipulations: he had to "include all the Avengers, Loki, a midway battle between the good guys, and finish with an epic showdown with the bad guys."[11] Whedon also had to contend with the DOD looking over his shoulder and requesting changes at times. As described in a liaison office report in April 2011, the army had read the initial draft of the screenplay and its rewrites and were ready to approve support of the project. The documents show that the army believed it was "represented well in the character of Captain America" and notes that following its feedback to producers, which included the request that the film strengthen the connection between the "legacy Army" and "today's soldiers," the OCPA-LA agreed to requests for production support, including filming access to the "White Sands Missile Range and a company of Soldiers for the climactic battle scene." In their assessment, the "film [was] being designed as a blockbuster release; U.S. and worldwide audiences [were] expected to be sizable," and the film supported its mission of "Maintaining Our Combat Edge," presumably in the popular imagination.[12]

The updates in the army's Hollywood office reports continue through the start of filming to the summer of 2011, when the military's representatives were on the set in Cleveland, Ohio, for the filming of the final battle scene, noting that "support is being provided by the 391st Military Police Battalion US Army Reserve (25 Soldiers, 5 Vehicles)."[13] Unlike other military-supported projects where the reports continue through postproduction and mention the DOD's viewing of the rough cut and hosting promotional screenings, the updates on *The Avengers* stop in August 2011, just as the climax was being shot. While the Pentagon is credited for its production assistance at the end of the movie, Whedon contradicted the credit on the DVD commentary of the film, saying, "There was no army involvement as there's no army story line."[14] Claims of an erroneous DOD credit were furthered by Phil Strub, who, in an interview with *Wired* shortly after the film's release, said they had refused to cooperate on *The Avengers*, explaining, "We hit [a] roadblock and decided we couldn't do anything."[15]

Strub's and Whedon's claims that the DOD did not assist the film are false; the Humvees and soldiers provided by the US Army Reserve do briefly appear in the final battle sequence, and it seems the US Air Force granted the producers access to F-22s and F-35s so they could be recreated in CGI and appear on the deck of S.H.I.E.L.D.'s flying aircraft carrier.[16] It seems, then, that the Pentagon initially supported the film but then walked away mid-production due to problems it had with the developing script, a conclusion bolstered by Whedon's own admission that he was still rewriting the screenplay as *The Avengers* started filming, due to his "inability to get things right the first time."[17]

Comments by Strub in interviews help flesh out exactly what the military found problematic. In *Wired*, he noted, "We couldn't reconcile the unreality of [the film's] international organization and our place in it. To whom did S.H.I.E.L.D. answer? Did we work for S.H.I.E.L.D.?" In another interview a year later, Strub reiterated that the difficulty in delineating S.H.I.E.L.D.'s authority and relationship to the Pentagon meant that the military did not work on *The Avengers*: "We were really excited about the movie. But the more we tried to reconcile the S.H.I.E.L.D. hierarchy—this all-powerful, international paramilitary organization who can do anything in any sovereign nation—we couldn't fit the US military into it. It just wasn't meshing. So we had to say no."[18]

As Spencer Ackerman writes, "The ambiguity around what exactly S.H.I.E.L.D. is" has been a "vexing complication" in both the comics and the films:

> If it's an American governmental agency, what kind of constitutional authority does it exercise over the military? If it's an international body, as the movie text suggests and Strub determined, are U.S. military personnel and equipment on loan to it through some kind of United Nations Security Council resolution? The questions may seem picayune, but they're precisely the stuff that can cause an image-conscious military to yank its cooperation from a movie.[19]

And yet Ackerman's sentiment does not fully explain the Pentagon's concerns. If the inability to reconcile S.H.I.E.L.D. with the Pentagon's chain of command was so problematic, then why did they agree to support the film before pulling out halfway through? Surely the DOD knew all along that S.H.I.E.L.D. operated internationally in a range of sovereign countries. In its comic book incarnation, S.H.I.E.L.D. is identified as an American intelligence agency, but one with a global reach and a high level of sophistication because it specializes in superhuman and extraterrestrial threats. While it isn't explicitly above the Pentagon in the hierarchy, it operates independently and exclusively of the DOD, often making decisions with huge consequences without consulting any government agency beforehand. If the characterization of the S.H.I.E.L.D.–DOD relationship was the real showstopper, then Strub and the army would never have approved support for the film in the first place.

What Strub really appears to be saying in his interviews is that S.H.I.E.L.D., as depicted in later drafts of *The Avengers*, is both technologically and politically *more powerful* than the Pentagon, and this made the military look weak to the point of irrelevancy in comparison to S.H.I.E.L.D. and its team of superheroes. Indeed, Strub's comments echo the Pentagon's PR objections to previous films where the script showed the military to be ineffective, such as in *Independence Day* and *Clear and Present Danger*, where, in the former, the air force battles a massive alien invasion, and in the latter, it's a black ops team fighting a Colombian drug cartel. On both films, Strub's office had issues with the military's forces looking toothless in response to the threat.[20] Likewise, Jeremy Latcham, the executive producer of *The Avengers*, confirmed to us that Strub would not provide assets for the helicarrier scenes used in the movie unless S.H.I.E.L.D. became a subset of the DOD and Nick Fury reported to someone inside the US government. In other words, Strub wanted S.H.I.E.L.D. to be a part of, not superior to, the Pentagon, but "our vision of S.H.I.E.L.D. was not really compatible with that," said Latcham. "While we went back and forth on this point, we ultimately concluded that the assets we were going to get from them were not worth the changes we would have needed to make to the script, so we just told them we were going to pass." Instead, Latcham employed a private company called Red Air, based out of Ohio, to fill out the deck of the helicarrier, "and that was our workaround for not giving DOD access to the Avengers script like they wanted."[21] As Strub also elaborated in a radio interview, "It came down to the relationship between the US military and the S.H.I.E.L.D. organization, which just, with its all-powerful international capabilities and weaponry that far exceeded our own, that we just couldn't figure out a way to dovetail those two. It just wasn't workable. So that was where we fell out with the *Avengers* picture."[22]

The specific scene that seems to have provoked the final falling-out sees S.H.I.E.L.D.'s leadership launch a nuclear missile at New York City when it appears the Avengers are unable to repel the alien invasion. The missile never hits the city; it is intercepted midair by Iron Man, who flies it through the wormhole that facilitates the invasion and uses the bomb to destroy the alien mothership.[23] The idea that someone other than the Pentagon could unilaterally decide to nuke an American city—even as an act of defense against a destructive alien attack—appears to have been the deal breaker for the DOD. Strub even alluded to this specific scene as being the reason they withdrew from *The Avengers*, explaining, "It's one thing, like in *Transformers*, where you have this unit of mostly soldiers and one airman, and they report to the chairman. It's a fictional military organization, but it's not outside of the system, as compared to S.H.I.E.L.D. S.H.I.E.L.D. is this all-powerful entity that can, you know, nuke New York City."[24]

The final cut of *The Avengers*, then, bears very few signs of the DOD's influence, as Captain America is only connected to his US Army roots in one rapid sequence of flashbacks while he wails on a punchbag. Whatever scenes were written in to "strengthen the connection of the legacy Army to today's soldiers" do not appear in the finished film, and the National Guardsmen only appear on-screen very briefly during the final battle and have no dialogue or significant role in the action (unlike the NYPD, who are shown heroically rescuing fleeing citizens while Captain America battles the aliens nearby). If we interpret S.H.I.E.L.D. as a more effective alternative to the DOD, as an organization that deals with the problems that the Pentagon cannot solve, then *The Avengers* becomes somewhat of an anti-establishment narrative—not because the government is depicted as evil or corrupt, but rather because it challenges the supremacy of the American military, depicting it as too weak or limited in its abilities to protect the globe, let alone New York City, from intergalactic threats. Indeed, while the military, especially the US Air Force, have prominent roles in *Iron Man* and *Iron Man 2*, they are almost entirely absent from *The Avengers*, and this omission could in itself be seen as an anti-establishment statement. The military's only notable visual presence in the final battle is a handful of soldiers being briefly shown during the invasion, which makes them look weak and irrelevant by comparison to S.H.I.E.L.D. and our superheroes. Similarly, at one point during the battle, two NYPD cops exchange the following dialogue: "We need to get out! They gotta bring the National Guard!" "National Guard? Does the army know what's happening here?" This line emphasizes how the conventional authorities—the military and the police—are unable to adequately respond to the aliens, demonstrating how S.H.I.E.L.D. is not just an alternative to the DOD but far superior to them.

While *The Avengers* is not a full-blown, anti-establishment narrative since S.H.I.E.L.D. is still presented as a military-like organization that incorporates superheroes into its structure and works with international governing bodies to save the day, the notion that there may be authorities to which the Pentagon is subservient provoked the DOD to withdraw its support. This marked the beginning of the deterioration of the relationship between the Pentagon and Marvel Studios until the release of *Captain Marvel* in 2019. This may have been for the best, however, because even though the Pentagon would provide some assistance to *Captain America: The Winter Soldier*, the MCU's Phase Two movies mark a pointed shift in tone and more consistently explore anti-establishment themes, which the DOD would have found difficult to support by nature.

Iron Man 3 (2013)

In *Assembling the Marvel Cinematic Universe*, Jennifer Beckett argues that the MCU's Phase Two movies, and in particular *Winter Soldier*, reflect citizens' growing concerns that the government had been granted too much power in the name of national security. After the events of *The Avengers*, "not only has S.H.I.E.L.D. been granted enhanced powers and a greater budget at a time of heightened security risk, its power also stems from an increased and tacit civilian support for counter-terrorism measures." As subsequent events unfold, viewers begin to wonder if the organization can be trusted. As these films mirrored the expanded powers "afforded to the CIA and NSA in the post-9/11 world," Phase Two movies, she writes, addressed cultural anxieties about the "ability of real-world security agencies to police themselves and the need for greater transparency and oversight."[25]

As the first film in Marvel's Phase Two development, *Iron Man 3* indeed marks a departure from the franchise's establishment narratives that were privileged in Phase One. In February 2012, the producers of *Iron Man 3* asked the DOD's permission to tour some military locations, including MCB Camp Lejeune and specifically its MOUT (Military Operation in Urban Terrain) facilities, for potential filming.[26] In the end, however, they never submitted a script or made a formal request for support, and the film was made without any military involvement. This lack of assistance resulted in a film that—like *The Incredible Hulk*—contains numerous critiques of the MIC, especially with regard to the War on Terror and the Pentagon's notion of a "clean war," which, as described in the previous chapter, seeks to downplay, or even eradicate, negative images of combat in order to sell the concept to both the public and recruits thinking about enlisting.

One of the most significant aspects of *Iron Man 3* is that it depicts Tony Stark as suffering from PTSD and anxiety attacks as a result of the events at the end of *The Avengers*, where he fights in a nuclear war in order to stop an alien invasion and even travels through space-time, nearly dying in the process. Stark refuses to discuss his troubles and seeks refuge from his emotional pain by developing and advancing his Iron Man technology, building suits that function via remote control and can split up and reassemble on demand. There is none of the hard-drinking, womanizing playboy of the original *Iron Man*, as Stark—who models himself as the smartest guy in the room—cannot wrap his head around what happened or quite how he survived, leading to his isolation and confidence crisis. Tony's suits become "an extension of his psychological trauma," because, "as a result of his PTSD-induced intimacy issues," Tony "often controls his suits remotely in an effort to convince Pepper that he is present when he is unable to be near her"—both physically and metaphorically.[27] This assessment is further supported in one particularly emotive scene, when he and Pepper are asleep in bed and Tony is enduring a nightmare flashing back to the events in New York. Triggered by the implants in Tony's arms, one of his robot suits approaches the bed and menaces Pepper, nearly attacking her because it perceives her to be the threat causing Tony's anxiety. This scene illustrates not just the radical shift in Stark from a carefree billionaire to a man carrying the mental scars of battle but also how the emotional consequences are rippling out and affecting his loved ones.

This depiction of the emotional impact of combat is more realistic and sympathetic than can be found in many DOD-supported productions and inverts the row between Marvel and the Pentagon on the set of the first Iron Man movie. There, an argument between Favreau and Strub saw a glib reference to military suicide nixed from the film because the Pentagon wished to avoid any allusion to the topic,[28] but in *Iron Man 3*, the mental health problems suffered by many combat veterans are a core part of the narrative, albeit in a nonmilitary character. This portrayal was praised for its depth and accuracy by *Psychology Today*, which concluded that Stark "appears to meet the full criteria for posttraumatic stress disorder," but he "either does not know enough about PTSD or he is in denial, refusing to recognize his own problem, which is a common occurrence among some of those who suffer similarly in real life."[29] Likewise, Andrea Letamendi, a clinical psychologist specializing in PTSD, opined that *Iron Man 3* was an important cultural entry because of the way it worked to "normalize the experience of disorders and destigmatize mental illness."[30] "Tony's struggle with anxiety is poignant," she writes, because it reminds viewers that a "brilliant, powerful, and tough guy can be vulnerable, scared, and confused" and because the film helped educate viewers about the most common symptoms of PTSD: recollections, such as nightmares and flashbacks; hyperarousal, resulting in insomnia or states of agitation; and the avoidance of physical or emotional triggers associated with a traumatic event—all of which Stark experiences.

Iron Man 3's PTSD subplot clearly challenges the status quo of the Pentagon and the media's depiction of "clean wars," but the film is even more representative of an anti-establishment narrative when it explores the notion of the MIC's villainy through the character of the Mandarin. In *Iron Man 3*, as Tony is suffering from the emotional aftershocks of the events in *The Avengers*, a new threat emerges. A terrorist mastermind known as the Mandarin (Ben Kingsley) begins to hack into live TV broadcasts to criticize the United States for its cultural and military imperialism and to take credit for a wave of recent bombings, which he dubs as revenge attacks. In response, the US president announces that War Machine will be deployed into action, but he explains that the hero has been rebranded as Iron Patriot and been given a red, white, and blue paint job. As Rhodey explains to Stark, "It tested well with focus groups . . . 'War Machine' was too aggressive. This sends a better message." This rebranding is mocked by both Stark and the media commentators featured in the film, a move that sardonically highlights the propaganda that the military tries to export in an effort to make war more palatable to the public. Adding to this point, in the same scene where he discusses his rebranding, Rhodey leaks classified information to Stark about the Mandarin's terror campaign, saying there have been nine bombings but the public only knows about three. Rhodey tries to justify the military cover-up, adding, "The Pentagon is scared. After New York, aliens, they need to look strong." This line may be a direct reference to the real Pentagon's paranoia about how they were depicted—in comparison to S.H.I.E.L.D.—in *The Avengers*, but it also critiques the military's withholding of vital information from the public in its efforts to boost its own image as an effective and competent organization capable of public protection.

As the Mandarin's attacks continue, one bombing seriously injures Stark's former bodyguard and driver, Happy Hogan (Jon Favreau), putting him in a coma. As Tony leaves the hospital after visiting Happy, he is surrounded by journalists barking questions, and he responds by threatening to kill the Mandarin, even giving out his home address to goad the Mandarin into a fight. Stark survives the eventual attack and sets out to uncover the truth about the Mandarin and his bombing campaign. Initially he expects the Mandarin to be from the Middle East, and when J.A.R.V.I.S. tracks the origin of the latest Mandarin broadcast, Stark asks him, "What are we talking? Far East, Europe, North Africa, Iran, Pakistan, Syria?" This is in keeping with the original plot envisioned by Favreau when working on the first Iron Man movie, where the Ten Rings insurgents who kidnap Stark were meant to be part of a larger network, and this was the first step in "building towards the Mandarin a movie or two down the road."[31] However, this expectation is radically subverted when it is revealed that the Mandarin is nothing more than a disgraced British actor hired to play the role of a terrorist mastermind by Aldrich Killian (Guy Pearce), a genetic scientist developing technologies to produce transhuman super-soldiers. As Stark puts it, the Mandarin is actually a "custom-made terror threat" who enables Killian to ramp up public fear so that he can sell his super-soldier technology to the Pentagon. In Killian's words, "I'll own the War on Terror. Create supply *and* demand." It also emerges that Killian has built his think tank on military contracts, which gave him access to wounded warriors whom he uses as guinea pigs for his experiments.

This plot twist is a cinematic assault not just on the Pentagon's cozy relationship with industrial corporations but on the entire War on Terror. It depicts the war as nothing more than a cynical money-making scheme and portrays the threat from terrorism as being a mass media shell game, artfully designed to stoke fear so the public accepts the policies and economics of "fighting the terrorists." The film, in other words, plays with the idea that the War on Terror is "hollow, dramatized and manufactured by media representations" in order to keep war manufacturers, tech companies, and politicians in power.[32] In real life, this concept was echoed by former national security advisor Zbigniew Brzezinski in 2007, when he wrote that the very phrase "War on Terror" is "meaningless" because it defines neither a geographic context nor an enemy. In fact, terrorism is just "a technique of warfare—political intimidation through the killing of unarmed non-combatants." The vagueness of the phrase, he writes, was deliberate because it "stimulated the emergence of a culture of fear," and because

> fear obscures reason . . . it [becomes] easier for demagogic politicians to mobilize the public on behalf of the policies they want to pursue. The war of choice in Iraq could never have gained the congressional support it got without the psychological linkage between the shock of 9/11 and the postulated existence of Iraqi weapons of mass destruction. Support for President Bush in the 2004 elections was also mobilized in part by the notion that "a nation at war" does not change its commander-in-chief in midstream. The sense of a pervasive but otherwise imprecise danger was thus channeled in a politically expedient direction by the mobilizing appeal of being "at war."[33]

Thus the concept that politicians and corporations may manufacture fear for power or profit rests, even more understandably, at the heart of *Iron Man 3*.

In total, then, *Iron Man 3* depicts the Pentagon as untrustworthy, especially as it lies to the public about events on the ground. The plot even takes aim at the Pentagon when Iron Patriot is sent into Pakistan to find the Mandarin but in reality is suckered into a trap laid by Killian that allows our arch-antagonist to steal the Iron Patriot suit and use it to launch a false flag attack on Air Force One. Whereas Iron Man is at best a metaphor for the military, Iron Patriot/Rhodey is its main representative in the Iron Man trilogy. This plot development, therefore, shows the Pentagon as foolhardy, accidentally enabling the real villain and chasing shadows while covering up the truth about the Mandarin's bombing campaign. Such depictions, in addition to the film's portrayals of postcombat mental illness and its more incisive critique of the military-industrial complex, makes *Iron Man 3* the most counter-establishment film in the Iron Man franchise. It invites viewers to see the continuing War on Terror as little more than a manufactured event to promote the bottom line of war profiteers—a far cry from the depiction of the war in Afghanistan in the original *Iron Man*, which is shown as a just war in a region full of anti-American terrorists.

Captain America: The Winter Soldier (2014)

Marvel's use of increasingly subversive themes continued in *Captain America: The Winter Soldier* the following year, becoming one of its most critically heralded films. Reviewers praised its willingness to embrace critical ideas and timely political themes, as well as its "more serious, mature and intense tone . . . inspired by [the] paranoid political thrillers of the '70s, making it the most radical departure from the tried-and-true MCU formula."[34] One reviewer described how "they have taken Captain America, the engagingly square strongman from the flag-waving '40s, and planted him in the black-ops cynicism of the present day, where the villain isn't some over-the-top mastermind but, in fact, the very military-industrial complex he's out to defend."[35] Another expressed how he "was legitimately shocked and impressed and fascinated" by a scene where "the movie clearly states that our modern intelligence apparatus and our whole system of national security was invented by some of the greatest villains of the 20th Century."[36]

The film's codirector Joe Russo explains that these messages were intended from the very beginning:

> [Marvel] said they wanted to make a political thriller. So we said if you want to make a political thriller, all the great political thrillers have very current issues in them that reflect the anxiety of the audience. That gives it an immediacy, it makes it relevant. So [we] just looked at the issues that were causing anxiety for us because we read a lot and are politically inclined. And a lot of that stuff had to do with civil liberties issues, drone strikes, the president's kill list, [and] pre-emptive technology.[37]

Russo also outlined how they adopted a similar structure to the 1970s conspiracy thriller classic *Three Days of the Condor*, which stars Robert Redford as a CIA analyst who discovers that his superiors within the agency have murdered his colleagues in an attempt to cover up their own participation in a rogue operation to seize Middle Eastern oil fields. As an homage to that film, Russo cast Redford in *Winter Soldier*, adding, "You could really call this movie *Three Days of Captain America*, if you wanted to. The structure is so similar. We felt like we had a decent shot at getting [Redford] because the script had a political component to it and we thought that might motivate him."[38]

Strangely, given its radical intentions, *The Winter Soldier* requested and qualified for some military support, as the DOD's database illustrates that some principal filming took place in Ohio, where "the National Guard allowed Marvel to build a few sets in a secluded area of the 22,000 acre Army National Guard base, Camp Ravenna, located an hour south of Cleveland. In return, the Guard received significant portrayal in the film. As always, there was no cost to the government, and when filming was completed, Marvel tore down the sets and restored the installation back to its original condition," noting that the entire process took place over the course of three weeks.[39] But despite the military's satisfaction that the movie portrayed the Army National Guard positively, *The Winter Soldier* contains numerous scenes and plot twists that—like *Iron Man 3*—have radical or critical implications for the MIC as a whole, making one wonder, like James Schamus on Lee's *Hulk*, if the Pentagon really understood the movie's intentions.

The film begins with Steve Rogers working for S.H.I.E.L.D. in Washington, DC, and befriending former USAF pararescueman Sam Wilson (Anthony Mackie) who invites Rogers to visit the local VA office, where Wilson works. Later in the film, Nick Fury sends Rogers and his team—including Black Widow—to recapture a S.H.I.E.L.D. ship that has been hijacked by pirates, but the mission almost goes bad and threatens the lives of the hostages. On his return to DC, Rogers confronts Fury, who reveals that the ship was an important part of Project Insight—the next stage in S.H.I.E.L.D.'s efforts to secure the Earth. Fury reveals that S.H.I.E.L.D. has constructed three giant helicarriers for "continuous sub-orbital flight" that are linked to satellites that identify targets. The helicarriers are equipped with "long-range precision guns [that] can eliminate 1,000 hostiles a minute. The satellites can read a terrorist's DNA before he steps outside his spider hole."

The three details underscoring S.H.I.E.L.D.'s next-generation approach to warfare—a drone aircraft delivering death from above, predictive analytics, and preemptive assassination—are all technologies and policies adopted by the US security state for use in the War on Terror and reinforce the Russos' claim that real-life anxieties were integral to the film. As Peter Bergen explains, the CIA's drone program began under the Bush administration in 2002, but it was President Obama who greatly increased its use in the War on Terror. By 2011, Obama was carrying out an average of one drone strike every four days, while under Bush it was about one strike every forty days. By 2013 (one year prior to *Winter Soldier*'s release), Obama had authorized 307 drone strikes in Pakistan alone, "six times the number of strikes carried out during President Bush's entire eight years in office." While Obama was able to drastically lower the number of civilian deaths caused by drone strikes in comparison to Bush, his strikes were highly controversial. Bergen, the director of the National Security Studies Program for the New America Foundation, explains that the president took it upon himself to act as the chief decision maker on whether individuals should be added to the "kill list" and that his regions for attack were "based merely on patterns of suspicious activity by a group of men, rather than on the identification of particular militants" in an area. Pakistani officials also (and correctly) believed the program was a violation of its national sovereignty, and thus its Parliament voted in 2012 to end any authorization for the program, a vote that the US government ignored.[40] In 2011, Obama's program came under particular scrutiny when an American citizen, Anwar Nasser al-Awlaki (a Yemeni American imam), was killed in a drone strike for allegedly serving as a senior recruiter for Al-Qaeda and for planning some of its terrorist operations. Al-Awlaki became the first US citizen during the War on Terror to be targeted by his own government without the rights of due process being afforded—a move that served to radicalize many other American Muslims, with the *New York Times* concluding that many of al-Awlaki's views on Islam and America carried "greater authority" *after* his death precisely "*because* America killed him."[41]

The concerns about the drone program's lack of due process and its targeting of militants based merely on "suspicious" activity features in Rogers's criticism of Project Insight when he says to Nick Fury that he thought, in America, "the punishment usually came after the crime," to which Fury responds, "We can't afford to wait that long." Fury adopts the logic of the Bush doctrine's preemptive, preventive warfare and the Obama doctrine of targeted killings without trial or even evidence, to which Steve Rogers objects. He accuses Fury and S.H.I.E.L.D. of "holding a gun to everyone on Earth and calling it protection." While Fury openly embraces morally compromised positions, our eponymous hero is a consistent voice of dissent, and the audience is clearly meant to sympathize with Captain America and the perspective he expresses.

Following this argument, Rogers goes to the VA office, where Wilson is hosting a support group for former service members, again incorporating themes of the emotional and mental struggles faced by combat veterans. As Wilson says, "We all got the same problems. Guilt. Regret." He goes on to explain that he lost his friend and wingman during a mission, adding, "After that, I had a really hard time finding a reason for being over there, you know?" Rogers asks him, "But you're happy now, back in the world?" to which Wilson responds, "The number of people giving me orders is down to about zero. So, hell yeah." This touching scene not only helps build the budding friendship between Rogers and Wilson; it is also a critique of the hierarchical military way of life and the emotional consequences of war. Even more so than in *Iron Man 3*—because this time it is ex-military characters expressing these thoughts and feelings—this is a much more sympathetic portrayal of military mental illness than is usually allowed in DOD-supported films. Perhaps the Pentagon's script reviewers overlooked the importance of this scene in what is mostly a comic action thriller, or perhaps the setting of a semifictional world that never makes clear which war Wilson fought in meant that they allowed the writers a bit more leeway to discuss themes that the DOD usually deems controversial.

Finally, as the movie progresses, Rogers's rejection of Project Insight eventually awakens Fury's curiosity, but Fury is met with obstacles during his investigation, including being stonewalled by World Security Council member Alexander Pierce (Robert Redford). His curiosity also leads to a series of people trying to assassinate him, including one where he is pulled over by DC Metro Police, to which Fury responds,

"Wanna see my lease?" in an obvious and satirical reference to racial profiling by law enforcement. After Fury is apparently assassinated by a masked superhuman known as the Winter Soldier (Sebastian Stan), Rogers and Natasha Romanov/Black Widow set about finding him and the other culprits to avenge Fury's death.

It eventually emerges that S.H.I.E.L.D. has been compromised and heavily infiltrated by Hydra—a high-tech Nazi secret society, who plans to use the Project Insight helicarriers and satellites to establish a worldwide dictatorship that murders anyone thought to be a potential dissident or opponent. This core plot twist reflects real-world concerns that extreme defensive or protective policies can become tools of oppression. The damage caused by proactive, preemptive warfare is amply demonstrated by the torture program, the drone program, mass surveillance, and the worst abuses of the Patriot Act, all of which have their metaphorical equivalents in *The Winter Soldier*. While it could be argued that it is S.H.I.E.L.D. who are infiltrated by Nazis seeking to take over the world, the film draws a parallel with the real CIA and DOD by name-dropping Operation Paperclip in a scene where Rogers and Romanov discover an AI recreation of the Hydra scientist Arnim Zola (who featured in the first *Captain America*) in an underground bunker. Paperclip was an actual operation where thousands of Nazi scientists and intelligence officers were recruited by the United States after World War II to help them defeat the Soviet Union. Thus, the dangers of a rampant security state willing to incorporate dangerous players to achieve their endgame are illustrated and critiqued in *The Winter Soldier*.

The climax of *The Winter Soldier* sees Romanov, Rogers, and Wilson counter-infiltrate S.H.I.E.L.D. to destroy Project Insight and dismantle S.H.I.E.L.D. from within. This includes Romanov dumping all of S.H.I.E.L.D.'s and Hydra's secrets online, mirroring major leaks by whistleblowers such as Chelsea Manning and Edward Snowden. The Snowden leak of thousands of documents recording the mass surveillance operations of the National Security Agency (NSA), including the collection of private citizens' bank accounts, medical records, and all electronic communications, perfectly mirrored Hydra's plan to use all possible data to identify Project Insight targets, leading to comparisons between Snowden's leak and Romanov's. However, this element was already in the script months before Snowden's leak first made the papers; as Joe Russo put it, "It was all leading up to Snowden. It was all in the ether [already], it was all part of the zeitgeist. The Snowden stuff actually happened while we were shooting."[42] Captain America thus goes from being a defender and symbol of the military and the security state in the Phase One films to an insurgent who destroys it. This character arc alone qualifies the film as an anti-establishment film, but combined with pointed dialogue citing specific, real-world objections to the security state, *The Winter Soldier* is one of the sharpest, most politically radical entries in the entire MCU.

Captain America: Civil War (2016)

The final film discussed in this chapter was again directed by Anthony and Joe Russo. *Captain America: Civil War* continues the subversive thread of its predecessor, basing its plotline on the 2006–2007 *Civil War* story line from Marvel Comics, which features a group of young superheroes trying to increase their fame while battling a group of villains in Stamford, Connecticut, during the filming of a reality television show. The battle accidentally leads to the death of six hundred people, including nearby schoolchildren, when the character Nitro explodes. The Stamford incident thus turns public opinion against the new superheroes and causes the government to pass the Superhero Registration Act. The act requires all enhanced individuals to register their real names with the government and to act under its official regulations. In the comic, Iron Man becomes the increasingly authoritarian figure that supports the registration, leading him to eventually take over as the head of S.H.I.E.L.D. and to build an intergalactic prison to house superheroes while they await trial for not registering. Meanwhile, Captain America emerges as the strongest opponent of the act, highlighting the conflict between freedom and security that is the dominant underlying theme in the story.

The Marvel Cinematic Universe loosely adapted this story line for *Captain America: Civil War*, but it is the events that unfold in *Avengers: Age of Ultron* that serve as the Stamford equivalent. As the Russos and writers Stephen McFeely and Christopher Markus explain in the director's commentary of the film, many viewers and creators were beginning to question the amount of civilian destruction unfolding in the MCU. The writers no longer felt like that element could go unaddressed, especially after the battles in New York and Sokovia. Part of the problem stemmed from the fact that, in keeping with the concept of the clean war, these films, along with others in the DCEU, presented mass destruction with little to no acknowledgment of implied deaths. As Bruno summarizes:

> In *The Avengers* (2012), an army wreaks havoc on New York, without any deaths implied nor shown; in *Man of Steel* (2013), a suburb and a city are torn apart, all with conveniently located occupants seemingly avoiding death; in *Iron Man 2* (2010), drones shoot bullets at a full convention center with no escapees struck; in *Batman Begins* (2005), a mostly empty monorail train is derailed without displaying death; in *The Dark Knight* (2008), a hospital is bombed without establishing the people inside of it; in *The Dark Knight Rises* (2012), bridges collapse without cars falling off; in *Justice League* (2017), there is wholesale destruction without establishing any setting whatsoever. . . . Similarly, in *Avengers: Age of Ultron* (2015), the film quite literally goes out of its way to imply that the Avengers have evacuated and saved an entire city's worth of civilians, only to reveal later in *Captain America: Civil War* (2016) that there were indeed many casualties during the film.[43]

Markus explains in an interview with *Collider* that if this is a realistic world, somebody's eventually got to say: "You tore down half of New York. Why are we happy about that?" We dropped helicarriers on Washington, DC. . . . Stop dropping helicarriers on my fucking head."[44]

In response to the invisibility of its own, written destruction, *Captain America: Civil War* leads by addressing the reality of civilian casualties during war when Wanda Maximoff saves both Captain America and a crowd of innocent bystanders by deflecting an explosion caused by a suicide bomber upward into a building, only to kill a number of

Wakandan civilians in the process. In an attempt to hold the Avengers accountable for their actions, General Ross, who has now been promoted to secretary of defense, champions the Sokovia Accords.

According to Ross, the Avengers are dangerous because they are enhanced individuals who constantly ignore sovereign borders and operate with unlimited power and oversight. "World governments can no longer accept this arrangement" because the heroes mark a decided challenge to their own sovereignty in a region. To rein the superheroes in, 117 nations agree to ratify the accords, which dictate "that the Avengers shall no longer be a private organization. Instead, they'll operate under the supervision of a United Nations panel, only when and if that panel deems it necessary." The Avengers are split on whether they should sign and submit to the Accords. As Vision states in the film: "Our enhanced nature invites challenge, and challenge invites conflict, and conflict invites catastrophe. Oversight cannot be dismissed out of hand." Even Tony, the narcissist who told Nick Fury in *Iron Man 2* that he didn't want to join his "super-secret boy band," changes his mind in *Civil War*. Stark is now riddled with guilt because, at the start of the film, the mother of a young man killed in the Sokovia attacks confronts Tony, arguing that he is responsible for her son's death. Thus, Stark begins the MCU as an exceptional individual and, as such, a metaphor for US exceptionalism; he goes where he wants and sets and chooses his own missions. After suffering from the emotional consequences of combat himself, however, he becomes more skeptical toward the use of superpowers and ultimately becomes the strongest advocate for oversight. While Tony, under this paradigm, may seem like a radical for no longer advocating for US exceptionalism and submitting to international oversight, Captain America is depicted as equally rebellious for rejecting the accords outright.

Indeed, Captain America, the more traditionally rank-and-file member of the team, does not want to submit to the UN at all. He tells the Avengers, "We try to save as many as we can. Sometimes that means we can't save everyone and if we can't be OK with that, maybe next time nobody gets saved." He also convincingly argues that panels, like the UN, "run on agendas." "What if they send us somewhere that we don't want to go and what if there is somewhere we need to go and they won't send us? The safest hands are still our own." This transformation of Captain America, who began the MCU as the most wholesome of US soldiers but then evolved into a figure of rebellion against the security state, should not be surprising. While the US Army originally saw Captain America as a positive cinematic representation, there were hints of his subversive side all along. In the first *Captain America*, Rogers is asked, "Do you want to kill Nazis?" and he responds, "I don't want to kill anyone. I don't like bullies. I don't care where they're from." It is this ethic, rather than any particular loyalty to the United States, that is carried forward throughout the franchise. While Rogers is seen battling on the side of the Allies against the Nazis and Hydra in *The First Avenger* and working for S.H.I.E.L.D. in the second film, he is consistently skeptical toward and defies authority—ignoring orders in *The First Avenger* so he can rescue a group of POWs and later working to discover Fury's secret weapons program. In *The Winter Soldier*, when Rogers realizes that S.H.I.E.L.D. is becoming the bully, he uncovers Hydra's infiltration and destroys the S.H.I.E.L.D. organization. Rogers evolves from merely disobeying orders in order to do good to using his superpowers to take down a center of power. The audience is encouraged to see Rogers's actions, including his use of force, as legitimate even though it is directed against the established authorities. In *Civil War*, this rebellious streak simply continues as Rogers rejects the demands for oversight, insisting that the Avengers can identify bullies for themselves rather than be told who they can and can't target by the UN.

According to the film's writers, it was important to make the split among the Avengers feel personal and legitimate. McFeely states that he wanted people "walking out of this movie going, Tony's right. And half the other people going, Steve's right. That would be a dream if we got a 49-51 split. Because the question is a legitimate one. Do they need oversight or not? And as soon as you imply oversight [is the answer] . . . Steve [makes] an excellent argument [against it]. And yet, things have happened that you can't deny." Markus adds that part of the challenge of the movie was "not making Tony clearly wrong as he seems to . . . be in the comic book." There he grows increasingly authoritarian and even builds a prison to house unregistered superheroes. We had to "give him his own personal reason," Markus states, "so that he's coming from a place where you understand why he would make this decision."

Despite its sympathetic portrayal of Stark's decision, *Captain America: Civil War* is still an anti-establishment narrative (as evidenced by the writers' hope that audiences would favor Captain America if only by two percentage points). This is, after all, a Captain America movie and not an Iron Man or even an Avengers title—a point furthered by the Bucky Barnes subplot. More specifically, when the UN meets in Vienna to ratify the accords, a bomb explodes killing several leaders, including King T'Chaka of Wakanda, and it appears as if Bucky, Steve's childhood best friend, is the bomber. T'Chaka's son—the Black Panther—refuses to wait for the UN's Task Force to act and instead vows to kill Bucky himself. Rogers also goes against the Task Force's wishes and tries to bring in Bucky "because [he's] the one least likely to die trying" and because the Task Force is authorized to shoot Barnes on site. Rogers therefore decides to act independently, recruiting some of the Avengers to aid his cause. When this plan is discovered, Stark then assembles his own team to capture the newly dubbed renegades at the Leipzig airport, where the teams fight until Romanoff allows Rogers and Barnes to escape, and the rest of Rogers's team is captured and detained at Raft prison.

Later in the film, Tony learns that Barnes is actually being framed for the Vienna bombing by Helmut Zemo, a former member of Sokovian intelligence who is seeking revenge on the Avengers for the attack that caused him to lose his family (a plotline that addresses concerns that wars merely radicalize their victims and create more wars). When Stark relays the information to Ross, he refuses to act on the intelligence because he is upset with Tony for the Leipzig incident, and thus Stark goes to strike a truce with Rogers and Barnes behind Ross's back. By the film's end, Stark realizes the limitations of the Sokovia Accords, which force the Avengers to act on what the government knows/cares to acknowledge about any given situation, and in this case the decision is based on flawed intelligence. Both Stark and Rogers also come to better understand the dangers of being placed under Ross's control. In the film's directors' commentary, Ross is described as having developed into a more statesmanlike figure but who, "at the end of the day . . . is still trying to control superheroes [to accomplish the military's aims]; he's just found a better way to do it." Although the film does not explicitly say so, it is also likely that even with the new intelligence that shows Zemo was responsible for Vienna, the public demands that Barnes be punished for the crime are too strong for Ross and the UN to ignore, and they would thus punish Bucky for the crime, even though he did not commit it.

Steve's decision to reject the Sokovia Accords is justified by the film's end. Indeed, Nathan Bosma and Adam Barkman argue that in *Civil War*, it is Captain America, not Iron Man, that wins the film's moral high ground. Using Immanuel Kant's philosophical positions, the pair argue that it is wrong to use a person purely as a means to an end, "without respecting that person, as an end in themselves, independently of that purpose." In other words, if the United Nations wishes to ask all superheroes to give up their secret identities and/or to only work at the behest of the government, "this doesn't give people the dignity they deserve and thus Cap can disobey the government with a clear conscience." Additionally, when the government demands superhero submission to the Sokovia Accords, they are asking for the Avengers to become merely a means to defend the world and nothing else: the government has no respect for them as people with the potential desire to disagree and to act otherwise; therefore, Captain America is right to reject the accords, a position that even Stark comes to see as the better one.[45]

Conclusion

Using Di Paolo's schema, *The Incredible Hulk*, *Iron Man 3*, *The Winter Soldier*, and *Captain America: Civil War* all qualify as anti-establishment films, while *The Avengers* contained sufficiently anti-establishment elements that the DOD took the unusual step of walking away mid-production.

Across the films analyzed in this chapter, the military and even S.H.I.E.L.D. are variously portrayed as reckless, immoral, hopelessly outgunned, incompetent, infiltrated by evil Nazis, and/or obsessed with PR manipulation. Meanwhile, the MIC is shown to be full of profiteering liars, and the wider security state is depicted as the worst possible threat to human life and liberty (albeit with help from a secret society of Nazis). While a large majority of Hollywood's output manifests pro-establishment stories, the characters and values in the films discussed in this chapter demonstrate that sometimes studios grant their filmmakers the freedom to explore more radical ideas and counter-establishment narratives. This is even true at the biggest studios who run the most risk if they alienate their audiences and thus generate lower box-office revenues due to subverted or failed expectations.

Additionally, it is clear from the contrast between the films examined in the first two chapters of this book that it is far easier to produce an anti-establishment story when the US government, especially the DOD, are not involved. Fundamentally the Pentagon operates as a politically and creatively conservative force in Hollywood, deploying production assistance only on products that glamorize or bolster support for existing centers of power or when the producers are willing to commit to rewrites to remove content deemed contentious or controversial by the DOD. Box-office receipts for the more radical MCU films show that the market can function as a counterforce to the Pentagon's cultural conservatism, however. According to figures from Box Office Mojo, *Iron Man 3* took over $1.2 billion worldwide, slightly more than *Iron Man* and *Iron Man 2* combined. In the Captain America franchise, *The Winter Soldier* earned more than $700 million, while *Civil War* grossed $1.1 billion, compared to just $370 million for *The First Avenger*. While *The Incredible Hulk* was something of a flop at just $264 million, at the time of its release, *The Avengers* became the third-highest grossing film in cinema history, and Disney's highest-grossing film ever, breaking the $1.5 billion mark. While some of these increases in revenue for later MCU movies can be attributed to a growing fan base and brand loyalty, there is no indication that employing more counter-establishment narratives and character arcs lead to reduced box-office receipts. These figures show that there is a mass market for films containing subversive ideas and plot points, especially when fronted by some of our favorite superheroes.

Collectively, these anti-establishment films also highlight the tension that often exists between superheroes and military power. In both *The Incredible Hulk* and, more prominently, the Captain America narratives, exclusive sovereignty in the hands of the state is decidedly problematic, as evidenced by the Nazi's genocidal efforts or in Hydra's infiltration of S.H.I.E.L.D., both of which show "that state coercive 'protection' keeps the populace safe or endangers it, contingent on who the enemy is defined as, and who gets to do the defining." Thus, these superhero narratives emphasize the importance of a system of checks and balances to state and military power because states often fail to act in the public interest. Indeed, "full state monopoly over coercion protects the populace only insofar as the individuals in power are good natured and wise,"[46] and this is one major reason why the real US military is so invested in its benevolent image on screen. In films like *The Incredible Hulk*, when the military's good-natured image breaks down, viewers are left championing Banner because they recognize he is the only character powerful enough to stop the destructive force of the US military. In Ang Lee's *Hulk*, viewers are far more apt to root for the military's success in containing Banner, who clearly represents a public threat, thereby reinforcing the legitimation of the military and its use of violence, precisely because it is seen being used in a benevolent manner by the film's end. The same rhetoric certainly applies to the world of war outside of Hollywood, as the state and the military are more apt to receive public support if they are seen using their power in protective rather than aggressive manners, and this is one reason why the military is so attentive to its image in popular culture. It needs the movies to help build and maintain trust with viewers.

Nonetheless, there are limitations to the radical nature of the films analyzed in this chapter. It should be noted that *Iron Man 3*, despite its critique of the American military-industrial complex, has also been accused of pandering to the Chinese government. According to Box Office Mojo, the film's stellar revenues were boosted by over $120 million in China alone, compared to just $23 million for the first two Iron Man films in the same territory. This strong performance in China was aided by a close cooperation with the Chinese government that saw censorship board officials invited to the set to monitor some of the filming. The Chinese cut of *Iron Man 3* includes product placement for popular Chinese brands, and the Mandarin was transliterated in the film to "Man Daren" to remove any Chinese association from the villain. The producers even shot a scene specifically for the Chinese cut that featured movie stars Fan Bingbing and Wang Xueqi as a medical team who carry out the surgery on Stark to remove the shrapnel embedded in his chest in the original *Iron Man*. As one journalist noted, "Some of the film's most over-the-top dialogue comes when the two discuss how the world's expectations and the life of Marvel's lucrative hero hinge on them and their unique Chinese medical abilities."[47] Somewhat paradoxically, then, US audiences were encouraged to read *Iron Man 3* as a substantially counter-establishment film, but with a few judicious edits and additions, the film was read as a pro-establishment film for Chinese audiences, showing the complexities of cinematic production in a global economy.

Second, all of these films contain the underlying militaristic value of resolving conflict through violence. The first two phases of the MCU split the audiences' sympathies, however, in terms of who legitimately uses violence against whom and to what ends. While *Iron Man*, *Thor*, *Iron Man 2*, and aspects of *The Avengers* conform to the model for a large majority of Hollywood productions in that they promote the state's use of violence, *The Incredible Hulk*, *Iron Man 3*, *The Winter Soldier*, and *Captain America: Civil War* all skew sympathy in favor of insurgent characters who are in some way battling against this system.

Additionally, even in anti-establishment narratives, contemporary superhero movies still feature conflicts that are resolved by an elite individual, or a set of exceptional individuals. The problems depicted in these films range from the realistic to the fantastical, but in every case the solution is an extraterrestrial demigod, a super-soldier, or a billionaire genius in a flying suit of armor. There are no mass movements or acts of democratic will depicted in these stories, with the possible exception of the UN's Sokovia Accords, which half of the Avengers rebel against and viewers come to see as unwise. The only collective action is carried out by a gang of elite superhumans, while ordinary people are reduced to passive spectators. In a May 2017 episode of *Real Time with Bill Maher*, Maher called out this element of superhero movies, linking its implications to the 2016 presidential election:

> If you're asking, what's the problem? The problem is that superhero movies imprint this mindset that we are not masters of our own destiny, and the best we can do is sit back and wait for Star-Lord and a fucking raccoon to sweep in and save our sorry asses. . . . Forget hard work, government institutions, diplomacy, investment. We just need a hero to rise, and so we put out the Bat Signal for one man who could step in and solve all of our problems very quickly. And that's how we got our latest superhero: Orange Sphincter.

Maher went on to compare Trump to Batman, arguing that Orange Sphincter "is a billionaire socialite from Gotham," adding, "[It] all would be funnier if so many people in this country didn't really believe in Orange Sphincter, didn't really believe that he possesses super deal-making powers and a superior brain that can solve in minutes issues that have plagued the country for decades."[48]

In a similar vein, Allan Austin argues that superhero films

> reflect, all too sadly, the ways in which Americans struggle to think their way to new solutions for the threats posed by the twenty-first century world . . . So long as Americans remain unable to imagine something better (or even different), they will be susceptible to trading security for freedom, to sustaining policies that seem more apt to perpetuate war than end it, and, ultimately, repeating a destructive cycle that offers nothing new moving forward.

And it's true that *The Winter Soldier*, which ends in S.H.I.E.L.D.'s destruction, offers no better alternative to replace it. The CIA simply steps in to play a more prominent role in the franchise, starting with Everett Ross's appearance in *Captain America: Civil War* and his more prominent role in *Black Panther*. Thus, while Marvel may look at the War on Terror "in some ways differently than DC, both ultimately end up in the same grim place: extralegal vigilantes—euphemistically labeled superheroes—will have to police the world to make it a better place by providing extralegal and clandestine security to Americans. The public will just have to trust them to do the right thing."[49]

“HI. I’M FROM THE MILITARY. SPACE IS THE NEXT FRONTIER”

NASA, SPACE FORCE, AND THE FUTURE OF THE GALAXY

3

“Now, here’s a story that I think you might really enjoy,” Jeremy Latcham said teasingly over the phone. “I got a call from Rick Loverd at the Science and Entertainment Exchange sometime after *Avengers* 2, who said that a lieutenant general from the United States Air Force wants to come by and talk to me about . . . the future of the space industry.”[1] Intrigued, Latcham agreed to the meeting, which was eventually composed of seven military members led by Lt. Gen. Steven Kwast of the Air University in Maxwell, Alabama. In the meeting, which Latcham describes “as one of the craziest experiences” of his life, Kwast walked in and said:

> Hi, I’m from the military. Space is the next frontier. It is imperative to the United States government that we have our values represented in space and not those of our adversaries. We ask that as Hollywood plots the future of movies and you delve into outer space, that you look to include American values and American points of view in space. We believe that democracy and capitalism and the idealism of the American dream are imperative

Parts of this chapter previously appeared in Tricia Jenkins and Tom Secker, “Superheroes, Movies and the Future of Space: NASA, the United States Space Force, *The Avengers* and *Captain Marvel*,” *Journal of American Culture* 43, no. 4 (2020): 285–299.

to have represented in space because that's really where the future of humanity lies.

"That is heavy. That's a lot, dude," Latcham joked with Kwast, but then Latcham proceeded to explain that the third and fourth Avengers movies would revolve around "a bad guy from outer space named Thanos, who does not share our values and wants to wipe out 50 percent of the world's population because he thinks it'll make society run smoother." In the films, Thanos runs counter to Captain America's point of view, which is that "every single person is worth saving, no matter who they are, where they're from, or what their background is. If we lose even one person, it wasn't worth it. And so *Avengers* 3 and 4," Latcham continued, "is basically a battle for the future of humanity against an adversary from space who doesn't understand America." "And [Kwast] was like, 'Excellent, my job here is done. Here is my card. Thank you,' and he left." Latcham said he thinks about that conversation a lot:

> I mean, it wasn't *that* cut and dry, but it was really fascinating that the military basically came to Hollywood with a message of "space is the future for humanity; minding its fate is going to matter; this planet's not going to make it forever, so when we go there, it needs to be American ideals that are in charge. Anything you can do to help support that mission, we appreciate."

As this book illustrates, Kwast and Latcham are just two players in a much broader government-entertainment complex, but their meeting is revelatory in two ways. One is that a movie's military-related ideology is not always influenced through the DOD's production assistance program. Sometimes it is encouraged through private meetings for which almost no one has a formal record. Kwast's concerns also highlight a second point, which is the growing importance of space to the American military and the way it is imagined in popular culture. With NASA's Mars Curiosity rover, the establishment of the US Space Force, China's first spacecraft landing on the dark side of the moon, and Elon Musk's SpaceX tourism program, the mid- to late 2010s have proven to be an exciting renaissance in space exploration. But while the mysteries of the universe have long captured the public's imagination, the role of space in American society has always been contentious, or at least multifaceted.

In one stream of thought, space mostly represents wondrous opportunities for peaceful exploration and scientific discovery that may ultimately enhance human existence and understanding. For example, in his book *Why Mars?* Henry Lambright argues that the government has poured several billion dollars into Mars exploration since the 1960s because it may reveal whether life has ever existed on another planet and because its robotic exploration is necessary before human exploration.[2] In the second train of thought, space functions as an extension of the territory that governments must colonize in the name of national security. For example, in its 1952 series on space, *Collier's* magazine warned readers that dangerous foes who established a space station "could actually subjugate the peoples of the world," and thus the United States must immediately embark on a long-term program to "secure Western 'space superiority.'" This latter sentiment was also echoed in the film *Destination Moon* (1950), which features industrial executives agreeing to finance a lunar expedition once a military general explains that "the first country which can use the moon for the launching of missiles will control the earth."[3]

No two organizations better represent these differing visions of space than the National Aeronautics and Space Administration (NASA) and the newly developed sixth branch of the US Armed Forces—the United States Space Force (USSF).[4] Founded in 1958, NASA is the federal agency responsible for the civilian space program and its aeronautics and aerospace research. According to its mission statement, NASA is dedicated to the "peaceful" exploration and research of space, as it seeks to advance scientific understanding of "the Earth, the solar system, and the universe"; to use that knowledge to preserve the planet's environment; to provide educational opportunities for inquisitive minds; and to advance technologies that will further space travel.[5] In contrast, the US Space Force, founded in December 2019, was designed to ensure that the United States has "unfettered access to and freedom to operate in space." The Space Force's Strategic Overview explains that because space is used for financial networks, communications, and global surveillance, "potential adversaries have recognized the U.S. military's dependence on space for modern military operations and the advantages space provides to joint and coalition forces." National adversaries, the overview claims, are trying to "exploit possible US vulnerabilities in space," making space "a warfighting domain." As a result, the DOD feels it must secure its free operation in space, in order "to deter aggression, to defend the homeland from attack, to project power abroad," and "to defeat adversary space and counterspace threats." The USSF, currently housed under the domain of the US Air Force, has therefore been established to organize, train, and equip US military space forces to engage in "both combat and combat-support functions."[6]

Superhero movies are fertile ground for exploring different visions of the role of human society in space. Stark Industries, for instance, offers an example of what a private company can accomplish in aeronautics when unfettered by government bureaucracy and how its relationship with the armed forces can enhance national security. The MCU's vision of Tony Stark was even inspired by real-life billionaire Elon Musk, to whom Robert Downey Jr. turned in order to get into character for the first *Iron Man*. As Alex Hern writes, "Musk's enthusiastic embrace of technology for technology's sake and his desire to push the limits of what was possible for private enterprise" made him the closest "real-world analogue for Marvel's billionaire arms dealer."[7] In other superhero narratives, space is often associated with ill-intentioned inhabitants who seek to conquer Earth (such as Thanos, Loki, or General Zod), while in yet others, the solar system contains wondrous materials that hold the potential for human enhancement (think of the Infinity stones or the Tesseract's promise of unlimited clean energy and its portal to other dimensions) if used by the right hands.

Given this history, this chapter explores how the ideologies that govern space and its relationship to scientific discovery and national security play out in three government-assisted films: *The Avengers*, *Man of Steel*, and *Captain Marvel*. Together, these movies reveal how the government-entertainment complex works to shape the narratives and/or reception of blockbuster movies, but how, despite NASA's influence on a project, the genre still privileges the DOD's vision of space as the high ground in military combat. It also reveals how *Captain Marvel*'s robust relationship with the USAF helped lay the groundwork for public support of the US Space Force when the branch officially launched just nine months later. Because it has been widely ignored in scholarly circles that examine state influence on cinematic production, this chapter also explores how NASA's approach to Hollywood collaborations differs from the Pentagon's by drawing on interviews with Bert Ulrich. Ulrich acts as NASA's entertainment liaison officer and explains why both the agency's culture and its lack of hardware often prohibit it from having the same kind of influence over movies as the DOD, thereby limiting science's more peaceful role in superhero stories.

NASA Enters the Movies

Bert Ulrich has served as NASA's multimedia liaison chief since 2005. When we interviewed him for this book in late 2019, Ulrich told us NASA did not have a formal entertainment program until the mid-1990s, when, under the Clinton administration, it hired a political appointee named Bobby Faye Ferguson.[8] Ferguson formalized the agency's motion picture partnerships partly because the help that NASA had just provided to *Apollo 13* (1995) "was sort of doled out piecemeal by different offices without any coordination," said Ulrich. Ferguson headed NASA's program until 2005, assisting several popular films, including *Armageddon* (1998) and *Space Cowboys* (2000), but she eventually left to run the multimedia liaison efforts for the Department of Homeland Security, and Ulrich, who had long been working at NASA on branding and logo issues, assumed her role.

According to Ulrich, NASA's entertainment program was initially modeled after the Pentagon's, and it, just like the DOD, offers two types of assistance to filmmakers. Basic assistance provides space-related imagery or video footage to any filmmaker wishing to acquire the service, while full cooperation involves providing filmmakers with technical expertise and/or filming sites at a NASA facility, so long as the producer already has distribution in place. Ulrich's annual reports show that several superhero movies have turned to the agency for image clearances and space footage in recent years, including *Iron Man*, *Justice League*, *Thor*, *Ant-Man*, *Aquaman*, and *Avengers: Age of Ultron*, highlighting the number of these films with space- and STEM-related themes.[9] *Guardians of the Galaxy*, in addition to NASA footage, was also granted permission to use the "meatball logo" on a few props in the movie.

When NASA engages in full cooperation on a project, a Space Act Agreement must be signed by all parties. This agreement requires a film producer to submit a draft of the NASA-related portion of the script in advance of filming so that the agency can either "(a) approve the script as it pertains to the portrayal of NASA, its scientific programs and research, and NASA employees (including astronauts)" or (b) "provide written comments in accordance with NASA Responsibility," highlighting script concerns. Any future script revisions that "substantively change NASA's portrayal in the film" must get agency approval. NASA must also grant written permission for its symbols to appear on sets, costumes, and/or promotional and advertising material. Finally, the Space Act Agreement states that if during the editing process, the film changes its narrative in such a manner to "degrade or diminish the goodwill associated with the NASA Symbols (e.g., portrays NASA as an evil, inept or corrupt agency), NASA shall not be deemed to have given the production company approval for use of those symbols in the film" and a dispute resolution shall apply.[10]

Although NASA's program was modeled on the DOD's, from our conversations with Ulrich, his approach to film production appears far less controlling than the Pentagon's. He states that his office is mostly trying to inspire people to learn more about space and the sciences through film. He is less interested in shaping scenes, lines of dialogue, or entire narrative arcs to glamorize its scientists, advance its research agendas, or even adhere to hard and fast rules about scientific facts. For example, NASA scientist Jim Green advised filmmakers of *The Martian* (2015) that the dust storm featured at the start of the film was scientifically improbable and that it would be more accurate to feature an electrical storm as the film's catalyst. When the filmmakers insisted on sticking to the original story line, NASA simply acquiesced rather than pull its support over notions of technical accuracy because the film, as a whole, was a great vehicle for getting the public excited about the exploration of Mars. When movies don't foster excitement for space exploration, NASA simply denies full cooperation. Ulrich noted that the movie *Life* (2017), starring Ryan Reynolds, was denied the use of NASA's logo because the script revolved around a sample from Mars that evolves into a homicidal life form, killing almost everyone aboard the International Space Station (ISS) before making its way to Earth to presumably wreak further destruction. The idea that space is full of murderous microbes did not, in Ulrich's opinion, further inspire people to explore the universe, but even here, he told the filmmakers they could make their own NASA logo for the film, so long as it didn't "look like ours."

When comparing himself to Phil Strub, Ulrich admits that he has a profoundly different philosophy about assisting movies. For Ulrich, the point of his work is not to create "propaganda for the agency. The point of [our work] is to inspire people. You can instill messaging . . . and that's fine if they take it. But if they don't take it, who cares? I mean they're there to make a movie and . . . we're there to inspire the public, and we have to think with the public in mind." Ulrich also said that, unlike Strub, he would never send filmmakers scene ideas aimed at telling them how to portray NASA, especially in fictional story lines. "We don't tell [filmmakers] you should do this or that. . . . I believe in freedom and artistic creativity," he states. He does admit, however, that he is picky about material that is based on actual people or events. For *Hidden Figures* (2016), both Ulrich and an official NASA historian worked closely with the director/screenwriter, Ted Melfi, to correct many of the inaccuracies found in the original script. A similar situation arose on *First Man* (2018). Ulrich states,

> We knew Neil Armstrong over the years. And the initial script we got from Josh Singer just wasn't what we knew of Neil. And they

> were like, "Oh, it's when he was young; he was different then," but we were not so sure. So we said, "You have to go to the families, you have to make sure they're fine with the script, and then you can come back to us."

After working heavily with Armstrong's sons and wives, the screenwriters eventually decided to tone down and evolve their original depiction of the astronaut, which, according to Ulrich, made him look extremely cold. Ulrich joked, "I mean, he looks more tortured now [in the film], which I'm sure was somewhat true," but the final character was more in line with what people thought of him, "which was good. And so, I think in those situations, that's where we really try to help out."

Overall, Ulrich is very enthusiastic about working with Hollywood and seems far more relaxed in his approach to script oversight. Under the Space Act of 1958, NASA is authorized to use its resources for public outreach, in order to build awareness of both the agency and the space industry more broadly. Ulrich believes that Hollywood is one of the most impactful ways the agency engages in that outreach, noting that "movies are a really important way to inspire people" because they get "people really interested and engaged in [the] sciences and engineering" and help motivate kids to enter STEM careers. "So," Ulrich continued, "we've just really embraced it," adding that NASA has "been very lucky" in recent years, because there have been several highly acclaimed films that have positively highlighted the agency and its work, including *The Martian*, *Hidden Figures*, and *First Man*. Ulrich, like Paul Barry, the former entertainment liaison officer at the Central Intelligence Agency, also recognizes that his agency will never possess the power to strong-arm production companies into making significant script revisions like the Department of Defense, even if it wanted to. Barry once remarked in an interview,

> The only real leverage I have [with filmmakers] is the ability to grant access to our Headquarters (filming or to meet personnel) or permission to use our official seal, which incidentally is protected under the 1947 National Security Act. But the reality is that it is easier

> and less expensive for Hollywood simply to recreate a facsimile of our lobby (signature shot) elsewhere. The military branches, of course, have much greater leverage [to negotiate scenes] because they can provide equipment (e.g. aircraft carrier for *Pearl Harbor*, jets for *Top Gun*, helicopters in Morocco for *Black Hawk Down*, etc.) [that can be difficult or very expensive to obtain elsewhere].[11]

NASA, Ulrich acknowledges, finds itself in the same position, and so, even if it wanted to strong-arm reluctant producers into making the agency look indispensable, it would not possess the power to do so. Sometimes, however, offering access to unique locations is enough to help promote the agency through Hollywood, as its work on *The Avengers* reveals.

NASA and *The Avengers*

In our interview, Ulrich acknowledged that the superhero genre is "a different world" from "hardcore science fiction" and that it is "hard to standardize our relationship with Hollywood because each project has its own requirements and its own way of dealing with stuff." NASA, he said, will support fantasy films, as long as they are not "too misleading for the public" and encourage the study of space, as evidenced by its collaboration with *The Avengers* in 2012. According to Ulrich, Latcham had contacted NASA, asking to shoot at one of its facilities—a request that was initially denied because the film did not contain any kind of NASA story line. "You know we are not a soundstage," argued Ulrich. "You can't just film any sort of movie here, so the producers just said, 'OK, we will build a NASA story line into the movie for you,' and they did." This is because Joss Whedon really wanted to film *The Avengers*' opening scenes somewhere "epic" that would create a sense of grand, visual scale to help set the tone for the film,[12] and NASA's Glenn Research Center was perfect for the job.

According to NASA press releases, Marvel filmed these scenes in August 2011 at Glenn's Space Power Facility's vacuum chamber and assembly high bay, as well as in an open field near Plum Brook

Station—both in Ohio. Roughly fifty tractor-trailers hauling film equipment were brought to the facility, where more than three hundred actors and crew members filmed the movie's scenes.[13] SPF facility manager Jerry Carek added that "about 20 Glenn civil servants and support service contractors were also involved in the preparation of the set," and workers were invited to attend a special screening of *The Avengers* on May 5, 2012.[14] The result of this collaboration is a lengthy sequence at the start of the film that prominently features NASA in a Joint Dark Energy Mission, working alongside S.H.I.E.L.D. to experiment on and understand the Tesseract—a potential source of endless clean energy that also acts as a portal into other dimensions. In the film, NASA is featured as an important and equal partner to S.H.I.E.L.D. and as the government agency best suited to understand the power of the Tesseract and to "harness energy from space."[15] Inside the B-2 Space Power Facility, NASA's banner flies at the same height as the S.H.I.E.L.D. banner to indicate its equality in the Avengers universe. There is also a shot of a sign outside of the facility that briefly establishes the Tesseract experimentations as some kind of joint NASA–S.H.I.E.L.D. project, where NASA is listed as the first partner on the sign (see figures 3.1, 3.2, and 3.3).

The film's Space Act Agreement details that Marvel Studios paid roughly $150,000 for its location privileges, with Carek stating, "This is how we survive, by allowing the private sector to use the facility as needed. Their contributions allow us to stay in operation."[16] And indeed, according to a 2015 NASA inspector general's report, the Plum Brook Station is a white elephant, consisting of five major facilities, two of which—the Hypersonic Test Facility (a wind tunnel) and the Cryogenic Components Laboratory—had not been used in four years and another of which—the Combined Effects Chamber designed for large-scale experiments with liquid hydrogen—has never been used.[17] While this money was a nice boon to the Plum Brook Station, $150,000 was a pittance compared to NASA's overall 2011 budget of $18.4 billion, so it stands to reason that NASA's public affairs office was far more interested in the collaboration for the film's promotional potential.

At first this may seem counterintuitive because despite the fact that

Figure 3.1: The Joint Dark Energy Mission sign featured at the start of *The Avengers*.

Figure 3.2: Astrophysicist Erik Selvig works at the NASA B-2 facility with NASA and S.H.I.E.L.D. banners in the background.

Figure 3.3: NASA's banner and logo hung equally with S.H.I.E.L.D.'s in *The Avengers*.

NASA is portrayed as an important government partner in the Joint Dark Energy Mission, its Tesseract studies accidentally leave the world open to invasion, first by the demigod Loki and then, consequently, by generic alien monsters. While NASA is not portrayed as evil by any measure, it could be argued that its failure to understand the Tesseract opens the door to a massive threat and that the film's space themes, which revolve around an alien invasion story, run counter to NASA's preferred image of space as full of desirable opportunities for discovery and learning.

That doesn't mean, however, that the film fails to promote scientific research or to depict scientists as inspirational figures. After Loki and his giant army have invaded Earth, the film culminates in a large battle sequence, where the film's astrophysicist, Erik Selvig (Stellan Skarsgård), proves instrumental in saving the planet. More specifically, as Loki and his space invaders enter Earth through the Tesseract's portal, the Avengers are shown fighting (and losing) the battle until Black Widow talks to Selvig on the rooftop of the Stark Industries headquarters. Selvig was first introduced in *Thor* as Jane Foster and Darcy Lewis's astrophysics professor, and in *The Avengers* he works at NASA on the Joint Dark Energy Mission. While Selvig is then mind-controlled by Loki for most of the story, when he recovers his mental agency, he tells Black Widow that he built a fail-safe to allow the power source of the wormhole generator to be cut. While it is Black Widow who actually brandishes Loki's scepter to pierce the energy shield surrounding the machine to shut it down, it is Selvig who builds this function into the generator and then tells Black Widow what to do. In other words, it is Selvig's scientific knowledge that defeats a superhuman threat and turns the battle's tide without ever wielding a weapon. It is a quiet but inspiring scene, where a lone scientist figures out the answer while all of our superheroes are flying around fighting aliens to little avail. Perhaps, for very thoughtful viewers, the scene may have encouraged them to consider how science, more so than violent conflict, may thwart or avert security threats. As Black Widow states in the final battle scene, "Maybe it isn't about guns."

Still, the film is limited as an unbridled celebration of science, in no small part because of the film's genre demands. As action blockbusters, Marvel films must usually deliver spectacular combat sequences where our heroes can showcase their CGI superpowers, not their prowess at scientific and empirical thinking (although this sometimes happens in *Iron Man* and *Ant-Man*). Vivian Sobchack writes that the rise of superhero films—which has come at the expense of science fiction film production—also signals the culture's current preference for magical rather than rational thinking. A preference for magical thinking, she writes, usually arises in a culture that is under significant and prolonged duress and attempts "to reduce uncertainty and enhance one's sense of control instead of dealing rationally with the complexity of real-world problems."[18] Given that many scholars have linked the rise of superhero films to the posttraumatic society induced by 9/11,[19] it is easy to see why superhero stories favor magical thinking over the slower, empirical narratives of science fiction, even though the latter might help us arrive at more peaceful solutions to world problems. For example, screenwriters might explore science as an alternative tool to thwart security threats, since warfare, over the centuries, has largely been about access to resources. If science can help populations reduce their demand for oil by developing renewable energy sources or can help fight drought to reduce mass migrations, then science can help limit the potential violent conflicts caused by resource competition. But fantasy and action genres do not engage in this type of exploration. They are about wizards, spells, or superpowered individuals that obliterate threats in large-scale battles to win the day.

Given this framework, it is unsurprising that NASA's relaxed approach to Hollywood in conjunction with superhero genre demands led *The Avengers* to marry science with magical thinking as the answer to world threats, instead of just science alone. While it is Selvig who figures out how to close the wormhole, it is still the use of violence and weapons of mass destruction that defeat the incoming and already arrived alien forces. In particular, while the Avengers are unleashing their powers against Loki's forces, the World Council orders the launch of a nuclear missile to destroy the city of New York against Nick Fury's will. Tony is able to redirect that missile into the wormhole just before it closes, where it explodes on the other side of the portal, destroying the aliens and saving human lives. As such, the climax to *The Avengers* embodies both of the dominant ideologies governing the role of space, as the scientific research that Selvig conducts on the Tesseract helps society better understand the nature of the universe, while his epiphany about the fail-safe simultaneously provides a complement to S.H.I.E.L.D.'s efforts to secure space in the name of national security. It should be noted, however, that Selvig's triumph in knowing how to close the wormhole is given less than a minute of screen time, while the spectacle of the war waged between the Avengers and Loki rages for most of the third act. Thus, the role of science in conflict resolution plays a far more marginal function in *The Avengers*, where the conflict conclusively resolves through Iron Man's use of the nuclear missile. The film's element of scientific achievement is also diminished at the end of the film, when Selvig admits that NASA and S.H.I.E.L.D. scientists are still too limited in their understanding of the universe to be wise stewards of the Tesseract and chooses to hand it back to Thor as he returns to Asgard.

Despite these limitations, NASA greatly benefited from the release of *The Avengers*, which broke various international and domestic box-office records, earning an extraordinary $207.4 million within the first three days of release.[20] On a basic level, Marvel Studios generated behind-the-scenes footage and interviews for NASA to use to promote the Plum Brook facility, which has largely relied on private industry interest to remain financially solvent. The film's depiction of NASA and its heroic scientist also promoted a positive image of the agency, and the film allowed NASA to develop a relationship with Marvel Studios that helped it promote excitement for and understanding of the space industry in years to come. For example, NASA used its Mission Control in Houston to provide an uplink of *The Avengers* to astronauts living on the International Space Station. Claiming that the screening was one "that would make Tony Stark envious," the publicized transmission boasted both NASA's real-life space prowess via the uplink and raised awareness about the ISS more broadly.[21] A similar tactic was repeated in 2016, when the popular characters Rocket Raccoon and Groot from Marvel's *Guardians of the Galaxy* were featured on the mission patch for all payloads servicing the ISS. The patch served as the payload insignia to draw attention to the science experiments that were conducted at the ISS as part of the National Lab in 2016. These experiments included the delivery of a magnetic levitation device to study bone loss, a furnace aimed at improving the quality of semiconductor materials synthesized in space, and equipment to study how stem-cell–derived heart cells matured in microgravity. Marvel Custom Solutions created the patch (see figure 3.4) for the Center for the Advancement of Science in Space (CASIS), which manages the National Lab under a contract with NASA. According to Ken Shields, CASIS's operations and educational opportunities director, "A major mission for us . . . is to find unique and innovative ways to bring notoriety to the International Space Station National Laboratory and the research that is being conducted," and "there are very few brands in the world who have as large an impact as Marvel." While the patch was the fourth designed to represent ISS payloads, it was the first to use Marvel characters, and CASIS planned to use Groot and Rocket Raccoon to help them launch a STEM-based educational initiative in 2017 as well.[22]

In 2014, NASA's Jet Propulsion Laboratory (JPL) also worked with

Figure 3.4: The official 2016 ISS mission patch featuring Groot and Rocket Raccoon. Source: https://www.theverge.com/2016/7/22/12256986/nasa-mission-patch-iss-guardians-of-the-galaxy.

Marvel on a traveling exhibition that premiered at Discovery Times Square in New York City on May 30 for a six-month engagement. The immersive experience allowed visitors to explore the superhero universe by participating in a simulated recruitment where they trained as agents of S.H.I.E.L.D. "While movie magic [was] the exhibit's main attraction," JPL "provided content that would enhance the authenticity of the experience and pique visitors' interest in real-world science and technology. The exhibit's NASA-supplied material . . . focused on topics such as the electromagnetic spectrum, black holes as powerful energy sources, and aerospace materials used in creating Iron Man's armor."[23] Deeper connections to NASA content were also planned for the exhibit's companion website.

In 2018, NASA's relationship to both space exploration and Marvel characters was further solidified when fans finished watching the trailer for *The Avengers: Endgame*. In that teaser, Tony Stark is shown stranded in space, telling Pepper Potts that he has run out of water and food

Figure 3.5: Screenshot of the tweets exchanged between NASA and Robert Downey Jr. on December 15, 2018.

and that he is almost out of oxygen. Fans then took to Twitter, asking NASA to help Tony, resulting in a fun, trending exchange where NASA gives some basic rescue advice, to which Robert Downey Jr. replies that it's "always good to know @NASA has your back" (see figure 3.5). Marvel Studios then thanked NASA for their suggestions, tweeting, "Appreciate any help you can provide."[24] Such Twitter exchanges may seem silly, but Ulrich implies that NASA's social media presence is key to energizing young people about the space industry, and the Avengers movies have helped connect younger Marvel fans with the agency through such platforms.

Finally, when asked about the effects of NASA's collaboration with Marvel when *The Avengers* was released, Ulrich stated that "2012 was kind of a magical year for us" because the shuttle program had just ended several months prior and "everyone thought that NASA was dead." In 2012, however, three things helped NASA reenergize interest in space exploration. The first was that social media was really taking off that year, helping NASA reach young people interested in STEM careers. The second was the Curiosity mission, which NASA launched in Times Square. Using the Toshiba Vision screen to broadcast images from the rover on Mars, NASA enjoyed the presence of thousands at the launch party, who all started chanting "NASA" at one point during the evening, and "all of the sudden NASA became kinda sexy" again. The third element was the release of *The Avengers*. While Ulrich can't say *The Avengers* is *the* reason why "NASA became really exciting to the public in 2012," he acknowledges that it was a major part of the general public's renewed interest in space. And that interest in space exploration has only continued to grow. "There is so much content about NASA out there now," Ulrich stated, noting that in 2018, the agency worked on 174 documentaries, up from 120 just a few years prior.[25] But while this section showcases NASA's overall vision of space as a territory ripe with discoveries that can enhance life at home, it is not the vision of space that dominates the superhero genre. Instead, most films promote a far more hawkish view of space, as evidenced by DC's *Man of Steel* and the MCU's *Captain Marvel*. Both of these films demonstrate how unimaginative superhero films have been in envisioning solutions to world problems outside of military violence—even when they involve extraterrestrial threats—thanks, in part, to producers' continued reliance on DOD production support.

Man of Steel (2013)

Man of Steel debuted just one year after *The Avengers* and shares many of the same plotlines: a superhero must fight off a colonizing force that originates from space, a few scientist characters assist in defeating the villains, but the story still resolves in a climactic, violent battle that again utilizes a wormhole to eliminate the invading foes. However, because *Man of Steel* received heavy support from the DOD and almost none from NASA, it, unlike *The Avengers*, prominently features the American military as one of the keys to defending the planet and as a trusted partner to Superman, the advanced alien from Krypton raised from near birth in Smallville, Kansas. *Man of Steel* also works to subordinate science-based conflict resolution in favor of a militarized response, depicts space as an important theater of command, and, given the film's imagery, suggests that the next 9/11 may well come from the skies, and thus the United States would be well advised to augment its weaponry in order to defend itself.

Produced by DC Entertainment, Legendary Pictures, and Syncopy and distributed by the overall DCEU masters, Warner Bros., *Man of Steel* was the first attempt to both ape and rival the MCU with the DC Extended Universe. While the previous attempt to reboot Superman—2006's *Superman Returns*—was a moderate critical and commercial success, it wasn't quite enough for Warner, so it scrapped plans for a sequel and moved on to another full reboot of the Superman character and franchise. Though they were initially delayed by the 2008 screenwriters' strike, they had started taking pitches from comic book authors, Hollywood writers, and directors by the summer on how to restart the film series. As comic book writer Grant Morrison put it after pitching his views to the studio, "I told them, it's not that bad. Just treat *Superman Returns* as the Ang Lee *Hulk*." Also referring to how Marvel had rebooted the Hulk with 2008's *The Incredible Hulk* just five years after Lee's version, comic writer Mark Waid commented, "*The Hulk* has proven the audience will forgive you and let you redo the franchise. You can reboot from scratch."[26]

In 2008, during story discussions for *The Dark Knight Rises*—the final installment of Christopher Nolan's Batman trilogy—writer David Goyer told Nolan of an idea he had for a Superman movie set in a modern context. Nolan was taken by the idea, so he pitched it to Warner, who was impressed by both the story idea and the runaway success of *The Dark Knight*, which came out that summer. They hired Goyer to write and Nolan to produce, before bringing on Zack Snyder to direct. Nolan favored a stand-alone film that wouldn't be connected either to his own Batman series or to a Batman reboot, saying that the characters should be kept separate because "each serves to the internal logic of the story. They have nothing to do with each other."[27] However, Warner wanted *Man of Steel* to be able to launch an interconnected cinematic universe to rival the MCU. While the connections between the films in the DCEU are looser than those in the Marvel equivalent, for the first several films, and particularly in *Batman v. Superman: Dawn of Justice* (2016) and *The Justice League* (2017), all the story lines and characters exist in the same shared universe. It wasn't until late 2018, in the run-up to the release of *Aquaman*, that DC decided to start stepping away from a single, interconnected universe and embrace more varied standalone film projects like *Shazam!*

While *Superman Returns* is a follow-up from the Richard Donner originals from the 1970s and 1980s, the Nolan/Goyer version of Superman is a total reboot. *Man of Steel* makes no references to the events of the original movies and provides a reworked origin story for the Superman character, albeit one based on preexisting Superman lore. It is also thematically and tonally very different, as it situates Superman in a dark, gritty post-9/11 world, much like the Nolan Batman trilogy, where Superman is less a Jesus-like figure of hope so much as a brooding, mysterious, scary alien. In both Goyer's and Donner's versions of the story, Superman is sent to Earth from Krypton while he is a small baby, but the exact circumstances differ significantly. In Donner's version, Krypton is undergoing a major geological crisis, so Jor-El and Lara Lor-Van pack up their only son, Kal-El, in a small spacecraft and send him into the solar system so that he can survive. In *Man of Steel*, there is also an environmental crisis, but it has led to a civil war on Krypton between the established powers and the insurgent General Zod, who attempts a coup in the midst of the planet's core collapsing due to excessive mining and resource exploitation. Krypton's demise leads Jor-El to imbue his baby son with the DNA codex of the Kryptons and to send him to Earth so that their genetic legacy might continue. When General Zod manages to escape Krypton just as it implodes, he spends the next few decades searching for Superman and the codex so that he can recreate his species. After finding Kal-El, Zod then decides to colonize Earth so that the Kryptons can have a viable homeland.

While in the original Superman films our hero is an arrivant—a messianic other who arrives on Earth and offers hope and optimism in the cynical post-Watergate, post-Vietnam period—*Man of Steel* is much more pessimistic and militaristic. This tone is emphasized in a scene after the thirteen-year-old Clark rescues a crashed school bus full of his classmates, and one of the children's parents goes to see the Kent family, clearly shocked by Clark's ability to push the bus out of a river. Following this exchange, Jonathan Kent (Kevin Costner), Superman's adoptive father, admonishes Clark, telling him, "You have to keep this side of yourself a secret. . . . When the world finds out what you can do, it's going to change everything. Our beliefs, our notions of what it means to be human, everything. You saw how Pete's mom reacted, right? She was scared, Clark." Kent's remarks reveal that even though space exploration has worked to discover if humans are alone in the universe, people may not be ready to cope with finding extraterrestrial life. Thus, they may work to destroy Superman in order to quell their fears of the unknown, so he encourages Clark to hide his superpowers. Later in the film, Kent even allows himself to die in a tornado rather be rescued by his son, because other people would see the rescue and expose his son's superpowers. This contrasts starkly with the original *Superman* (1978). In a scene where Lois Lane asks Superman, "Why are you here? There must be a reason for you to be here," Superman responds, "Yes. I'm here to fight for truth and justice and the American way," to which Lois quips, "You're gonna end up fighting every elected official in this country!" While corny and somewhat satirical, this scene illustrates how the original Superman was a symbol of positivity in a pessimistic world, while in the *Man of Steel* version, he is simply another reason for people to be afraid and confused in a world full of fear and confusion. Unlike in Donner's *Superman II*, which resolves when Superman robs Zod and his cohorts of their superpowers in the Fortress of Solitude, in *Man of Steel*, Superman actually commits murder, snapping General Zod's neck in order to save human lives. As Goyer acknowledges, this ending upset a lot of Superman fans because historically, in the comics, there has been an editorial mandate that states "Superman doesn't kill, it was a rule." They knew about the no-kill rule, Goyer stated; "we just thought but sometimes, whether it's a soldier or people in law enforcement," people have to kill in order to protect others, and thus the creators took a major narrative risk, hoping it would equate to larger box-office rewards.[28]

At first, it seems counterintuitive that the DOD refused to support Donner's earlier, more hopeful and patriotic versions of Superman but offered assistance to *Man of Steel*.[29] However, *Man of Steel*'s portrait of the military and its underlying, fearful worldview were more in line with the Pentagon's rhetoric (which consistently claims that fatal threats lurk around every corner) than the somewhat irreverent, tongue-in-cheek portrait of the military in the Donner movies. For one, *Man of Steel* exploited the fear of another 9/11, as General Zod, in his attempts to colonize Earth, begins to wipe out its population through strikes on both Smallville and Metropolis. The battle scenes that ensue are highly referential of the attacks on the World Trade Center. For example, *Variety*'s Justin Chang wrote that one of the most notable features of the film was the way Snyder "channels the specific terror and chaos of 9/11; you see it in those brief scenes of small planes hitting skyscrapers, and in the lingering shots of ash-covered Metropolitans being pulled, traumatized but hopeful, from the rubble." Peter Debruge wrote that he was jarred by the film because in one battle sequence, Snyder "cycles through a series of street-level closeups, showing the faces of random Metropolis citizens (whom we all read as New Yorkers, obviously) moments before a huge space laser starts destroying skyscrapers." In the following montage, Snyder observes those same characters fleeing "from the clouds of dust and rubble" and "from the expressions on the extras' faces to the ground-level view of such a cataclysm, these images directly reference/rip off the footage captured—and endlessly repeated on-air—by news crews following the collapse of the World Trade Center."[30] By utilizing the imagery of 9/11, then, *Man of Steel*, much like *The Avengers*, exploited domestic viewers' fear of another terrorist attack, but unlike *The Avengers*, it suggested that the best response to such an attack would be a military one. Thus, in *Man of Steel*, it is Superman, working alongside the American military, who resolves the conflict, whereas in *The Avengers*, it is Selvig who is able to figure out how to close the wormhole to stop Loki's invasion, while Tony finishes things off by diverting a nuclear bomb.

Part of the reason the military plays such a strong role in *Man of Steel*'s resolution is that the DOD helped shape the content of the film. While Phil Strub was originally opposed to assisting the script, calling it "hopeless" and "stupid,"[31] he eventually sat down with the writer and over the next seven months negotiated a series of script changes that enhanced the military's role and image in the film.[32] One major concern that the DOD had involved the depiction of its hardware as inferior to Zod's. Space invasion stories often prove problematic for the DOD because by their very nature, they feature an opposing force with more sophisticated weaponry that often, and easily, wipes out military forces. This is true in *Man of Steel*, which does not adhere as closely to the concept of the clean war as many of the other films discussed in this book. When the DOD is called upon to help defeat General Zod, viewers see his forces obliterate military aircraft with American service members on board, making it clear they have died fiery, painful deaths.

With DOD guidance, however, the filmmakers still found a way to glamorize nearly every branch of the armed forces. In one early scene, the adult Clark Kent is working on a fishing trawler, trying to maintain his anonymity, when a nearby oil rig explodes in an obvious reference to the 2010 Deepwater Horizon oil rig explosion. Clark goes to help, and when the Coast Guard arrive, they are shown bravely landing on a helipad in the midst of furious flames in order to pick up several survivors rescued from the oil rig by Clark. Superman then holds up a collapsing section of the rig's structure while the helicopter takes off—showing the hero working side by side with the Coast Guard to save lives. The scene reinforces notions of American exceptionalism by juxtaposing both our Kansas-raised superhero and the military forces who aid him.

More profoundly, in the scene when Zod deploys "the World Engine" to begin a terraforming process, the USAF launches a suicide attack at Zod's ship to distract him while Clark destroys the machine. Their plan is to use a C-17 to drop Superman's original Kryptonian ship onto Zod's, colliding their Phantom Drives to create a singularity/wormhole to suck Zod's forces back out into space. Strub wanted to make sure the point of these scenes was not to show how weak the military is in comparison to Zod but rather "to portray (via CGI) the heroic sacrifices of fighter pilots to divert the Kryptonians from the C-17, because the destructive capability of the Kryptonians has already amply been demonstrated."[33] Strub also insisted that all of the fighter craft featured in this scene be from the air force and requested a special emphasis on the F-35—the most expensive fighter jet in the entire US arsenal. The DOD's attempt at generating military pride from this scene backfired, however, after several journalists pointed out that the F-35s were appearing in a superhero movie before they were actually able to fly in combat, due to numerous delays, faults, and glitches. Nonetheless, these scenes work to depict the military as brave and willing to make profound sacrifices for the greater good, while showing off some new hardware to boot. This is seen most prominently in the character of Colonel Hardy (Christopher Meloni), who voluntarily flies his fighter craft into Zod's ship just before telling another character that "a good death is its own reward."

Other changes secured by the DOD include a scene that occurs after General Zod and his forces arrive in a gigantic spaceship and demand that the Earthlings turn over Kal-El/Clark Kent or be destroyed. A journalist who thinks that Lois Lane knows who Kal-El is announces as much during a TV interview, causing the FBI to turn up at the Daily Planet, where Lois works. The original script portrayed this as a violent raid carried out by either special forces or SWAT teams. The DOD's notes say, "There must be no 'Tier 1 Operatives' or any other special operators/SWAT police, etc. Only a few (no 'army of') FBI agents in suits. And they must not be 'storming through the cubicles' as if they're conducting a drug bust in a thuggish way."[34] They also objected to a military character acting as though he has law enforcement authority, and to the FBI producing handcuffs when they take Lois Lane away. As a result, these scenes were changed so that the audience never sees a raid, and the FBI's presence at the Daily Planet offices is only briefly referred to when the editor, Perry White, calls Lois and tells her, "The FBI is here, throwing around words like treason." The FBI also arrives outside Lois's apartment during the call, but we do not see them carrying out a thuggish raid; they merely detain her as she tries to escape down a back alley. These script changes protected the image of the military, who is fully removed from the Daily Planet scenes, and also the FBI, whose real-life special agent Dale Shelton was also a consultant on the movie.[35] The revisions helped both agencies sidestep any hint of citizens' civil liberties being infringed upon during the War on Terror, an especially important move given the passing of the Patriot Act in 2001.

In one of the final scenes of the movie, the DOD also requested changes, as a military general is shown using a drone to find Superman, who, like Tony Stark, proves an ally of the United States but one unwilling to be subsumed by its chain of command. In this scene at the Institute for the Search for Extraterrestrial Intelligence (SETI), Clark crashes the drone in front of General Swanwick before they discuss how to develop a mutual trust moving forward. In his notes, Strub comments, "While we're not thrilled with the portrayal of the US military relentlessly spying on Superman, we can live with this scene, provided that Superman describes the drone as 'one of your spy camera drones,' to make it clear that it is not armed." They then went on to demand that dialogue making fun of the general's hat was removed and "replaced by something that doesn't appear to trivialize him." The DOD also asked to show more of a meeting of the minds between the two, with Strub suggesting that Superman tell the general that before the Zod attack "you hadn't earned my respect. You have now," and then he extends "his hand to offer a handshake, and the General, after a pause, takes it warmly and says something grudgingly, like 'OK, that's good enough for now.'" While the filmmakers did not take up the suggested dialogue word for word, they did make the changes regarding the unarmed drone, rewrote the scene to include the ethos of mutual trust the Pentagon desired, and removed all of the jokes about the general's hat.

In return for these changes, *Man of Steel* benefited from full military support, including weeks of filming at Edwards AFB, with access to hangars and permission "to construct a guard shack, arm & security fencing and base camp" for that period of shooting. The DOD also provided "approximately 200 military extras at EAFB to portray military members from various services," and allowed for aerial photography and the filming of taxiing, takeoff, and landing of various military aircraft, including C-17s, C-130 large transport planes, and UH-60A Blackhawk and CH-47D Chinook helicopters. The California National Guard provided many of these aircraft along with M1-A1 and M2 tanks and Stryker vehicles, while the Army Reserve provided armored security vehicles. Two F-35 multirole fighters stationed at Edwards were also used for filming, as were emergency vehicles and fuel trucks. The contract signed between the DOD and the producers also granted filmmakers permission to bring their own aircraft onto Edwards, in the form of a "Hughes 500 'Little Bird' helicopter; Camera ship helicopter (AStar), and Lear jet."[36] Other government agencies also helped make *Man of Steel* into a rich visual spectacle, including the Canadian Armed Forces, the US Coast Guard, and the National Guard.

While *Man of Steel* received criticism for its ending, dialogue, and acting performances, it was widely praised for its action sequences and musical score by Hans Zimmer. It was also a box-office success, taking in over $116 million on its opening weekend in the United States and a total of $668 million worldwide, according to figures from Box Office Mojo. The military also recorded its success, with a report from the entertainment liaison office noting that the "film began its run with a massive $125.1M, breaking the record for the biggest June opening weekend ever, ahead of *Toy Story 3*'s $110.3M bow in 2010." They also noted that "among 2013 films, *Man of Steel* had the second-best debut of the year behind *Iron Man 3*, which started with $174.1M in May."[37]

A comparison of *The Avengers* to *Man of Steel* yields several important conclusions. First, while the DOD fell out with *The Avengers'* producers because they couldn't find a way to make themselves seem as powerful as S.H.I.E.L.D. (see chapter 2), in *Man of Steel* they are shown working side by side with Superman, in part as a result of extensive script revisions enforced by the Pentagon. Both films feature an extraterrestrial army attacking Earth, reinforcing the concept of space as more advanced high ground for combat missions. In *The Avengers*, however, the final showdown is partially resolved when an astrophysicist explains how to shut off the wormhole machine and therefore stops the invading alien forces. In *Man of Steel*, the roles are reversed. Due to the bulk of the film's government assistance coming from the DOD, it resolves in a climax that uses military violence. This is not to say that science does not play a role in *Man of Steel*. Jor-El serves as Krypton's chief scientist, and when Superman and Lois Lane are trapped aboard Zod's ship, Jor-El's hologram helps Lane change the ship's atmosphere from a Kryptonian to an Earth-based one, in order to make Lois and Superman stronger while simultaneously weakening Zod. The plan is a good example of how scientific understanding can be used to mitigate threats without the use of guns and bombs. Likewise, Jor-El tells Lois about the importance of the Phantom Drives in defeating Zod, knowledge that she passes along to Kal-El, who understands how to technically carry it out. Nonetheless, none of the reviewers saw *Man of Steel* as a celebration of scientific understanding. Instead, the film was called everything from "annihilation porn" to cinematic "shock and awe" and "an uneasy attempt to milk 9/11 imagery for excitement and suspense."[38]

Finally, despite the fact that *Man of Steel* features an attack from the skies, the film debuted a few years too early to directly bolster the emerging zeitgeist that emphasized the importance of space to military combat and to the air force more particularly. Indeed, despite the fact that the army, navy, air force, and coast guard all are featured in *Man of Steel*, it was the National Guard—not the air force—that spent roughly $10 million of taxpayers' money on a Soldier of Steel recruitment campaign. That campaign featured two theater spots that played during the film's release, an official workout plan for men and women interested in bulking up like Henry Cavill, and flyers sent in the mail to potential recruits. Its goals were to link Superman to National Guardsmen and to exploit the popularity of Superman to encourage seventeen- to twenty-four-year-olds to learn more about becoming citizen-soldiers.[39] For example, in one of the theatrical spots, viewers are told that Guards are soldiers of steel who are "seemingly ordinary people . . . perhaps in this very theatre," who "know the uniform they wear makes an extraordinary difference" and are "capable of extraordinary feats." The visuals intercut between clips of Superman from *Man of Steel* and shots of National Guardsmen rescuing American citizens trapped by floods and earthquakes to draw explicit parallels between the superhero and the "citizen soldiers of the National Guard" (and to downplay the fact that Guard soldiers can be recruited and deployed into combat zones). The promo finishes by saying, "Learn how one American icon inspires another" and directed audiences to the Guard's soldierofsteel.com website, which now redirects to the Guard's recruiting website, www.nationalguard.com.[40]

As Ryan Pumory writes, at the time of *Man of Steel*'s release, the National Guard was undergoing significant changes. Prior to September 11, 2001, the Guard served a largely "noncombat, supporting role in US military operations." Enlistees essentially played the role of "weekend warriors," living at home instead of on bases and working in the army part-time rather than full-time. Because of the strain of both the Afghanistan and Iraq wars, however, the Guard was soon asked to play an increased role in combat missions, with at least 370,000 Guard soldiers having been deployed to those regions after 9/11. With the global financial crisis of 2008 and over $75 billion worth of military budget cuts in the subsequent years, the military grew further reliant on the Guard, which conveniently and simultaneously experienced large spikes in enlistment in 2009, due to a "weak economy, high unemployment, and the high cost of college tuition." By the time *Man of Steel* was in full development, Secretary of Defense Leon Panetta, speaking at a 2011 National Guard conference, said that the Guard is now firmly established "as a *vital operational arm of our military* . . . a force far different from the strategic reserve many envisioned during the Cold War." Just one year prior to *Man of Steel*'s release, the office of the National Guard bureau chief was also elevated to serve on the Joint Chiefs of Staff by the 2012 National Defense Authorization Act.[41]

These cultural shifts help explain why the National Guard—even though it is never mentioned in *Man of Steel*—invested in Superman as a symbol of a new type of citizen-soldier, and why, despite the heavy depiction of the air force and its portrayal of space as an important

Figure 3.6: "Soldiers of Steel" recruitment ad featuring Superman. Source: https://www.military.com/undertheradar/2013/06/soldier-of-steel-can-superman-recruit.

theater for command, the air force did not use *Man of Steel* in its recruitment drives (for fear of the military competing against itself). By *Captain Marvel*'s release just five years later, however, the military's aims and objectives had shifted yet again. In 2016, the air force began pushing for the robust training of personnel for space-related combat missions, and by 2018, President Trump officially ordered the founding of the US Space Force, commenting, "Our destiny beyond the Earth is not only a matter of national identity, but a matter of national security."[42] Similarly, three-star air force general Chris Bogdan said that space is the "new warfighting domain. Our job is to try and help the Department of Defense to become space warfighters."[43] While *Man of Steel* and *The Avengers* depicted 9/11-style attacks coming from space and prepared the public for a renewed emphasis on US military responses to those threats, the timing of *Captain Marvel* and its links to the US Air Force helped solidify, more than any other film, the image of space as the latest territory in military expansion and offered preemptive support for the founding of the US Space Force.

Captain Marvel (2019)

Featuring many of the same tropes and values as *Man of Steel*, *Captain Marvel* was heavily supported by the DOD and generated similar military-sponsored promotional campaigns. In 2016, the USAF began running Entertainment Industry Leader Tours (also known as Civic Leader Tours or CLTs), where dozens of Hollywood writers, directors, and producers are taken to air force facilities in order to encourage them to produce more air force–friendly stories and/or to foreground it in their movies. The inaugural tour took Hollywood leaders to Alaska for several days, visiting Eielson AFB in Fairbanks and Joint Base Elmendorf-Richardson in Anchorage. The tour promised to provide participants "with an overview of US Air Force airpower entities located in Alaska, with the goal of introducing common work practices, missions and operating challenges in the Arctic environment to enhance future film and storytelling abilities in a realistic manner."[44]

By spring 2017, the USAF entertainment liaison office had already begun planning for its next tour and were exploring its Space Command as a likely location, as an April report noted that air force project officer Leslie Finstein and Lieutenant Schirner were in contact with Mike Pierson of Space Command's Public Affairs office, regarding the possibility of a CLT. "Mr. Pierson offered an exciting range of options to include, but not limited to" NORTHCOM's Modular Air Force Firefighting unit and its Tactical Air Control Party at Fort Carson. While a tour of Nellis AFB was initially under consideration, the staff agreed "that Space Command may have more to offer."[45] Forty-five air force staff members then went on an "idea generation tour" to Colorado Springs in June 2017 to prepare for the CLT the following month and nail down exactly what they wanted to show to Hollywood creatives. Documents from both tours refer to the entertainment liaison office's general mission "to project and protect the image of the United States Air Force within the global entertainment environment" and a file on the Space Command CLT outlines how the tour was envisioned as a "three day, two night trip to Colorado Springs, Colorado to showcase the vital role Space Command plays in our nation's defense. Attendees will visit Cheyenne Mountain, Schriever AFB, Peterson AFB, Fort Carson, and the beautiful Air Force Academy campus. The trip aims to inspire realistic storytelling of Air Force people, missions, and assets in the entertainment industry." Coming off the heels of the bitter and vicious 2016 election campaign, which had exacerbated the political polarization in the United States, among the notes for participants in the Space Command tour was also a request to "please leave politics at home. Your US Air Force is non-partisan, even in this political climate. Please don't put Air Force members in awkward situations by bringing up the topic."[46]

Despite this, the choice of Space Command was clearly political, as it aimed to promote the idea of space as the ultimate high ground and future territory for US military expansion. This agenda was a high priority for the air force, which in 2016 had just launched its own AF Space Force Mission—a training program to help the Space Command ready its airmen for space-related combat. In its mission overview, or white paper, Gen. John Hyten, commander of the AF Space Command, wrote:

> Space as a global commons is vital to commerce and is an essential element of Joint Warfare and global stability. Space is no longer a sanctuary where the United States or our allies and partners operate with impunity. Although Air Force Space Command (AFSPC) has a long history of providing space capabilities vital to the defense of our nation, the training and skills that sustained our space operations for the last several decades are not the same skills we need to fight through threats and win in today's contested, degraded and operationally limited (CDO) environment. To ensure our forces are prepared to operate in this new reality, AFSPC must transform our culture and build the expertise and skills necessary for our space forces to operate freely, and if necessary, defend themselves in the global commons of space.[47]

Given that the 2017 CLT tour of Space Command came just one year after the Space Force Mission was established and almost a year prior to President Trump's declaration on TV that he was ordering the Pentagon to create the US Space Force as a new military branch, it stands to reason that the tour was intended to build both public and administrative support for an expansion of the air force program through Hollywood.[48] Undoubtedly, *Captain Marvel* presented a unique, high-profile opportunity to propagate the idea of space as an important theater for combat (as well as the air force's unique ability to win those wars), with the movie releasing just nine months before the official launch of the USSF. An air force summary of support to *Captain Marvel* highlights how the Space Command CLT led to the film's producers asking for military support, and lists the film's key themes and messages, noting, "Captain Marvel may be fiction but her story represents generations of real women who broke through barriers to serve their nation in air, space, and cyberspace."[49]

Indeed, among the dozens of Hollywood insiders who attended the Air Force Space Command tour in 2017 were Anna Boden and Ryan Fleck, the cowriters and codirectors of *Captain Marvel*, as well as Mary Livanos, an associate producer on the project. Other Marvel Studios mainstays also participated, including location manager Illtyd Jones; screenwriter Jonathan Spaihts, who penned *Doctor Strange*; and executive producer Jonathan Schwartz, who produced *Captain America*, *Guardians of the Galaxy*, and *Captain Marvel*. No Marvel Studios creatives attended the 2016 tour in Alaska, so the Space Command CLT represents the rebirth of the military-Marvel relationship that had worked so well for both parties during the Phase One films, but which broke apart on *The Avengers* and was effectively suspended following *The Winter Soldier*. Other superhero genre creatives on the 2017 CLT included Adam Cozad, the screenwriter behind *Suicide Squad 2* and writer/producer/comic book author Marc Guggenheim, who has worked on everything from *Supergirl* to *DC's Legends of Tomorrow* to the *X-Men Origins: Wolverine* video game.

From Boden and Fleck's participation in the CLT to *Captain Marvel*'s release in March 2019, the air force provided a full range of military assistance to the film. As part of her character research, for example, Brie Larson, who plays the lead Carol Danvers, spent several days at Nellis AFB, Nevada, "where she was introduced to fighter pilots and weapons systems operators." She spent an hour flying in an F-15 and played out a simulated battle to get a feel for what real fighter pilots go through, which Larson said was "awesome. In particular, doing a barrel roll and feeling the G-forces later became pieces that were really helpful when we were making the movie . . . I knew what that felt like." The director of the air force's entertainment liaison office, Lt. Col. Nathan Broshear, also noted that Larson wanted to have dinner with the female pilots "and spend the evening with them to trade war stories, so to speak. And then every night that's kind of what she did. She spent time with those fighter pilots and got a chance to know who they are and how they tick."[50] Larson also spent a lot of time with Brig. Gen. Jeannie Leavitt, a pioneering aviator, the air force's first female fighter pilot, and the first female commander of Fifty-Seventh Wing at Nellis. Leavitt consulted on the movie and was one of the inspirations for Captain Marvel's backstory, with Livanos, the film's associate producer, commenting on how the 2017 CLT indirectly led them to Leavitt. In an interview, Livanos explained that Leavitt spent time with her, Fleck, and Boden,

> telling us more about her experience coming up through the ranks and becoming a pilot back in the late '80s, early '90s, and the trials and tribulations that she faced. She's a huge inspiration for the character of Carol Danvers. She just has an unwavering steadfast spirit. Really, all of the pilots that we met during our time at Nellis were just high-achieving individuals who don't settle. We found them to be huge inspirations, and we were just blown away by all the people that we met during our time there.[51]

When it came to filming *Captain Marvel*, the producers did not ask to shoot at Space Command but were granted access to Nellis and Edwards AFBs, where they shot flight sequences and most of the flashbacks that tell the story of the protagonist's history in the air force. As well as providing aircraft and military extras, Maj. Stephen "Cajun" Del Bagno worked as an on-set technical advisor, "helping us make sure that we were portraying air force pilots in the right way," said Livanos.[52] Del Bagno also made a cameo appearance in the film as a tertiary air force character in one of the flashback scenes—as did Leavitt and Maj. Matt "Spider" Kimmel—and Del Bagno's call sign Cajun appears in the background in several scenes. Shortly after completing work on the movie, Del Bagno died in a training accident, leading to Larson and others posting tributes on social media, the producers emailing their condolences to the air force, and ultimately the filmmakers dedicating the movie to him in the closing credits. They also credited the 412th Test Wing at Edwards Air Force Base, the 144th Fighter Wing at Fresno Air National Guard Base, California, the 309th Aerospace Maintenance and Regeneration Group at Davis-Monthan Air Force Base, and the 57th Wing and 56th Fighter Wing at Luke AFB, Arizona.

When the film released, the DOD provided promotional support to the film via social media, television broadcasts, and numerous articles on sites like *Air Force Times* and Military.com. When Larson appeared on *Good Morning America* to debut the film's trailer, she did so from the Air and Space Museum in an event "worked by [the] LA/NYC teams" of air force public affairs, resulting in Leavitt appearing at the museum alongside Larson to help promote the movie.[53] The museum also hosted two preview screenings attended by dozens of military officials, and the day before the premiere, a DOD document records that the "Air Force hosted the co-directors at the Pentagon," where Boden and Fleck "attended office calls and had lunch with Air Force leaders. They also participated in a personal development session" for public affairs officers from the air force and the DOD.[54] On the day of the premiere, dozens of airmen attended the red carpet, and the Thunderbirds performed a flyover to help add to the elite glamour of the event. Leavitt also attended the premiere and was interviewed on the red carpet, praising Larson for "how interested she was in being very genuine in her character" and promoting the "new opportunities" waiting for women in the air force.[55] Meanwhile at the Disneyland resort in California, there was another flyover by the 144th Fighter Wing of the California Air National Guard with the PA system announcing to visitors, "In just a few minutes, the skies above the Disneyland resort will roar with the awesome power of a F-15 fighter jet formation . . . We hope you enjoy this exciting aerial exhibition and we invite you to cheer for these exceptionally skilled pilots." The next announcement then drew parallels between superheroes and the military, saying, "In honor of our great service members from the United States Air Force, and to celebrate one of the universe's most powerful heroes, Captain Marvel, please look up at the skies above."[56]

Much like the National Guard did with *Man of Steel*, the air force saw *Captain Marvel* as a great opportunity for boosting recruitment, especially with women, and organized a tie-in recruitment campaign called Origin Story. Partnering with the advertising agency GSD&M, the air force produced video spots that were distributed through movie theaters, YouTube, and social media platforms. These were designed to capitalize on both the release of *Captain Marvel* and International Women's Day (the date of the film's release) to recruit more women into the air force. The videos exclusively feature female airmen and equate them with superheroes, as a voiceover intones, "Every superhero has an origin story. We all got our start somewhere. For us, it was the US Air Force." Likewise, Marvel Entertainment broadcast a livestream of the film's premiere from the red carpet, and their hosts interviewed some of the airmen present, asking questions including, "Every hero has an origin story, what's yours?" However, some of these female-oriented recruitment efforts provoked criticism when the Origin Story video spots were released just days after air force veteran senator Martha McSally testified that she was raped by her superior officer while in the air force. In an interview for the Wrap website, professor Kara Ellerby outlined, "Even though they have been including more women and promoting them into positions of power in different branches and in the Pentagon, that hasn't really stymied the issue of sexual violence. There is still something very deep-seated in the culture of the military that's damaging to women."[57]

Nonetheless, *Captain Marvel* helped promote the glamour, bravery, and prowess of the US Air Force, while the film itself promoted the service's agenda of depicting space as an important combat frontier. The opening scene features Carol Danvers in hand-to-hand combat training with commander Yon-Rogg (Jude Law) of the Kree—a highly militarized alien race. At this point in the story, Danvers is assumed to be Kree, known by the name Vers. Before long she and the rest of her unit are deployed to a border planet on the edge of Kree space, Torfa. They are meant to rescue an undercover Kree operative who has infiltrated the planet to gather intelligence on the invading army of Skrulls—a rival alien race with shape-shifting abilities. The operation turns into an ambush leaving many of the Kree soldiers dead and Vers kidnapped by a Skrull commander named Talos. The Skrull are trying to get information on a faster-than-light drive, and as they probe Vers's memories trying to find out what she knows, Vers has flashbacks to her past on Earth, when she was an air force test pilot in the 1980s. Vers eventually breaks free from her restraints, defeats the Skrull soldiers, and uses an escape pod to flee their ship, crashing landing on Earth, leading to further chases and battles with the Skrull that in turn garners the attention of S.H.I.E.L.D. and its young agent, Nick Fury. This opening act is fast-paced and dominated by violence and the struggle for territory. Vers is told by Yon-Rogg that the Skrull have taken over Torfa and that they have infiltrated Earth, and that they are a threat to the human race. The entire vision of space offered by the first segment of *Captain Marvel* is one of war and colonization, and much like *Man of Steel*, the moral of the story is that the only way to meet these challenges is through military violence.

The second act of *Captain Marvel* sees Vers team up with Fury to figure out what's really going on, but first they test each other to ensure they aren't a shape-shifting Skrull in disguise. In a bar, Vers quizzes Fury on his background, and Fury explains he was in the army and then became a spy before joining S.H.I.E.L.D. "Been riding a desk for the past few years, trying to figure out where our future enemies are coming from. Never occurred to me that they'd be coming from above," he states. When Fury then asks Vers to prove that she's not a Skrull, she simply extends her arm and fires a photon blast from her hand, destroying an innocent nearby jukebox. While this scene is one of the more comical in the film, it replicates familiar ideas—that outer space is full of potential enemies and that casual violence is a way to overcome obstacles, and even to build trust with your own kind. Vers then examines a crystal she recovered from a Skrull that contains recordings of her extracted memories, which leads her and Fury to a nearby air force installation that houses Project Pegasus (see figure 3.7)—the same project mentioned in the NASA scene at the start of *The Avengers*. An on-screen graphic informs us that this is a joint NASA–USAF facility, which is the only mention of NASA in the entire film. NASA did not provide any support to *Captain Marvel*, so this fleeting reference is merely an echo of their input on *The Avengers*, as they'd already been tied to Project Pegasus in MCU lore.

It turns out that Pegasus is an energy research project based around the Tesseract, and that a woman Vers had seen in nightmares is Dr. Wendy Lawson, whose role in Pegasus was to try to develop a faster-than-light engine. Vers learns of her own history as an air force test pilot named Carol Danvers, and she remembers flying a craft equipped with Lawson's experimental engine when they were attacked by a Kree fighter craft, crash-landing on Earth and leading to Danvers being presumed dead. She also learns that her superpowers derive from when she destroyed the engine to prevent Yon-Rogg from taking it after he shoots them down. The explosion of the engine, combined with being rescued by the Kree and given a transfusion of their blood, turned her from a human into a superpowered part-human, part-Kree. Once more, violence and destruction dominate all the dramatic conflict in the film. Likewise, space, through Danvers's gradually revealed backstory, is depicted as full of warlike creatures we are not adequately prepared to defend ourselves against. While in the original comics Danvers's backstory is that she was a crack air force test pilot before becoming security chief for NASA, in the film adaptation her NASA role is removed and the story is oriented entirely around her military experience.

The final act of the film continues to embody these militaristic values, as Danvers and Fury set out to find Maria Rambeau—a fellow former air force pilot and the last person to see Lawson and Danvers alive before the test flight. In one flashback scene establishing the close friendship between Rambeau and Danvers, Rambeau asks, "About to show these boys how to do it. You ready?" Danvers responds, "Higher, further, faster, baby"—incorporating one of the air force's mottos directly into the film's dialogue. Rambeau also has a daughter

Figure 3.7: Title card announcing Project Pegasus and a joint NASA–USAF program.

who spends her entire time on screen wearing a conspicuous US Air Force T-shirt—an obvious recruitment plug. This has echoes of another alien invasion movie, *Battleship* (2012), where the army leaned on the producers so that the "Wounded Warrior character was expanded significantly from the original cameo appearance to a major character instrumental to defeating the invading aliens and saving the planet—all while wearing an ARMY t-shirt." The army document goes on to say that "the $200 million project is a pro-military chest-thumper with corresponding recruiting benefits."[58] It is likely that the choice to dress Rambeau's daughter in an air force T-shirt originated with the military Hollywood office, especially given one heavy-handed scene that was shot at military housing on Edwards AFB. Rambeau's daughter is helping Danvers redesign her space suit uniform, and Danvers ends up copying the symbols and colors from the daughter's T-shirt, explaining, "We're on the same team." Following a plot twist where Talos reveals that the Kree are the evil alien race trying to wipe out the Skrull, Danvers switches sides to help the Skrull, and the climax of the film sees a large space battle in Earth's orbit where Danvers—now in full air force colors—destroys a Kree bomber and several other ships after fully gaining control over her superpowers. This forces the Kree to retreat and allows the Skrull to escape genocide. The film ends with Fury drawing up initial plans for his initiative to help ward off future alien invasions, which he names after Danvers's air force call sign: Avenger.

At almost every step in the plot, Danvers's/Captain Marvel's violence is rewarded and shown to be righteous, allowing her to rediscover who she is and triumph over the enemy. It could be argued that it is not merely Danvers's skills and experience from her time in the air force but primarily her superpowers that enable her to flourish and overcome the antagonists, and thus *Captain Marvel* does not foreground the military to the extent that *Man of Steel* does. However, the role of the air force, and by implication the forthcoming USSF, in the climactic victory against the Kree is emphasized by Rambeau's part in the unfolding struggle. While Danvers leads the assault on the Kree battalion of spaceships, Rambeau pilots an experimental craft stolen from Project Pegasus to not only aid in the battle but also help the Skrull refugees escape. Rambeau accomplishes this despite having never piloted the ship before, emphasizing the excellence of her USAF training, how it has equipped her for even interstellar battle, and how it is not just the half-alien Danvers who can take the fight to space-based threats but regular military service members too.

As aforementioned, the film's release in March 2019 came right between President Trump's announcement of the creation of the Space Force as a separate military branch in 2018 and its formal creation in December 2019 and functioned as a powerful recruitment tool for both the USAF and USSF. As *Air Force Times* reporter Stephen Losey put it, somewhat tongue-in-cheek, "When Captain Marvel is released March 8, supervillains across the galaxy are about to learn that an airman is the last person that you wanna cross."[59] Figures from Box Office Mojo show that *Captain Marvel* reached a vast audience, taking in over $426 million in the US and over $701 million in foreign markets for a worldwide total of over $1.12 billion and becoming the first female-led superhero film to pass the $1 billion mark.[60] The film also helped encourage women to apply to the Air Force Academy with air force statistics showing the branch enjoyed both the highest number and highest proportion of female applicants to the academy in five years in the wake of the film's release. The Origin Story promotional campaign also "received 173,000 visits, 11 million views of the video itself, and 200 million impressions overall," with Lt. Col. Jacob Chisolm, deputy chief of strategic marketing at the Air Force Recruiting Service, praising the film for doing much of the campaign's heavy lifting.[61] Perhaps the most obvious vindication of *Captain Marvel*'s ability to function as a military recruitment tool is that Leavitt was promoted to become commander of air force recruitment following her role consulting on the film.[62]

In the end, then, *Captain Marvel* functions not only as a powerful piece of military recruitment propaganda but also as a strong advocate for the militarization of space. Aliens are shown to be either deceptive or violently threatening, necessitating a forceful response. Space itself is shown to be little more than another war-fighting domain, as we learn almost nothing about the Kree or Skrull civilizations except for their capacity for violence and deceit. Their technologies, political systems, and religious and philosophical beliefs are never explored; they are simply two warring factions whose conflict spills over onto Earth. As such, *Captain Marvel* is equally as or even more militaristic than *Man of Steel*, and far more so than *The Avengers*. In the latter, it is the marriage of science and violence that repels hostile alien hoards, while in *Man of Steel* NASA is name-dropped in one line of dialogue, and Jor-El uses some scientific prowess to help defeat Zod. In *Captain Marvel* NASA is sidelined almost completely, and ideas of science and discovery are largely irrelevant to the development of the plot and the resolution of the conflict. The film also took the concept of military combat in space seriously. Indeed, all three of the films mentioned in this chapter depict villainous threats coming from more advanced, extraterrestrial forces, helping the American public—as well as the global community—prepare for a future where combat is not just limited to air, land, and sea and where specialized military forces are necessary for space combat. And this concept had continued to be echoed in entertainment offerings like Netflix's *Space Force* (2020), a spoof-like comedy about the establishment of the branch starring Steve Carell. *Space Force* lampoons the unit's prowess, the presidential motivations for establishing it, and military officers themselves, but it also articulates the need to compete with Russia and China to establish US dominance in space.

Conclusion

We do not wish to claim that the trend of favoring space as a new military combat zone that promises spectacular battles with alien forces is unique to the superhero genre, or the sole result of the military's influence in moviemaking. This trend can be seen in a range of sci-fi products. Both the *Star Trek* and *Star Wars* franchises have undergone reboots, beginning with 2009's *Star Trek* and 2015's *The Force Awakens*. Both have largely abandoned their established role as space operas in favor of becoming action stories set in space. The original *Star Trek* TV series, the spin-off films, and late twentieth-century TV incarnations such as *The Next Generation* (1987–1994) and *Voyager* (1995–2001) typically feature a nonviolent response to the challenges faced by the crews of Starfleet ships. They incorporate elements of diplomacy, scientific discovery, or technological innovation; intelligence tactics such as subterfuge or manipulation; or heroic risk-taking or self-sacrifice to solve problems. The more recent versions, in contrast, are increasingly dominated by lengthy battles, either between huge fleets of spaceships or between characters using high-tech, futuristic weaponry. The climax of the CBS series *Star Trek: Discovery* (2017), much like the climax of *Star Wars: The Rise of Skywalker* (2019), for example, is a vast, sensory-overloading battle involving hundreds of spaceships, despite both productions working with NASA and neither working with the DOD. Such trends have been noticed by scholars as well as fans, with Sobchack lamenting that recent science fiction films have lost much of their "cultural ballast," since now they too often devolve "into lengthy but meaningless chases" and "endless battles."[63] As Geoff King also adds, "In an age in which the big Hollywood studios have become absorbed into giant media conglomerates, the prevalence of spectacle and special effects has been boosted by a growing demand for products that can be further exploited in multimedia forms such as computer games and theme park rides," yet another reason that helps explain the role of industry trends in determining genre shifts and cinematic content.[64]

The decline of the classical sci-fi genre, however, is much more convenient for the DOD than for NASA, as the two institutions are in competition for funding and authority from Congress. Films depicting the challenges of space requiring a violent, military response help maintain the Pentagon's role in the forefront of politicians' minds. Not since the days of the space race and the Apollo program have NASA's budgets and perceived importance come close to rivaling the Pentagon's, and the decline of classical sci-fi stories mirrors the decline of political enthusiasm and funding for peaceful space exploration, which peaked in the 1960s (see figure 3.8).

That said, it can be argued that one contributing reason for the prominence of space stories steeped in violence rather than in exploration and discovery has to do with NASA's more laissez-faire approach to Hollywood production. Internal documents from NASA's Multimedia Liaison Office confirm that they provided help or engaged in promotional outreach on *John Carter* (2012), *Man of Steel*, *The Dark Knight Rises*, *The Winter Soldier*, *Teenage Mutant Ninja Turtles* (2016), *Wonder Woman*, *Dark Phoenix* (2019), and HBO's *Watchmen* (2019), but all of these products, with the exception of the "mystery box" series *Watchmen*, feature dramatic conflicts that are primarily resolved through violence. If NASA exerted more influence on the content of these films then perhaps some of them would—like *The Avengers*—have incorporated a more blended approach to story writing and explored other ways for their protagonists to overcome obstacles aside from blasting vast swathes of urban jungle. Without the same assets to leverage as the DOD, however, NASA, especially, under the more laissez-faire approach of Bert Ulrich, seems unlikely to aggressively promote scientific understanding as key to human conflict resolution in popular entertainment.

Finally, while many of these stories feature alien threats, the DOD and its Space Force are not really concerned about having to do battle with extraterrestrials at this time. As Arthur Asa Berger writes in *Popular Culture Genres*, alien beings (like Thanos, the Kree, or General Zod)

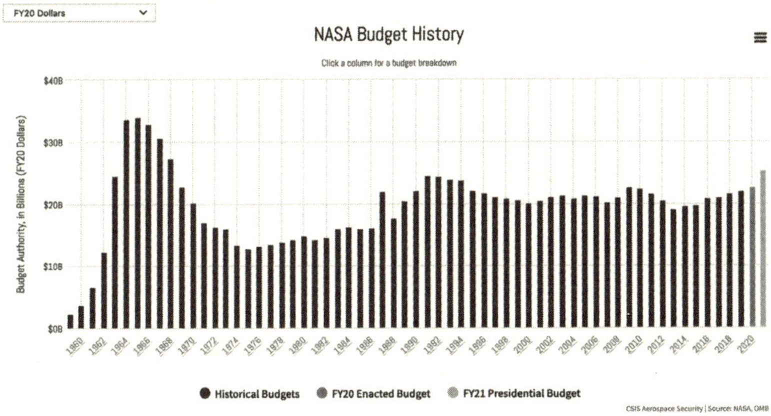

Figure 3.8: The history of NASA's annual budget. Source: https://aerospace.csis.org/data/history-nasa-budget/.

instead represent "a fear of foreigners, anxiety about contamination of national values, racial parity and related concerns." Aliens, in other words, simply represent people from other regions with values, beliefs, and religions that "pose a threat to our way of life, which is, of course, the right way."[65] This xenophobic view of space is represented in Lt. Gen. Steven Kwast's comments to Latcham, the movies discussed in this chapter, and in the rash of other military-supported alien invasion films throughout the 2010s, including *Battle: Los Angeles* (2011), *Transformers: Dark of the Moon* (2011), *Battleship* (2012), *Pacific Rim* (2013), *Independence Day: Resurgence* (2016), and *Transformers: The Last Knight* (2017). In each of these films, the aliens function as metaphors for countries and peoples perceived as a threat by the US military and security establishment. In most of them, the DOD is shown leading the way in fighting back and protecting the Earth as a whole. The implication in these narratives reflects the US security state's suspicion that someone—be it the United States, China, or another nation or international conglomerate—is going to begin colonizing space and disrupting our satellite communications, which begs the question of viewers: wouldn't you rather it was the United States leading the way? And wouldn't you rather the DOD establish an early foothold so as to maintain American primacy across the solar system before those dastardly Chinamen get there first? Indeed, as other nations—most notably China—grow to economically rival the United States and develop their own ambitious space programs, it is likely the threats these nations pose are behind the Pentagon's and Hollywood's hostile, militaristic views of space. Unfortunately, this view conflicts with the notion of space as a neutral territory full of wondrous opportunities for scientific research and exploration, but, as the next chapter reveals, one quasi-government agency is helping Hollywood value science more than in years past.

4 You Can't Just Fall off a Planet

Assembling the Science and Entertainment Exchange

In 2007, Marvel debuted a new traveling exhibition at the Ontario Science Centre in Toronto. Featuring thirty hands-on "action centers," the exhibit aimed to introduce visitors to a variety of scientific principles in a fun and engaging manner. A station featuring Doctor Octopus—a Spider-Man nemesis who wields four robotic tentacle arms—launched a discussion on prosthetic limb development. The blind superhero, Daredevil, illustrated how sightless creatures navigate with echolocation and acoustics, while a station featuring Professor X explored DNA and genetic mutation. By using popular superheroes as a gateway into science, the exhibit taught visitors about arachnology, magnetism, engineering, hydraulics, chemistry, evolution, sound waves, visual perception, and more.[1]

The Marvel Superheroes Science Exhibition is just one example of the ways that science and superhero stories have long been intertwined. As comic creators invented heroes who could speed through objects, teleport, become invisible, and fly, they turned to science to explain these characters' origins. The Flash, for example, derived his powers from a chemical spill exacerbated by a lightning strike; Spider-Man is the result of a radioactive spider bite;

Part of this article previously appeared in Tricia Jenkins and Tom Secker, "Science, Superheroes and the Science and Entertainment Exchange," *Journal of Science and Popular Culture* 4, no. 1 (2021).

the Fantastic Four are made super by exposure to cosmic rays; and characters such as the X-Men are explained by "genetic mutations," which Stan Lee used to describe "myriad abilities ranging from psychic powers to teleportation to weather control."[2] Superhero characters often feature as scientists too. Outside of Tony Stark and Bruce Banner, T'Challa, in the *Black Panther* comics, is not just a powerful warrior but an accomplished scientist, a role that his sister, Shuri, more prominently adopts in the movie. Mr. Fantastic (Reed Richards) holds PhDs in physics and electrical engineering; the Flash (Barry Allen) works as a forensic scientist; and Dr. Jon Osterman, who rushes into an intrinsic field generator for something he left inside his lab coat, emerges as the superpowered Doctor Manhattan. Furthermore, several characters such as Captain America and the Hulk are themselves the result of scientific experiments, with Jason Bainbridge summarizing that, in total, MCU heroes are "usually the product of science, augmentation or experimentation in pursuit of progress and protecting the state."[3] Given superhero films' strong ties to science, this chapter examines the role of the science advisor in the genre, as well as the work of the Science and Entertainment Exchange (an arm of the National Academy of Sciences) to demonstrate how both groups are trying to modernize scientists' image and popularize scientific concepts through these movies. In doing so, these groups are also offering important and alternative narratives to those more violent plot points proffered and preferred by military entertainment liaison offices.

The Role of the Science Advisor in Hollywood

While superhero films are far more grounded in action-adventure and fantasy than they are in science fiction, they are still rooted in scientific concepts. And as modern audiences have grown more sophisticated, filmmakers have become increasingly reliant on scientific advisors to make the science in these films more plausible. As scholars such as Scott Frank, David Kirby, Kevin Grazier, and Stephen Cass have all demonstrated, scientists play at least six important roles in Hollywood cinema. The first involves the fact-checking of scripts and/or the creation of technobabble for writers to make scripts sound more authentic.[4] The second is helping shape a film's mise-en-scène, as set designers and directors are often unsure about how to create scientific spaces on screen.[5] For example, Mark Wise from Caltech helped the producers of *Iron Man 2* visually explain how Tony creates a new element to repair his heart's arc reactor. According to Marvel producer Jeremy Latcham, "Mark came out to our offices with a few graduate students and walked us through how an element would be created, how the Large Hadron Collider works, how you would fire the particles, and how you might miniaturize the collider, since the one in France stretches for miles, and we needed this thing to go around Tony's basement." Such consultation was invaluable because Mark "helped solve a creative problem that no one on our writing or production staff had the technical expertise to even know how to start addressing," said Latcham.[6]

The third role that science consultants play in the filmmaking process is to "enhance the plausibility of cinematic events within the film's logic." Plausibility, Kirby writes, is about helping maintain an audience's suspension of disbelief, which, when lost, can affect a film's ability to make money.[7] Indeed, science consultants are often tasked with making "things that are referentially unreal (dragons, fake volcanoes, incredible hulks) into objects and situations that seem perceptually real." They must also bridge "veritable truth" and "dramatic truth," where dramatic truth is the version of a scientific truth "that is entertaining and commercially viable," in other words, the one that appears on screen "once it is filtered through . . . time and budgetary constraints" and the "personal preferences of the director or the filmic requirement to keep things visually appealing."[8] In the case of *Thor*, director Kenneth Branagh wanted to incorporate the disc-shaped planets that populate the comic series, even though they are implausible because planets are sphere-shaped for gravitational reasons, said Kevin Hand, a planetary scientist from NASA's Jet Propulsion Laboratory, who consulted on the movie.[9] He was not really bothered by this vision of a dramatic truth; however, the fact that the writers were also considering a fight scene where a character eventually falls off the edge of a planet disturbed him and the other advisors greatly. According to Sean Carroll, a theoretical physicist who also advised on the film, "We were like, what is pulling that character off of the planet? It's the planet's pull that keeps you on a planet; you can't fall off a planet even if you try!" Carroll said that the science advisors "really advocated that that scene be changed in the movie, and thankfully, Kevin Feige agreed with us," understanding that this would be one time where "bad science" might actually take viewers out of the narrative "because even if they aren't trained in physics, [viewers] will still smell something wrong."[10]

The fourth role of the science advisor involves using science to create opportunities for narrative drama or conflict, while the fifth is invested in how Hollywood positions science in a cultural context, or rather, how it helps people envision what scientists look like, what kinds of science people should prioritize, and how science works as both a process and an "ideological status."[11] This fifth role was flagged by the University of Southern California's Clifford Johnson, a Black British physicist, who has consulted on multiple MCU properties, including *Agent Carter*. Johnson explained in our interview that while he made detailed suggestions on every script of the series' second season, "to the point where bits of dialogue, chalkboards of equations, lab designs, and machines that they designed, all came from me," the most impactful result of his work was that the writers created an African American character who is a scientist on the show "because they had met me." According to Johnson, it had not occurred to the writers "to have that kind of character. But it ended up being a major character around whom they were able to revolve not just a lot of scientific aspects but other questions about what it's like to be a scientist of African descent. I mean, the show is set in the 1950s," he said, "but a lot of the questions [about race] are still relevant today." Indeed, Johnson believes that his inspiration behind Dr. Jason Wilkes (Reggie Austin) probably had more impact on the audience and its vision of what science and scientists look like than did the fact that he gave the writers pages of technobabble for their scripts.[12]

Finally, Kirby argues that studios often feature their science consultants in publicity materials or at press events, usually to claim legitimacy for the science they present on screen.[13] While this role is more relevant to documentaries or science fiction films, Johnson revealed that Marvel asked him to appear in several videos on YouTube, where he explains the science of zero matter and extra dimensions to enhance the legitimacy of *Agent Carter*.[14] These types of collaborations can also promote the work of scientists too. After James Kakalios, a physics professor at the University of Minnesota, worked with the creators of *Watchmen* at Warner Bros., he asked the studio if he could employ some of the film's footage in a YouTube lecture, where he explains the science behind Doctor Manhattan's appearance and powers.[15] That video, released in 2009, has since garnered 1.86 million views, and according to Latcham, Kakalios calculated how many Intro to Physics lessons he would have to teach in order to match that reach, realizing that it would take several careers' worth of lectures to replicate.

The Role of the Science and Entertainment Exchange

Zack Stenz, the screenwriter of *Thor* and *X-Men: First Class*, notes that too often Hollywood creatives employ "schmience"—a "wonderfully vaudevillian term" that sums up Hollywood's attitude that "actual science is nothing but a burden that a storyteller should ignore or fast-talk his or her way around with semi-plausible sounding gobbledygook." Even science fiction writers, Stentz argues, feel comfortable making up whatever "scientific rules and concepts they feel serve the storytelling need of the moment," even though this is absurd since "a writer on a legal show would never think of creating a new Constitutional amendment to let a heroic lawyer win a case." In order to help writers avoid these pitfalls and solve problems through more scientifically plausible means, Stentz recommends the Science and Entertainment Exchange (SEEX).[16]

Until the creation of the SEEX in 2008, there was never a formal process for connecting scientists with filmmakers even though science advisors have been working on films for decades. Currently, the director of the exchange is Rick Loverd, who, in addition to writing the comic series *Beserker*, worked as a writers' assistant on NBC's *Friday Night Lights* (2006–2011) and crafted narratives for Marvel's Avengers S.T.A.T.I.O.N. Exhibition, currently housed in Las Vegas.[17] In essence, the SEEX serves as the nonprofit Hollywood outreach arm of the National Academy of the Sciences (NAS), which itself was formed in 1863 by Abraham Lincoln. The NAS aims to provide accurate, nonpartisan information to both Congress and the public through its network of scientists and the peer-reviewed research they produce. It is a highly prolific institution, issuing a dissertation-length document every business day of the year on topics as varied as the economics of immigration, the dietary needs of farm animals, and the safety of abortions.[18]

Unfortunately for the NAS (and the public), most of its science reports are dense and dry, so in order to help popularize its science, the academy—with the help of filmmakers Jerry and Janet Zucker—launched the Science and Entertainment Exchange. The goal was to allow any writer, director, or producer of a book, video game, feature film, or television series to connect with cutting-edge scientists just by dialing 1-844-NEED-SCI? So far, the program appears successful. In just twelve years, the exchange has collaborated on roughly 2,600 films, books, games, and television series, including *Frozen* (2013), *Godzilla* (2014), *Ghostbusters* (2016), and *Big Hero Six* (2014). In regards to superhero stories, its work can be seen in *The Flash* (2014–), *Watchmen*, the Avengers movies, *Black Panther*, each of the Thor films, *Ant-Man* (2015), *Ant-Man and the Wasp* (2018), *Doctor Strange* (2016), *Daredevil* (2015–2018), *Agents of S.H.I.E.L.D.* (2013–2020), *Agent Carter* (2015), and several others.

Like government agencies with entertainment offices, the Science and Entertainment Exchange is invested in its outreach program because of its potential to recruit viewers to STEM careers and to promote science more broadly. As Susan Carol Losh demonstrates, scientists are often stereotyped as clever and hardworking in popular culture, and science careers are widely perceived as "prestigious," but scientists are also depicted "as socially inept," "eccentric," and often villainous.[19] Christopher Frayling demonstrates in *Mad, Bad and Dangerous?* that mad scientists or their creations account for 41 percent of the monsters and/

or villains appearing in nearly a thousand British horror films released between 1931 and 1984.[20] Likewise, Eva Flicker notes that male scientists usually emanate "an aura of absent-mindedness, extreme confusion, or even madness" and that "in the eagerness of [their] scientific curiosity," they often take the "risk of causing immense damage to humanity."[21] Images of scientists in popular culture are also overwhelmingly male, and science careers, though prestigious, are often depicted as "uninviting," partly due to their long hours in social isolation for little monetary reward.[22]

These images have real-life implications. As J. Burris and the Gates Foundation have separately argued, students in the United States are often underprepared for or avoid science concentrations, and women's participation in the fields of engineering and other hard sciences are still low when compared with that of men.[23] As a result, Loverd shared in his 2015 talk at the MindShare Convention in Los Angeles that part of his goal at the SEEX is to help Hollywood create images of scientists that will generate a wider interest in STEM, especially among young and female consumers. "There are so many great careers developing in STEM, computer programming, health care, AI, genetics, where kids just aren't going right now," he stated. "How do we share that with Hollywood writers . . . and get them to write for us?" Loverd believes the answer lies in connecting scientists with Hollywood creatives so that writers can begin to change their own perceptions. He reports that 80 percent of all Americans say they don't know a scientist and that most of the other 20 percent are thinking of their doctor when they say that they do.[24] "Why would writers be any different?" he asks. Thus by connecting his network with creatives through salons, guild-hosted panels, retreats, happy hours, and laboratory tours, Loverd hopes that writers, who write what they know, will begin to write something fresh.

Many readers may expect that the SEEX would also be invested, and even a stickler, for accurate science in films, but Loverd states, "We can't come in and be the scientific accuracy police; that will never inspire anyone. Story will always trump science, but science can improve story." In fact, Loverd states that the SEEX never even demands science in movies.

> Our staffers simply encourage scientists to convey the facts and share what they think is cool, interesting, or inspiring about them. By not explicitly telling storytellers what to do, but instead showing them what's on the cutting edge and introducing them to incredibly interesting people, we inspire writers to think differently. And, all on their own, the writers take what we've given them and begin to incorporate this new knowledge into their narratives.[25]

Johnson made a related comment when he said that too many science advisors simply feel like they need to "give a film a grade" based on its scientific accuracy. That kind of evaluation isn't always helpful, Johnson said, because "it discourages filmmakers from playing with science" if you are always just saying, "No, you can't do that."[26] Instead, he believes that scientists should help filmmakers engage with science more fully because ultimately it will help change and inspire the culture on a deeper level. "I'm trying to put science back into the general culture where it belongs," he stated. "It was marginalized, became a special interest group. We can't run a democracy that way."[27]

As a result of its work in Hollywood, the rest of this chapter draws on four case studies, as well as several interviews, to reveal how the Science and Entertainment Exchange works in Hollywood. It is largely thanks to the SEEX that the role of scientists as technical advisors has grown in the entertainment industry, allowing more filmmakers to draw from a different kind of expertise to add fresh ideas, production value, and authenticity (as opposed to strict realism) to their narratives. These advisors offer a valuable alternative (or at least supplement) to the plethora of current and former CIA, FBI, military, and police officers who have been the primary technical advisors in Hollywood movies for decades. Because many of the SEEX's science advisors do not work for the security state (the majority that we talked to are university professors), these advisors have also helped push more science-based story lines that have helped expand the superhero genre beyond its worn conventions of white men resolving conflict through military violence—tropes that dominated the early films of both the MCU and the DCEU. While violence will always be a part of superhero stories, the newer ones with strong scientific themes have proven to be viable commercial products and helped showcase that science and technology have a lot more to offer than just being tools for conquest and fighting. This is an important message for US viewers, in particular, where so many great scientists, engineers, and innovators end up working for private companies engaged in defense, such as Lockheed Martin, Raytheon, Northrop Grumman, or Huntington Ingalls Industries.

Changing the Face of Scientists and Popularizing Scientific Concepts: The *Thor* Series

When *Thor* (2011) debuted as the fourth installment of the MCU, it was the first to feature a hero from another planet, and thus Branagh and Feige believed that some of the 1960s comic's elements needed an upgrade to better suit a modern audience. One of the first changes they wanted to make was to the character of Jane Foster (Natalie Portman), transforming her from a nurse to a scientist. The filmmakers also wanted a way to explain how Thor is able to travel through space, understanding that a "rainbow bridge" might not serve as a sufficient explanation. To these ends, the SEEX put *Thor*'s filmmakers into conversation with several science advisors, including Carroll, Johnson, Hand, and Kevin Hickerson from Caltech.

According to Carroll, Marvel Studios needed help in determining which type of scientist Foster should be, as the narrative demanded that she conduct research in the desert and ultimately discover a wormhole. Carroll and Hickerson suggested that Foster feature as an astrophysicist (or as a particle physicist) searching for dark matter and then worked with the set designers to help create a realistic lab for her and her mentor, Erik Selvig. Hickerson, for example, fabricated a dark matter detector and a model of a liquid xenon detector for the scenes when Foster is trying to understand Thor's abilities.[28]

The pair also worked to popularize the concepts of dark matter and the Einstein-Rosen Bridge through their consulting roles on the film. In our interview, Carroll revealed that Feige was originally opposed to the idea of a wormhole to explain Thor's arrival on Earth because wormholes "were so 1990s." But when Carroll pitched the term Einstein-Rosen Bridge, the studio president loved the sound of it, asking to what it referred. The answer, ironically, is a specialized wormhole, but the updated term worked for the creators, and now millions of people have at least heard of what was a rather obscure physics term just a decade ago. Likewise, Hickerson, who researches dark matter, proposed it as an explanation for the composition of Thor's hammer (Mjölnir). Hickerson joked that because the composition of Mjölnir is a mystery and because no one really knows how wormholes work or what dark matter is composed of, he encouraged the filmmakers to combine all three concepts to explain the Thor universe, and thus, Foster uses her particle equipment in the series to detect a vibrant source of dark matter coming from both Thor's hammer and the wormhole through which he traveled.[29]

As early as *Thor: Ragnarok*, Johnson was also talking with filmmakers about the concept of neutron stars as a further explanation for Thor's hammer, which is most fully employed in *Infinity War*, when Thor visits one to forge his new weapon, Stormbreaker. As science writer Cassidy Ward explains, when stars die, they either explode or collapse into black holes, but neutron stars fuse all of their "innards" to iron and continue to collapse, "falling forever inward until their very positrons and electrons combine into neutrons." These stars become so dense that a teaspoon of their matter weighs a billion tons, and they spin faster and faster as they get smaller, sometimes more than a hundred times per second.[30] Watching *Infinity War*, it is easy to see how Johnson's discussion with the filmmakers influenced the story's development. When Thor, Groot, and Rocket Raccoon arrive at a galactic forge to make his new axe, the forge is orbiting a neutron star, and Thor must find a way to fire the forge by harnessing the heat contained within the star, in order to allow its energy to flow into the mold and melt the metal that will become Stormbreaker. Thor even has a line about his weapon being created "in the heart of a dying star."

Each of these advisors helped increase the scientific plausibility, and thus profitability, of the *Thor* series, and they successfully popularized scientific concepts too. Indeed, these types of story elements, which employ "loose science," often inspire scientifically inclined YouTubers to create video lectures that explain the "hard" science behind the MCU. To cite just one example, the channel Because Science! hosts of slew of videos that teach scientific concepts through the hook of the superhero story, including "How to Forge Thor's Infinity War Weapon," "What Kind of Symbiote Is Venom?," and "How Thanos Throws a Moon,"[31] thereby creating further, extratextual opportunities for STEM learning. This phenomenon is as old as the comics themselves. Ever since the 1960s, when comic book writers applied loose "scientific principles to explain fantastic phenomenon," fans have stepped in, writes William Svitavsky, "in letter pages and discussions elsewhere [with] scientific explanations as to how the Human Torch flies or how Spider-man sticks to walls."[32]

Thor, however, also helped the SEEX's goals of changing the face of scientists in popular movies. American women enter life and health sciences (like nursing) in robust numbers, but their participation in physical sciences and engineering fields has remained low.[33] Scholars argue that a prominent reason for this gender disparity is that girls and women perceive "science culture" as largely and inhospitably male,[34] and these perceptions have been generated, in part, by cinematic history, leading Jacques Jouhaneau—who studied sixteen thousand films—to declare that the "cinematic scientist is, above all, a hero of the male sex."[35] Jane Foster's character helped shift this narrative, and *Thor*'s marketing posters highlighted the science aspect of her character by lauding the hero as the God of Thunder and Foster as the Woman of Science (see figure 4.1).

Loverd also states that Foster's potential to encourage girls' interest in STEM careers was an important aspect to *Thor*, and one eventually exploited by Disney when it approached the exchange around the time of *Thor: The Dark World*'s release to help in the film's promotion.[36] As part of its initiative to encourage young women to consider STEM careers, the exchange worked with Disney, at the conglomerate's behest, to create the Marvel Ultimate Mentor Adventure, a contest that required girls to interview a female scientist and report back on what they learned. Ten finalists were then invited to Los Angeles to walk the red

Figure 4.1: Marketing poster for *Thor* highlighting Jane Foster's science career. Source: http://www.sneakpeek.ca/2011/03/thor-woman-of-science-and-goddess-of.html.

carpet at the film's premiere and engage in science-related activities around Los Angeles for a week. The contest also helped the exchange generate a new set of contacts and possible film advisors too.

Finally, if popular films work to contextualize science and scientists within society, it is important to note the cultural work that Jane Foster, Erik Selvig, and their assistants Darcy and Ian accomplish in *Thor*. As Matthew Nisbet et al. write, entertainment media does not present one common or unified description of the scientist, but there have been "several 'clusters' of images that are seen across time period, medium, and genre." Scientists, as mentioned earlier, are often depicted as evil or mad figures, operating outside the rules of normal society, but they are also depicted as powerless individuals that are manipulated or dominated into doing the dirty work for either big business or the military, such as those featured in *The China Syndrome* (1979) and *Silkwood* (1983). Still other images highlight the degree to which scientists differ from other people, being marked as either eccentric or extremely antisocial and thus not particularly relatable.[37] In contrast, the group of scientists featured in the Thor movies are a close group of friends with relatable, if quirky, personality traits. In a scene when Selvig meets Thor at a bar, the two share a boilermaker, which then evolves into a drinking contest to essentially see who is the mightiest Norseman. The two end up drunk, and in a comedic scene, Thor must throw Selvig over his shoulder and deliver him to Jane's trailer in a stupor.[38] Likewise, in *Dark World*, Jane is reintroduced to viewers on an awkward blind date, where she is trying to forget her old, godlike boyfriend who has essentially ghosted her, and later in the film, Darcy chides her for not knowing how to change her ringtone, even though she has three degrees. These details work to show scientists as endearing, normal people, helping viewers indirectly build rapport with the scientific community. Indeed, Kirby states that many science consultants champion plot elements indicating flaws in their characters, even if they involve issues like extramarital affairs, because they are important in humanizing scientists and making them more relatable to viewers.[39]

Furthermore, the work that Foster and Selvig are engaged in has to do with better understanding the nature of our universe. In the first

Thor movie, their work is not in the service of either big business or the MIC (although their research is eventually stolen by S.H.I.E.L.D.), and when Loki arrives to attack Thor in the film's final act, S.H.I.E.L.D. operatives actually run away in fear, while Selvig, Foster, and Darcy remain to protect the town. In *Thor: Dark World*, Selvig is first shown roaming around Stonehenge in a crazed, naked state, and he is institutionalized halfway through the movie as he tries to recover from the trauma of being mind-controlled by Loki in the previous Avengers installment. Clearly this plot element embodies old, negative stereotypes of the mad, white, male scientist, but unlike other movies, such as *Back to the Future* (1985), this arc is temporary, and by the end of *Dark World*, Selvig has regained his mental faculties and again the group plays a vital role in protecting Earth. When the film's villain, Malekith, tries to conquer the Nine Realms during a cosmic event called the Convergence, it is Selvig who discovers where the realms will align on Earth so that Thor can defeat him. As Thor fights various villains during the Convergence, it is Selvig's detection devices (and makeshift weapons) that somehow allow Thor to teleport Malekith to Svartalfheim, where Malekith's damaged ship falls on top of him, ending in his defeat. It is not exactly clear how the scientific equipment in the film functions, but despite the film's plot failings, it, like the original *Thor*, still works to depict scientists as smart, brave, and dedicated to preserving human lives outside of the framework of the MIC.

Ant-Man (2015)

Another MCU film that benefited from science consultants—both those arranged through the SEEX and independently—was 2015's *Ant-Man*. Critical responses for this film were somewhat mixed but mostly positive, conceding that the story of an ex-convict using an amazing shrinking suit to become a superhero called Ant-Man is a fairly ridiculous premise, even for Marvel. The *Hollywood Reporter* summed this up, commenting, "Although the story dynamics are fundamentally silly . . . a good cast led by a winning Paul Rudd puts the nonsense over in reasonably disarming fashion," while the *Los Angeles Times* praised

Ant-Man as "playful in unexpected ways and graced with a genuinely off-center sense of humor."[40] Unlike most prior entries in the MCU, *Ant-Man* operates on a fairly small scale (pun intended) and is more of a local, action-comedy heist than the usual tale of transhumans overcoming planet-threatening villains. It is also a good example of a Phase Two MCU movie that relies more heavily on scientific tropes for its entertainment value, although the MIC does play a role, in the villain Darren Cross.

The story begins with Scott Lang (Paul Rudd), an electrical engineer turned cat burglar who "hates violence," being released from prison for a recent heist. He links up with his old crew of ex-convicts led by his former cellmate Luis, charmingly portrayed by Michael Peña. Luis puts Scott, a security systems hacker, onto a job burglarizing a safe in the basement of a rich man's home, which turns out to be a setup orchestrated by tech industrialist and science genius Hank Pym, an ex-S.H.I.E.L.D. employee and the original Ant-Man. Pym (Michael Douglas) and his daughter Hope (Evangeline Lilly) recruit Scott to carry out a heist against Pym's former company, Pym Technologies, now headed by Darren Cross (Corey Stoll), a former protégé of Hank's. Cross has finally replicated the technology used by Pym to power the original Ant-Man suit—which shrinks the wearer down to insect size, making them the ideal infiltration and sabotage agent—in order to profit from the sale of his own highly weaponized version of the suit called the Yellowjacket. Before forming Pym Technologies, Hank worked for S.H.I.E.L.D. as a scientist, but after discovering its attempts to copy his private "particle shrinking technology" to use for offensive, military purposes, Pym quit the organization in disgust and vowed to never release his technology to the public. Pym explains to Scott that he is concerned that Cross will sell the Yellowjacket technology to Mitchell Carson, a former senior employee at S.H.I.E.L.D. "presently in the business of toppling governments," and warns that if he is not stopped, "Darren Cross is gonna unleash chaos upon the world."

Meanwhile, Cross unveils his Yellowjacket suit during a demonstration at Pym Technologies in a scene that is reminiscent of Stark's demonstration of the Jericho missile system at the beginning of *Iron*

Man. A video summarizing the potential uses of Cross's Yellowjacket technology was consciously designed to highlight how the film's villain is part of the weapons industry. Dark-toned motion graphics ape real-life promotional videos released by the likes of Lockheed Martin and Raytheon, while a grisly voice-over intones, "An all-purpose peacekeeping vessel, the Yellowjacket can manage any conflict on the geopolitical landscape, completely unseen . . . A single Yellowjacket offers the user unlimited influence to carry out protective actions and one day soon, an army of Yellowjackets will create a sustainable environment of well-being around the world." According to director Peyton Reed, they wanted to deliberately incorporate the visual style and doublespeak of the arms industry's PR efforts, commenting that the company who did the reel "really built something that felt like one of those . . . industrial military complex [films]," where the language implies that "we can't get away with things and there's too much surveillance in the world, [but] what if we could create a technology that gets past that surveillance, and we could do these awful things and take out people we don't like and remove certain governments? We liked the sense of dread that it gave us."[41]

If this story line of a scientific genius industrialist who loses control of his company to a former ally who then betrays him and plans to use his advanced suit technology for evil by teaming up with agents of chaos sounds familiar, then that's because it is the same basic plot as the first *Iron Man* film. Reed admitted that "there are a lot of parallels" between the films and explained that most of these elements were "baked into the original script" written by Joe Cornish and Edgar Wright.[42] This *Ant-Man* script was also initially developed at the same time as *Iron Man*, at the beginning of the MCU and during the height of the Bush administration's global War on Terror—a context that helps explain why both films focus on a struggle involving the MIC. However, there is a crucial difference between the protagonists across the two films, which lends *Ant-Man* a more radical, pro-science, and anti-military tone than that of *Iron Man*.

The profile of the villains in both films is remarkably similar, right down to the bald heads of both characters, but the profiles of our heroes are markedly different. While in *Iron Man* Tony Stark has the benefit of wealth and youth and being part of the American establishment, in *Ant-Man* Pym is an aging outsider fighting against the odds. Hope is a brilliant scientist still working at Pym Technologies but without much control over the direction of the company, and Scott is an engineer and hacker who is broke and jobless and whose ex-wife and daughter have moved on after he was sent to prison. As such, *Ant-Man* has a much more renegade, David vs. Goliath tone than the Goliath vs. Goliath feel of *Iron Man*, and our heroes are categorically opposed to the MIC rather than representatives of the "good" part of the industry, as with Stark. Indeed, when Scott originally suggests that the Avengers be called in to steal the Yellowjacket, Pym refuses, saying that he will never let his technology get into the hands of a Stark, quipping, "Besides they are probably too busy dropping cities from the sky" to help anyway—a reference to the events in *Avengers: Age of Ultron*.

Though this political radicalism is not drawn out in any great detail, the story dynamics of *Ant-Man* have the audience siding with the small against the big, both literally and figuratively. While in *Iron Man* Stark's technological innovations are essentially an advanced weapon that allows him to do battle with his enemies, in *Ant-Man* Scott's shrinking suit has no weapons aside from miniature frisbees that he can throw at objects to make them rapidly grow or shrink. He has no projectile armaments or bombs, and the suit has no flight capability. This stands in contrast to Cross's suit, which is armed with four weaponized "legs," flies, and can fire lasers at incoming threats (see figure 4.2). As Rocco Gangle writes, an object's design is a "mode of revealing" its makers' philosophies and truths because "final causes, or purposes, are essential aspects of all technologically-produced objects."[43] The fact that the Ant-Man suit has no weapons abilities reveals both Scott's and Pym's disdain for militarized violence and that they see technology as a primarily peacekeeping or defensive force. They are not, in other words, trying to employ large-scale violence (pun again intended) against threats like Cross; they are simply trying to use the suit to prevent others from causing destruction and chaos.

Much like *Thor*, *Ant-Man* also foregrounds female scientists not just

Figure 4.2: Toy replicas of the Ant-Man suit (*left*) and the Yellowjacket suit (*right*), highlighting their defensive and offensive designs. Source: ToyWhiz.com.

for their intelligence but also for their toughness and courage. Early on, Scott inquires why Hank isn't sending his daughter Hope, who is more technologically knowledgeable, a better fighter, and generally more competent than Scott, to lead the heist against Pym Technologies to destroy the Yellowjacket. Pym explains that decades ago he and his wife, Janet van Dyne, were a miniature superhero team, Ant-Man and the Wasp, but that his wife disappeared after using her shrinking suit to go subatomic, so she could infiltrate and sabotage a nuclear missile that was launched at the United States. Pym, still grieving over the loss of his wife and the damage that loss has done to his relationship with Hope, wants to protect his daughter and refuses to let her lead the heist. Nonetheless, Hope is shown to be a highly intelligent scientist and a tough, capable fighter who runs Scott's combat training in preparation for the break-in at Pym Technologies. Janet van Dyne's own heroic self-sacrifice is echoed at the end of the film too, when

Scott, as Ant-Man, is fighting Cross, who is threatening Scott's young daughter. When he cannot pierce the Yellowjacket suit's armor, Scott goes subatomic in order to slip between the molecules in the titanium. This results in Yellowjacket imploding, killing Cross and destroying the Yellowjacket technology (though Scott's intention is to disable the suit, not to murder Cross), but it also abandons Scott in the Quantum Realm. Once again, though, it is not the government or the military who save Scott but his own scientific ingenuity, as he jerry-rigs the Ant-Man suit to escape the Quantum Realm and return to his normal size.

Ant-Man benefited from the support of various government agencies, crediting the states of Georgia and California; the Georgia Film, Music and Digital Entertainment Office; the City and County of San Francisco and San Francisco mayor Ed Lee; and the US Department of the Interior at the end of the movie. They even borrowed a World War II Russian T-34 tank from the Military Veterans Museum in Oshkosh for the shot where Pym and Hope burst out of Pym Technologies during the climax of the film.[44] However, none of this support required the sort of script review and rewrite process demanded by the Pentagon and other arms of the security state, so the nonmilitarized use of science and the anti-authoritarian streaks in the *Ant-Man* script remained intact. Indeed, the lack of DOD involvement helps partially explain why the Ant-Man technology contrasts not just with Cross's use of the same underlying tech but also with the predominant depictions of technology in the early MCU, where it tends to be used for surveillance or militaristic ends. This shift is important because as Kirby observes, "filmic images can have an impact on the public's conceptions of science . . . from encouraging excitement to instilling fear about science and technology, and sometimes both."[45] *Ant-Man*'s image of science and technology falls into the "both" category because these tools are wielded by both our heroes and our villain, but for different purposes. Cross uses his scientific genius to create an advanced weapon with the aim of causing mayhem and making money, while Pym revives his version of the same technology in order to stop Cross's diabolical scheme. The takeaway for the public appears to be that science, and in particular technology, are morally neutral and their consequences largely depend on the motives and aims of the people using them. So while *Ant-Man* demonstrates that tech can be put to violent and morally abhorrent ends (and is thus something to fear), the film also demonstrates that the best (and perhaps, most exciting) answer to this problem is other scientists using advanced technology as an opposing force for moral good.

Like in *Thor*, the filmmakers of *Ant-Man* also made use of science consultants both provided via the Science and Entertainment Exchange and separately from it. For the scenes involving the large group of ants that assist Scott and Hank on missions, the filmmakers used independent consultant and entomologist Steven Kutcher, who has worked in Hollywood for several decades as an insect wrangler. In our interview, Kutcher lamented the film's reliance on CGI ants, positing that live ones would have heightened the film's production value as the live spiders did on *Spider-Man*.[46] Nonetheless, he consulted the film's producers and CGI artists on what different types of ants look like in terms of their texture and movements, providing photos and film footage of ants in various scenarios, so they could be replicated digitally. While Kutcher acknowledges that the film's digital artists performed solid work and that "if every film that was ever made had to be checked for proper science, it would not be as much fun," he did express regret that the film's ants "have no hair on them" because "anyone in entomology who knows anything about insects knows they have a lot of hair because that's how they sense things."

Spyridon Michalakis of the Institute for Quantum Information and Matter at Caltech was another consultant on *Ant-Man* who was connected to the filmmakers through the SEEX. A quantum physicist, Michalakis recalled on a Caltech blog that he was in an airport when he got an email from the exchange, asking him to consult on a new superhero movie: *Ant-Man*. "As I read halfway through the email, I grumbled to myself: Why can't I be the guy who works on *Thor*? Who is this *Ant-Man* anyways?"[47] After learning more about the character, however, his enthusiasm grew, and Michalakis went to Pinewood Studios and met with Rudd, Reed, the writers, producers, VFX specialists, and others. It was following this meeting that producer Brad Winderbaum asked

Michalakis to suggest the name for the tiny land where Scott ends up in order to defeat Yellowjacket, as well as terms for the process of how he got there. After Edgar Wright was replaced as writer/director for the project and Peyton Reed came on board, a major rewrite of the script was undertaken by Rudd and Adam McKay. Reed explained, "We wanted to introduce the microverse from the comics" but due to legal problems using the word, they needed a new name for it, and so Winderbaum asked Michalakis for his input.[48] Michalakis offered several suggestions including "going nano, going quantum, going atomic," or going into the "quantum realm," and thus the Quantum Realm in *Ant-Man* got its name.[49] The writers also incorporated the term "going subatomic," inspired by the physicist's input.

In his blog, Michalakis commented that the film "is actually good!" but in a separate interview he highlighted one of the main scientific inaccuracies in the movie, which explains that the shrinking technology works by reducing the spaces between atoms, thus making the overall object or person much smaller. Michalakis commented, "That's the least credible part. How does a 160-pound man ride on ants, if he hasn't somehow converted his mass into something else? You cannot just convert it into energy without containing it. Otherwise you have a nuclear bomb of unprecedented destructive power." However, he also praised the MCU films, saying, "Marvel really has gone out of their way to incorporate real, interesting science; I think they realize that so much real science almost feels like science-fiction," before summing up, "When I think about science outreach, I can't think of a more fun way to do it than with superheroes."[50] Michalakis's statement is again substantiated by the popularity of YouTube videos on science and *Ant-Man*, including "How to Control Insects Like Ant-Man" and "What Would Happen If You Were Shrunk?," the latter of which garnered 3.35 million views alone. Indeed, incorporating more scientific and technological elements has only increased the popularity of the films themselves (see box office data, below), while also promoting science and technology to a wider audience outside of classrooms and documentaries. As such, while Michalakis had mixed views of the technical accuracy of the film, he recognized that it is most fundamentally an entertainment product, and that its scientific value is in inspiring audiences to learn more (whether about ants or quantum physics) rather than beating them over the head with strictly accurate information. In terms of the Science and Entertainment Exchange's overall mission to bring more accurate science into movies, *Ant-Man* can only be seen as a partial success, but the exchange's secondary goals of challenging stereotypes about who scientists are and what they do, as well as encouraging people to learn more or even take up STEM careers, were well served by this smaller, but very significant, entry to the MCU.

Ant-Man and the Wasp (2018)

The renegade vibe and emphasis on more benevolent uses of revolutionary science carried over into the sequel *Ant-Man and the Wasp* and in some ways enhanced the approach to the ideas manifested in the first film. Following the Sokovia Accords and the events of *Captain America: Civil War*, Scott, in the sequel, is under house arrest and has been forbidden from using high technologies or contacting others who might be using them, while Hank and Hope are hiding out from the authorities in a custom laboratory that grows and shrinks at the touch of a button. Luis and the rest of Scott's gang are running a struggling consultancy specializing in building security, and the FBI frequently turns up at Scott's home to make sure he is abiding by the law. In particular, the lead FBI agent Woo (Randall Park) is shown to be both incompetent and an antagonist harassing our lead character, thus parodying the FBI's desired image as ruthlessly competent upholders of the law. Scott frequently confounds Woo, not through violence but through magical misdirection, a skill he has learned through an online magic school while under house arrest. While there are more villainous characters in the film, Woo is the only representative of the security state, and his depiction is sardonic and, in some respects, quite pathetic, as he becomes increasingly enamored with Scott as the film progresses, coming across as a slightly lonely man looking for an exciting person to befriend. On top of this, the primary mission our heroes take on in *Ant-Man and the Wasp* is not a battle against an evil superpowered villain; rather, it is a scientific challenge. After Scott's journey to the Quantum Realm in *Ant-Man*, Pym and Hope begin to wonder if their wife/mother, Janet van Dyne (Michelle Pfeiffer), could still be alive down there, and they start developing a plan to try to find her and bring her home. While there are a number of amusing chase sequences in *Ant-Man and the Wasp*, including vans and cars that grow and shrink with the flip of a lever, there are very few fight scenes, no gunplay, and very little weaponry, underlining how the film is again a departure from its more violent, militaristic, and weapons-centric predecessors in the MCU.

In the final scene of *Ant-Man*, Pym reveals to Hope that he and his wife had been building a Wasp suit for Hope's use, which has the same shrinking technology as the Ant-Man suit but also has wings allowing for flight capabilities. As Hope quips in response to the reveal of the suit, "It's about damn time." When *Ant-Man and the Wasp* begins, Hope tries to purchase a piece of equipment on the black market wearing the Wasp suit, so that she and Pym can complete the tunnel that will shrink an exploratory craft, allowing Pym to go into the Quantum Realm to search for Janet. In the midst of her meeting with black marketeer Sonny Burch (Walton Goggins) to buy the component, Hope is ambushed by Ghost (Hannah John-Kamen) and a fight ensues. We see Hope as the Wasp shrinking and growing, fighting and defeating Burch's henchmen and going toe to toe with Ghost, though Ghost escapes with the equipment. The film emphasizes not just Hope/the Wasp's scientific skills and intelligence, as in the first *Ant-Man*, but also her superhero and fighting abilities. However, this is the only major fight sequence in the film, so Hope's primary role in the story is as a scientist, once again teaming with two other scientists, Pym and Scott. As such, this is a much more rewarding and positive portrayal both of a female scientist and of a female superhero than in any prior MCU film, where the female characters are divided into either scientists such as Jane Foster in *Thor* or superheroes such as Black Widow. By combining the two in Hope/the Wasp, *Ant-Man and the Wasp* took a major step forward both in appealing to female audiences and in promoting the idea of credible, charismatic female scientists, and simultaneously maintaining the somewhat anti-establishment tone of the first *Ant-Man*.

Furthermore, it emerges in the film that Ghost is suffering from "molecular disequilibrium," a condition where her body is starting to disintegrate at a molecular level. She believes that the answer to curing her condition lies in the Quantum Realm, hence she steals the equipment Burch was going to sell to Hope. Pym, Hope, and Scott begin a search for the component, which leads them to Bill Foster, a physicist who worked with Pym on Project Goliath, an inverted version of the Ant-Man technology designed to turn people into giants. Foster is introduced to the audience while he gives a lecture to students on quantum decoherence, which was inspired by the writers talking with Michalakis after he was re-recruited to consult on the sequel. Foster leads our intrepid trio to Ghost, and using some cunning deception and misdirection, they manage to retrieve the component and complete the tunnel to the Quantum Realm. Their laboratory is yet another promotion of the virtues and skills of real scientists, as it combines highly innovative technology with ad hoc equipment and systems that have clearly been put together on a budget. Director Reed highlighted the difference between this and Stark's laboratory in the *Iron Man* films, pointing out, "It was important for me in the first and the second movie to delineate between Hank Pym's high technology and Tony Stark's high technology." He pointed out how the Pym lab in *Ant-Man and the Wasp* includes giant Duracell batteries, enlarged via the Pym particle technology, to help power the equipment, and when Pym and Hope use the Quantum Array to pinpoint Janet's location in the Quantum Realm, Reed explained, "There's a clunky, pieced-together, tactile quality to this thing; it's definitely not Stark Industries technology; it's something he has created, and it has a very mechanical feel."[51] While Stark's home lab and Stark Industries in particular are lavish, luxurious, and opulent, Pym's lab is much more cramped and cobbled together, more like a real science lab dependent on limited funding and resources. By having the audience's sympathies lie with fugitives from the law working in an improvised lab on a very limited budget, the film not only maintains the anti-authoritarian feel of the original film but also promotes a more realistic, less idealized image of scientific research and technological development than the Iron Man trilogy.

Additionally, when Pym goes through the quantum tunnel in search of Janet and shrinks down to the subatomic realm, he encounters several weevil-like creatures that menace the podcraft he used to travel. Michalakis consulted on this sequence and several of his ideas made it into the final film, including a suggestion that the Quantum Realm be visually depicted via "beautiful colors changing constantly to reflect transience." He also suggested microscopic creatures called tardigrades as something Pym could encounter in the Quantum Realm, saying, "They remind me of the massive worms from *Dune*."[52] However, physicist Sean Carroll, who recommended Michalakis to consult on the first Ant-Man film, told us, "There's nothing realistic about [that scene] whatsoever," adding, "There are such things as tardigrades and they're very tiny but they are not subatomic . . . there is nothing that's subatomic that's a living creature." (See figure 4.3). Nonetheless, he admitted, "That's OK, you can't shrink people either so, you know, you are imagining that whatever world the world of *Ant-Man* is in is very different to our world."

Finally, when Pym breaks through the void and arrives in the Quantum Realm, he is surrounded by flux, much as Michalakis described to the producers. He cannot find Janet and, confronted with a world he cannot comprehend, begins to lose his mind. Eventually, Janet, who has been surviving in the Quantum Realm for thirty years and absorbing its power, appears before him, helping restore his sanity, so they can both escape and return to the normal world. Meanwhile, Ghost has found the Pym lab and is battling Ant-Man and the Wasp, as she becomes desperate to find a cure for her condition. Reed commented on this setup to the ending, saying, "We talked early, early on about what is the third act, what is it going to build to, is it gonna build to a thing where the quantum tunnel opens and quantum creatures come over and start taking over San Francisco. That felt like the kinda stuff we've seen a million times." Instead, Pym and Janet emerge from the tunnel, and Janet uses her quantum superpowers to cure Ghost, liberating Ghost from her molecular condition before Janet reunites with

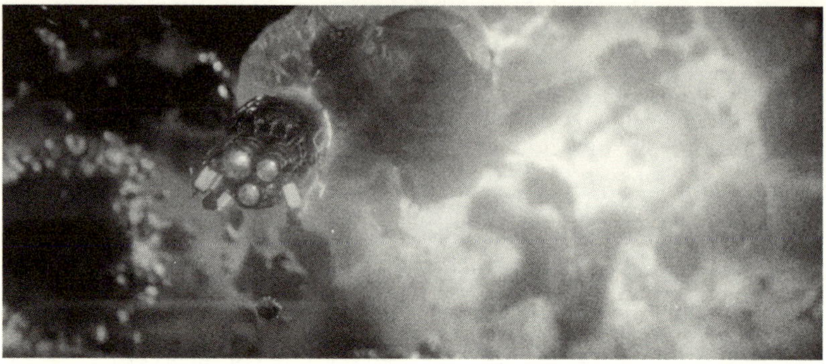

Figure 4.3: Hank Pym's pod menaced by tardigrades in the subatomic realm.

her daughter. Just as with Hope/the Wasp, Janet is both a brilliant scientist and a superhero, but instead of using her powers for violence, she uses them benevolently, to cure an antagonist suffering from a condition that would otherwise have killed her. As Reed outlined, "There is something evolved and something enlightened about Janet van Dyne. . . . We see that there is a decidedly more peaceful resolution to the situation. . . . The one thing I wanted to show here was this benevolence about Janet; she's become a very different type of hero."[53]

While the filmmakers took several scientific liberties, *Ant-Man and the Wasp* contains a lot of plausible science, including Foster's lecture on quantum decoherence and the existence of tardigrades (albeit in the subatomic realm). Much of the film's entertainment value also comes from Pym, Hope, and Scott's use of shrinking and expanding suits, cars, and even entire laboratories to evade detection, rather than on the spectacular, violent combat sequences so familiar to the genre. The directors also resisted the temptation to have fictional monsters escape from the Quantum Realm to provide a conventional threat that would have to be met with violence and opted for a more peaceful ending focusing on a benevolent hero who doesn't need to use violence, because her strengths are better suited to healing and other nonviolent means of overcoming obstacles. The film also subverts some of the stereotypes about science and scientists by depicting a laboratory in a more down-to-earth way, free from gleaming, expensive-looking equipment, and by depicting all four of our heroes as scientists, two of which are women. As Hollywood has embraced more depictions of female scientists, they have tended to cast sexy, younger women such as Jennifer Connelly (*Hulk*), Liv Tyler (*The Incredible Hulk*), Natalie Portman (*Thor*), Naomi Harris (*Rampage*), and Freida Pinto (*Rise of the Planet of the Apes*). While greater representation of female scientists in major movies is a positive development in cinema, this recent trend is not without complications. As one study of entertainment media depictions of female scientists observed,

> Glamour and attractiveness is a double-edged sword for representations of women in science. . . . Showing female scientists as "feminine" and "attractive" could be seen as a positive challenge to "manly"/"frumpy" stereotypes, or it could be seen as a way of undermining their professionalism and imposing an ideal of female scientists about appearance from which their male colleagues are free. It could also be argued that the emphasis on looks also takes the attention away from women's intellectual capabilities.[54]

The underlying assumption appears to be that in order to get audiences, especially young adults, to identify with scientific characters, those characters have to be relatively young and sexually attractive. *Ant-Man and the Wasp* helps subvert even this newer trend, however, because while Janet has a smaller role in the film than our three protagonists from *Ant-Man*, by casting Michelle Pfeiffer, the filmmakers showed a more mature female scientist in a very positive light, as intelligent, powerful, and kind. Her sexuality and attractiveness are entirely irrelevant to her role in the plot, subverting the assumptions of studio executives and the expectations of filmmakers and audiences. The MCU would take this stereotype-busting approach to portraits of scientists yet further with the character of Shuri in *Black Panther*.

Black Panther (2018)

Written and directed by Ryan Coogler, *Black Panther* debuted as the eighteenth installment of the Marvel Cinematic Universe and as the sixth movie in the franchise's Phase Three development. The story revolves around the struggle for the political control of Wakanda, a highly advanced African nation. The film's opening explains that the advancement of Wakandan society is partly due to the fortuitous landing of a giant meteor made of vibranium (a fictitious and very rare super-element) in its country thousands of years prior, but viewers also see that the Wakandans have proven exceptionally adept at the research and development of the material. As Coogler explains, a "key theme" in *Black Panther* is "tradition vs. innovation," most obviously in the arc of the protagonist T'Challa, who has to decide whether to try to replicate his father's isolationist reign over the kingdom or go his own way and start opening up the kingdom to the outside world.[55] We also see this theme in other core aspects of the story, including T'Challa's relationship with Shuri, his younger sister and the head of Wakanda's research and development division, and in the conflict with Killmonger, a Wakandan American who usurps T'Challa and takes over the throne, with the intention of using its technology as a springboard to fight against the global oppression of Black people.

While the political dimensions of *Black Panther* are addressed in chapter 5 of this book, in essence, Wakanda has remained undisturbed by outside colonizers wishing to plunder its resources and thus has been free to advance its society to a technological standard rarely seen in the MCU. Some of its technology goes beyond what even Tony Stark and S.H.I.E.L.D. have created, and much of it is used for benevolent purposes rather than for fighting various threats or—as in *Captain America: The Winter Soldier*—surveilling and oppressing the entire world. Instead, we see technology being deployed in the film for socially beneficent ends, such as efficient transport, high-yield agriculture, extraordinary medical care, advanced communication through holographic displays, and, of course, the Black Panther's suit, which allows T'Challa to absorb and release massive quantities of kinetic energy and enhance his strength and speed.[56]

Like in *Thor* and *Ant-Man*, Wakanda's visual, on-screen depiction is partly the result of conversations the filmmakers had with science consultants provided by the SEEX, including acoustics and sound expert Daniel Bodony and Stanford anthropologist Jim Ferguson.

Ferguson, for example, suggested several visual elements to make the fictional Wakanda authentically African, without duplicating any specific African nature or culture. Ferguson explained in our interview that he commented on a set of working storyboards, pointing out a few places where the filmmakers, who were following the original comic, were making an "African kingdom that didn't look very African." "For instance, they were setting up a whole scene involving an elaborate crypt for the ashes of the ancestors," he said. "I told them no one in Africa cremates and that putting the dead into the soil is a big deal," and thus Coogler changed the script because he "really cared about there being some relation between Wakanda and actual African modes of thought."[57]

In a lengthy phone conversation with Coogler and producer Nate Moore in early 2016, Daniel Bodony also discussed several elements of his work that had an impact on the finished film. He explained, "They were asking about the science and physics of vibranium in particular and sound and physics more broadly," including questions about how they could visualize sound. While Bodony was reluctant to "draw a straight line" between what he told Coogler and Moore and the content of *Black Panther*, noting that "making films like that involves hundreds of people," he highlighted several scenes that incorporated aspects of their discussion.[58] One specific concept they talked about was "acoustic cloaking," which occurs when materials are designed "to make it seem as if the object is invisible to sound." This concept appears early in the movie when the entire Wakandan nation is shown surrounded by an invisibility shield that prevents the outside world from seeing or hearing (and therefore discovering) their advanced civilization. While this technology is reminiscent of Stark's plan in *Avengers: Age of Ultron* to construct "a suit of armor around the world," the Wakandan shield is less a tool for repelling extraterrestrial armies and more of a device to prevent the outside world from realizing that Wakanda is the most highly developed society on the planet. By using cover and deception, they employ cloaking as a nonviolent form of protection and thus avoid the need to fight against possible colonizers. As such, their genius is not simply in generating such a radical technology but also in how and why they use it: it is not to dominate others but rather to sidestep the predictable efforts of others to dominate them.

Another key scene where Bodony was involved is one where Shuri is presenting T'Challa with the latest generation of equipment for him to use while under his Black Panther guise, including a new suit and a pair of trainers that prevent the user's feet from making noise while moving around. As Coogler points out, Shuri "makes fun of T'Challa for being stuck in the past," as our protagonist is unsure about adopting the new technology she has created for him, although she eventually wins him over.[59] Bodony helped with the visuals of this particular scene, explaining that he and Coogler talked about how you would design the surface of tires to be quiet and how that might transfer to Black Panther's special, silent shoes. A further topic Bodony discussed was how Coogler and Moore could visualize sound, outlining that "there are many scenes in the movie where you see a weapon that was used, or you see the interaction of some vibranium-powered object with another object, and several of those visualizations are similar to what we discussed—how very strong sound will distort light and bend it around and how you can visualize [sound] on the surface of a lake and make that three-dimensional" (see figures 4.4 and 4.5).

According to Bodony, the potential properties of vibranium made up around "30 percent of the conversation" with Coogler and Moore, adding that "by its name, it has some element of sound; we talked about using vibranium as an energy-storage device, absorbing the impact of a weapon, giving energy back in some other form, and using it [as a source to] power other things." This conversation about "how materials store energy and absorb it" is obviously reflected in Shuri's next-generation Black Panther suit, as it has the ability to absorb kinetic energy from enemy weapons, including bullets and even explosions, and then to disperse that energy in a sphere to strike at enemies. While this is a more militarized use of vibranium, the energy sphere that the suit projects is not lethal or projectile, and it is typically used to halt enemies in their tracks or to allow Black Panther to break free and escape when surrounded by enemies. Furthermore, it only functions if the enemy attacks first, allowing for the suit to absorb and store the

Figure 4.4: How sound vibrates in the world of *Black Panther*.

Figure 4.5: Another example of the visualization of vibranium's sound qualities.

energy from their blows before visiting that energy back on them. In short, it is more of a defensive than an offensive weapon, in keeping with the less aggressive or destructive depiction of technology through much of the story.

In total, Bodony had a very positive opinion of the finished film, praised its depiction of science and technology as a "counterbalance to James Bond–ish tech, where all tech is delivered by people who work in secret, to spy on others." And when it comes to the issue of the somewhat implausible technology that is featured in the story (such as the psycho-projection of someone in an almost physical object or the fact that Black Panther's suit can fit into a small matchbox), Bodony explains that he, like Clifford Johnson, is in total "favor of moviemakers pushing whatever thought process they want regardless of whether the science is there. My job is to figure out how things work; their job is to envision worlds that are different" from ours. He also noted that there is a distinction between films like the Alan Turing movie, *The Imitation Game*, and superhero movies, positing that "if the intent of the movie is [to be] a historically accurate depiction of what has happened then science accuracy is important, but in a thing like Marvel Comics, who cares, let them do their thing; the whole premise is fanciful."

Black Panther did not just embrace a highly imaginative and less militaristic approach to technology, however; it also raised important questions about who creates high technologies and for what purposes. Much of the Wakandan tech serves multiple purposes at once, from medicine to communication to more operational ends such as cover and disguise. In some cases, the Wakandans improvise, using their technology to do things other than its original design purposes, emphasizing not just how advanced their technology is but how innovative thinking and hands-on problem solving are central to the culture. Coogler drew attention to this, explaining, "A lot of things in African culture . . . have multiple uses. I like to think about the fufu dish in West Africa, how it's a food but it's also a utensil; we wanted everything to have multiple purposes and be contact-activated."[60] This attention helped generate a positive image of not just Wakandans but of scientists and engineers more broadly, emphasizing that not all scientists work on advanced weaponry (like Tony Stark and much of S.H.I.E.L.D.) but on everything from emergency medical equipment to improving farming methods. Perhaps the best example of this in the film is when Shuri uses Wakandan tech to heal Everett Ross after he has been shot in the back and paralyzed, and he recovers almost instantaneously with no signs of serious bodily trauma or injury. Bodony also praised this dimension of *Black Panther*, noting that these images "can only serve to improve people's perception of what scientists and engineers are." Indeed, Wakanda has no military-industrial complex, and while the end of the film does descend into a large battle for control of the country when T'Challa and his family return to try to defeat Killmonger, there are very few deaths on screen, in part due to the use of high technologies that are primarily defensive rather than offensive or are based in traditional, hand-to-hand combat rather than in large-scale destruction.

The character of Shuri also challenges many negative, simplistic, or restrictive stereotypes about science and scientists, as she is a teenaged African girl whose genius is at the center of Wakandan research and development. As Robyn Spencer writes in "Black Feminist Meditations on the Women of Wakanda," Shuri, "Wakanda's brilliant scientist and technological powerhouse, steals every scene she is in. She masterminds everything from T'Challa's fight strategy to the high-speed train system that will frame T'Challa and Killmonger's battle to the death. Her centrality and power is evident in the scene where she coaches Everett Ross (Martin Freeman) through his mission to short circuit Killmonger's plan while simultaneously fighting for her country, family and life."[61] At the end of the film, Shuri is also placed at the helm of the first outreach initiative that T'Challa implements on behalf of Wakanda, which takes the form of a STEM training center to empower those in the impoverished neighborhood of Oakland, California, where Killmonger was raised. Shuri also refuses to recognize Killmonger's authority after his successful coup d'état and instead heads the efforts to stage a countercoup and return T'Challa to the throne. As Coogler points out, each of these roles is "usually occupied by a white male, but it's a sixteen-year-old African telling everyone what to do."[62] Her technical and scientific genius, alongside her anti-authoritarian attitude and ability to take command at critical moments to do what's right, make her an attractive and inspirational character that upset conventional notions of "who does science."

Through characters like Shuri and T'Challa, *Black Panther* also works to effectively reverse decades of Western media representations of Africa, which, according to James Michira, have primarily showcased it as "The Dark Continent"—a place "where people thrive in backward traditions and practices, superstitions, as well as weird outdated and repugnant rites like female 'circumcision.'" Images of Africa as a place naturally prone to violence, war, savagery, and political instability; as famine and disease-ridden; as technologically backward; and as an undemocratic region, where people are incapable of governing without corruption or violent coups, have frequently appeared in Western media as well.[63] From what we see in *Black Panther*, however, Wakanda is a thriving, economically and politically stable society (at least until Killmonger arrives from the United States) and the most scientifically advanced nation on Earth. This reversal of Africa's image is profound because the notion of Western technological superiority—both in practice and in imagery and propaganda—has been used to justify the colonization of underdeveloped regions. As Zaheer Baber writes, in simplistic and often ahistorical discussions of colonialism, the scientific prowess of the West is used to ascribe a benign and "civilizing role to colonialism," "as it depicts a spread of technology from the 'core' to the 'non-scientific periphery'"—narratives that work to "contribute to colonial expansion and the legitimation of Western power" in colonized regions.[64] As a result, Wakanda's supreme technology is one of the most powerful tools the film uses to subvert colonial notions of Africa/Africans as inherently primitive and in need of saving, and because that message is never inverted throughout the course of the film, it makes it one of the most empowering elements of *Black Panther*.

Interestingly, *Black Panther*'s depiction of an African society that needs neither intervention nor aid from the outside world but rather has a lot to offer other developed countries is perhaps one reason why the CIA—which has a long history of damaging, colonialist intervention in Africa (see chapter 5)—felt it necessary to debunk or demystify the technological feats displayed in the film on its official website. In an article called "Wakandan Technology Today: A CIA Scientist Explores the Possibilities," the anonymous author spends his or her entire time either (a) presenting Wakanda's science as fictional fantasy (like its vibranium, virtual cars, or Lesotho blankets that generate holograms), (b) describing how the CIA already uses similar technology (like reflective panels to help reduce an object's visibility or clothes that can absorb shock), (c) explaining how the CIA would co-opt Wakandan technology for its own purposes, noting how the "world's spy agencies might like outfits that could reform on the fly in order to foil surveillance," or (d) explaining how the CIA would not have been fooled by Wakandan trickery. This last element is evidenced by the line that while in the movie "Wakanda keeps itself hidden from the rest of the world by a sort of invisibility cloak that . . . presumably blocks all sorts of radiation, not just light," "in real life," the CIA's satellites "would have picked up the heat, radio waves, microwaves, or other signs of a fully-industrialized country."[65] The operative word here is "presumably" because there is no indication in the film as to whether the Wakandan invisibility cloak does or does not block electromagnetic waves and the heat signature of their advanced civilization, and when Everett Ross, the CIA operative featured in the film, has the full extent of those advancements revealed to him, he is shocked and confused. Nonetheless, while the film shows the CIA as not fully aware of Wakanda's capabilities, the real CIA insisted that they would be.

One wonders why the CIA published this rather confusing piece of material, which, after all, addresses the fictional technology of a superhero movie. One motive was likely an effort to capture the interest of young STEM students by attaching the agency to a popular blockbuster movie in hopes of attracting the film's fans to a career in intelligence—yet another testament to the power of movies to recruit viewers to government agencies and/or science careers. It also seems plausible that the agency felt threatened by the fact that the CIA officer in the film is initially fooled by Wakanda's science and does not understand much of what he encounters when he reaches Wakanda. Indeed, Ross's depiction of an easily fooled, ill-informed officer, coupled with the idea that an African country might be more developed than the actual CIA in regard to its technology, seems to have struck a nerve that the agency felt compelled to address online. After all, if you are a young STEM genius, the film does not inspire you to employ your talents on behalf of the CIA, which looks hopelessly behind the times in the movie. The CIA's counter piece tries to correct that image, speaking volumes about the importance the security state places on the circulation of ideas in popular culture—even when, or especially when, it appears in a widely popular superhero movie.

Regardless of the CIA's odd response to *Black Panther*'s technology, it is clear that the film unwaveringly works to usurp colonial images of Africa as a backward continent and promotes new and positive images of scientists. As Johnson writes in "The Hidden Superpower of Black Panther: Scientist Role Models," *Black Panther* presents "vast audiences" with images of "black heroes of both genders using their scientific ability to solve problems and make their way in the world, at an unrivaled level," noting that such representations "have a positive effect on the interests, outlook and career trajectories of viewers." Johnson also writes that "improving science education for all is a core endeavor in a nation's competitiveness and overall health, but outcomes are limited if people aren't inspired to take an interest in science in the first place." He argues that there simply are not enough images of minority scientists in our popular culture to inspire members of underrepresented groups to enter STEM careers, many of whom "end up genuinely believing that scientific investigation is not a career path open to them." Thus, *Black Panther* could certainly help "erode the crumbling tropes that science is only for white men," and as more and more characters like Dr. Jason Wilkes appear within the MCU, Marvel Studios may be one of the leading players in helping change the image of scientists in the public imagination for people of color, in particular.[66]

Conclusion: The SEEX/Marvel Synergy

This analysis of the impact of science advisors on superhero movies, and in particular the influence of consultants provided to the MCU via the SEEX, illustrates how feasible depictions of science and technology are becoming more common in blockbuster movies and that the portraits of scientists themselves are becoming more positive and diverse. This is important. As Sidney Perkowitz writes in *Hollywood Science*, the quality of science education in the United States is "not uniformly high." While elementary students score above international averages in math and science, high school students score below average, with less than "one-fifth of seniors reaching scientific and mathematical proficiency at their grade levels." The current production of college graduates in STEM fields also trails the growth of jobs in these areas, with the difference made up by immigrants, and "the failure to convey science to the populace means a lack of a well-informed citizenry when it comes to the scientific issues confronting us all."[67] The consequences of this failure became especially apparent during the COVID-19 pandemic, where many American citizens came to deeply distrust both Dr. Anthony Fauci and the Centers for Disease Control and Prevention, rejecting their statements on how viruses transmit and on the effectiveness of face coverings and social distancing as preventative measures, leaving the United States to suffer the greatest number of deaths and national cases of the virus than anywhere else in the world at the time of this writing.

While Perkowitz notes that summer blockbusters may not play a strong role in depicting accurate, in-depth looks at scientific issues, they are still powerful vehicles for introducing principles like black holes or dark matter to the public, encouraging them to learn more and, most importantly, serving as powerful inspirational vehicles for young people considering future careers in STEM.[68] While it's too soon to tell how many Black scientists might result from the release of *Black Panther*, or how many female scientists Shuri, Jane Foster, or Hope Pym might inspire, Dr. Anya Johnson, a Black, female marine biologist, is already hoping for a "Shuri Effect," noting that "it gets heavy," feeling "the weight and honor of representing your people." "I probably spend more time choosing an outfit for visiting a high school assembly than I do for a date," she writes. "Because it's so rare for most kids to meet a black scientist, I feel compelled to try to convey a coolness that makes them think they could have a career in science without giving up who they are. . . . Now, I can wear sweatpants and just tell them to watch *Black Panther*."[69]

These case studies also reveal that technology has taken on a broader role in the MCU, as in Phase One, it was primarily a means of creating super-soldiers or of creating augmented weaponry, often in the form of armored suits. In Phases Two and Three, technology has been used for similar purposes, but its roles have expanded to include everything from trying to imprison a rampaging Hulk (*Age of Ultron*), to healing wounds that would have otherwise left one paralyzed or dead (*Black Panther*), to creating a means of exploring the subatomic world (*Ant-Man and the Wasp*). Over time, Marvel Studios has developed a closer relationship with the SEEX and the science consultants they provide, contributing to these distinct changes. In fact, Latcham notes that the SEEX is his favorite Hollywood outreach program to collaborate with, partly because its work is so education-focused, but also because of the way it helps him streamline production. On *Avengers 2*, for example, Latcham needed help with the scene where Vision is born, as they wanted to figure out how to essentially "print flesh on him." Within one hour, Loverd had him connected with Professor Anthony Atala at Wake Forest University, who "is doing cutting-edge research on growing organs, by using cells and something akin to a 3D printer." "I mean what a great organization that I could call and get connected to the best scientists in the world in an hour," Latcham said, adding that through that collaboration, the scene ended up with "something that feels real, cutting-edge, and futuristic but is totally grounded in real science."

By moving farther away from violence as the dominant means of resolving dramatic conflict and providing entertainment value, Marvel Studios and Disney have done nothing to harm their bottom line. While the Thor trilogy has always been the ugly duckling of the MCU in terms of critical responses, its worldwide revenues have grown with each film, from $449 million for *Thor* to $644 million for *Thor: The Dark World* to $853 million for *Thor: Ragnarok*—the most beloved installment of the series. Likewise, the Ant-Man films are somewhat lower-budget, they feature far less well-known heroes, and the second movie is almost wholly centered around a scientific challenge rather than defeating a villain, and yet they drew $519 million and $622 million, respectively. Meanwhile, *Black Panther* took in over $700 million in the United States alone, and a worldwide total in excess of $1.3 billion. The final Phase Three movie, *Avengers: Endgame*, which largely focuses on a scientific story line whereby our heroes travel through time to recover the Infinity Stones (albeit in service of a final showdown with Thanos), became the second highest-grossing film of all time with close to $2.8 billion at the box office and overshadowed only by 2009's *Avatar*.[70] These figures help demonstrate that using science consultants in the preproduction and production of films results in more technical dialogue, more plausible science, and a more varied depiction of scientists than was typical in twentieth-century cinema and that these elements do not harm the popularity of superhero movies at all. In fact, in all likelihood, these elements actually enhance it. After all, audiences have seen the Avengers assemble to fight villains in a city-scale battle on numerous occasions, and while that maintains a certain fascination for some, incorporating more science and technology into narrative arcs has given the Phase Two and Phase Three MCU movies other options in terms of both story and visual spectacle. The revenue figures for these films confirm that less violent or even nonviolent stories with an emphasis on scientific challenges and the virtues of knowledge and innovation are just as commercially viable as their more combat-filled counterparts, if not more so. Just as there is an appetite for more politically radical films, as we explored in chapter 2 of this book, there is a market for more socially radical films too.

To that end, it should be noted that none of the four films discussed in this chapter had production assistance from branches of the security state, which all but guarantees that technology is reduced to its capacity for augmenting or manifesting violence. The closest any of the four films came to such support was *Thor*, which hired former military technical advisors and is the most conventional and militaristic of the four films, albeit less so than *Iron Man*, *Man of Steel*, or *Captain Marvel*, all of which had Pentagon assistance. That said, *Black Panther*, *Avengers: Infinity War*, and *Avengers: Endgame* all feature violent conflicts at their climaxes, in keeping with the perceived expectations of the superhero genre, showing how genre limitations, yet again, impede the use of scientific themes and resolutions in summer blockbusters. However, by reforming the public image of science and scientists around less militaristic or even countermilitaristic uses of technology, these films still inspire kids with scientific talents to consider pursuing them professionally, and they now also encourage them to do so outside of the machinations of the MIC. The somewhat rhetorical question posed by these later MCU films asks: Would you rather be Justin Hammer: a cynical, slimy, and largely incompetent manufacturer of weapons, or Shuri: a cool, sassy, confident developer of benevolent technologies of many different kinds? Would you prefer to use your talents to subjugate the world by manufacturing chaos, like Darren Cross, or heal the world like Janet van Dyne? While some filmgoers will still be drawn to the more violence-based characters, the first (and more violent) generation of MCU protagonists such as Iron Man and Captain America have completed their stories and are being replaced by a more diverse range of icons, both in their ethnicity and gender but also in their approach to conflict, offering audience members a wider selection of potential inspirations and role models.

Despite the MCU embracing more scientific characters, however, we should still ask whether science and technology could have played even a larger, more radical role in the MCU overall. A look back on the first three phases of the franchise suggests that a quite different arc for the series was possible. In *Iron Man 2*, the SEEX helped come up with ideas for how Stark can create a new element to serve as an integral part of his chest plate, powering both the Iron Man suits and the electromagnet in his chest that prevents bomb shrapnel from reaching his heart. This is a miniaturized version of the arc reactor that we see at Stark Technologies in the first Iron Man film—a giant clean-energy generator initially developed by Howard Stark decades earlier, which apparently doesn't work that well, as Obadiah Stane derides it as "a publicity stunt" and quips, "We built that thing to shut the hippies up!" However, with the addition of the new element created in *Iron Man 2*, the reactor now functions perfectly, providing a vast amount of energy with virtually no pollution or resource depletion. This could have been a turning point for the MCU and Stark could have used the arc reactor technology to revolutionize the entire world, but instead he only uses it to power the Stark Tower in *The Avengers*. Stark then has the chest plate and shrapnel removed from his body at the end of *Iron Man 3*, and the arc reactor plays very little role in the MCU from that point forward. This is significant because the reasons behind Thanos's mass-murder plot in *Avengers: Infinity War* are the problems of resource depletion, pollution, and excessive consumption driven by overpopulation—all problems that could have been resolved, or at least counteracted, by the widespread use of clean energy provided by Stark's arc reactors. Had the MCU been braver and bolder in their imagination, a less violent and more scientific MCU could have been possible, and the greatest act of violence in the series—Thanos's instant murder of half of the population of the universe—might never have happened. Even without Thanos's insane solution to a very real set of problems, there could still have been plenty of room for dramatic conflict, as people jostled for control of the arc reactor technology and over its possible uses and ends.

Some may dismiss this as a fruitless thought experiment, while others would reject it because it would take away the need for the quite wondrous time-travel story line in *Avengers: Endgame*, which helped tie almost the entire MCU together in a spectacle of highly satisfying fan service, but there is more at stake. Had the world's most popular and successful film franchise committed to a more benevolent and less violence-centered view of the purposes and value of technology, it could have functioned as a beacon to the centers of power in the real world, encouraging them to move beyond the tribalistic scrap for control of resources and peoples. What better example could films set for the real world's billionaires than to show one of them developing a means for clean energy and then providing it to the world for free?

ALL NEW, BUT NOT THAT DIFFERENT?
DIVERSITY, POLITICS, AND THE SUPERHERO

5

In their book *All New, All Different*, Allan Austin and Patrick Hamilton trace the history of diversity in the American comic book industry. The pair argue that until the 1990s, most comic book series perpetuated worn ethnic stereotypes and/or worked to reinforce concepts of white hegemony. For example, during World War II and the Cold War, ethnic minorities most commonly functioned in comic books as villains, especially those of Japanese, Soviet, and Chinese descent. From the 1960s to the 1980s, writers tried to reach a wider audience by featuring multiracial teams or duos, as well as minorities like Luke Cage, the Falcon, and Black Panther in stand-alone titles. While these characters worked to bring greater representation to the industry, multiracial teams most often featured people of color in token roles; many solo titles employed negative racial stereotypes; and superhero duos privileged white hegemony through unequal partnerships, such as Iron Man and War Machine, where Rhodes literally works as Stark's employee. Allan and Hamilton argue that collectively these titles served audiences "longing for a fantasy of racial equality and harmony," while too often their narratives belied it.[1]

The 1990s saw more significant strides in racial progress, especially with the industry trend of "ethnic replacement heroes"—a practice where writers transformed an established white hero into a "nonwhite" one, such as when Eddie March or James Rhodes replace Tony Stark as Iron Man, Monica Rambeau adopts the Captain Marvel identity, John Stewart becomes the Green Lantern, or John Trujillo replaces the Black Condor. While these stories did not always succeed financially or culturally, they are often celebrated because the writers pushed the characters beyond "the flattened and distancing expectations of race," treated characters with great empathy, and carved out an authentic and nuanced heroic identity, even if it was based on a previously established, white-led title.[2] Today, this type of inclusivity continues, as evidenced by the Pakistani American Kamala Khan taking up the identity of Ms. Marvel. This richer history of diversity had led scholars such as Adilifu Nama to argue that superheroes of color now act as cultural ciphers and sources "of wisdom concerning notions of racial reciprocity, racial equality, racial forgiveness, and, ultimately, racial justice."[3]

In the cinematic realm, older trends of racial representation continue, although they too are changing. The DC Universe has long struggled with issues of diversity, "with the Christopher Nolan Batman trilogy and what has followed remaining predominantly white." When people of color appear in DC titles, they tend to play subordinate and stereotypical roles, such as Morgan Freeman's Lucius Fox, who, although he offers sage advice, decidedly serves Batman and accedes to his decisions. Likewise, while *Suicide Squad* was celebrated for its highly diverse cast, several reviewers argued that the film reduced Killer Croc, El Diablo, and Katana to shallow ethnic stereotypes, while *Justice League* replicated old race patterns by adding Cyborg as the token person of color in an otherwise Caucasian team.[4] Marvel, especially in recent years, has done better with diversity. While the Spider-Man films at Sony have been predominantly white, Marvel's recent reboots feature multicultural stars such as Zendaya and Jacob Batalon, while the animated *Into the Spider-verse* is almost entirely composed of a Black and Latinx cast. The MCU also includes racially diverse heroes, such as the Falcon, Iron Patriot, Gamora, Shuri, T'Challa, and others, and Simu Liu has recently been announced as the lead, Shang-Chi, in its upcoming movie about a Chinese hero (albeit one proficient in martial arts).

In terms of gender diversity, superhero stories follow a similar trajectory. Jennifer Stuller writes that "superhero comics have not traditionally been written with a female audience in mind," and even modern stories, "like those of classic world myth, continue to focus on male experience and fantasy." Just like men of color, women of all races are vastly underrepresented in superhero stories and are often confined to stereotypical roles, such as the supporting mother, the wife/girlfriend, the vixen, or the damsel in distress.[5] Similarly, in their 2007 study of television cartoons, Baker and Raney reveal that only one-third of superhero characters were female, that females acted as team leaders only 10 percent of the time, and that they were frequently depicted as more emotional and attractive than their male counterparts. Additionally, while only one-third of the characters were depicted as having a mentor, the females were twice as likely to have one, and all but one of the mentors were male.[6] Another study of mainstream superhero comics produced between 1993 and 2013 reveals that women represented fewer characters even in female-headed titles and that women in ensemble casts made up less than one-quarter of all characters and were drawn in just one-quarter of the frames. Nearly every issue depicted women as sexual objects, especially on the issue covers, as well.[7]

In film and television, women have recently made significant gains, with Wonder Woman, Captain Marvel, Jessica Jones, and Black Widow all featuring in solo titles. However, while Batman and Superman have enjoyed numerous incarnations on the silver screen for decades, Wonder Woman languished in development at Warner Bros. until Patty Jenkins's 2017 production. Likewise, even though Black Widow has been a member of the Avengers and debuted in *Iron Man 2* in 2010, she did not get a stand-alone movie until a decade later, well after Thor, Iron Man, and Captain America had had several installments of their own movies released. The WikiFandom list of the 129 heroic characters who have appeared in both the films and television series of the MCU also reveals that only forty-three are female, or just 33 percent.[8] As Carolyn Cocca summarizes, over the last seventy-five years, superheroes have been overwhelmingly portrayed as male, heterosexual, white, and able-bodied, even as an increasing number of female, queer, colored, and disabled superheroes have been emerging in print.[9]

One of the reasons that so few superhero films have featured female leads is that early attempts failed miserably at the box office, including *Supergirl* (1984), *Tank Girl* (1995), *Catwoman* (2004), and *Elektra* (2005), mostly due to the fact that "these films were poorly, shamefully, and embarrassingly produced."[10] The global box-office successes of *Wonder Woman* and *Captain Marvel* suggest, however, that viewers are interested in female-led superhero stories; they just want them to be good. The recent record-setting film, *Black Panther*, also highlights audiences' interest in movies led by people of color, and studios' desire to produce more diverse films has increased in recent years, largely in response to the Oscars So White and Me Too movements. As stated in *Superwomen: Gender, Power and Representation*, such diversification is important because limited portrayals of heroic characters "curtail imagination," forcing marginalized groups to either cross-identify with white, male heroes, or, far worse, to fail to imagine that heroic characters look like them. Diverse heroes, on the other hand, help viewers "to see that anyone can be a hero," and often build tolerance, acceptance, and empathy across all categories of identity.[11]

Of course, diverse representation is not without complications, as the most prominent examples of superhero stories with diverse leads still manifest many of the same societal values and political subtexts as more traditional films in the genre. *Wonder Woman*, *Black Panther*, and *Captain Marvel* were all heralded for employing leads outside of straight, white, able-bodied, American males, but none are truly radical in their politics, especially *Captain Marvel* (as we explored in chapter 3). Some of the same ideological compromises that turned *Captain Marvel* into an air force recruitment tool and a means of advancing a militaristic worldview of space also afflicted *Wonder Woman* and *Black Panther*, despite neither set of filmmakers working with the Pentagon. (*Wonder Woman* sought assistance from the British military, while *Black Panther* was made without support from any military or intelligence agency.)

Indeed, both films can be interpreted as discomforting promotions for the Atlantic hegemony, in spite of being led by characters who might be expected to oppose and resist that hegemony.

Rebecca Wanzo writes that comics and films always "hold progressivism and conservatism simultaneously," which helps explain why some communities become deeply attached to representations with flawed or even caricatured origins. As she states about the 2016 Netflix series *Luke Cage*, the show was based on a comic series about a wrongly incarcerated man who is experimented on in prison. Media reviews soon hailed "the bullet-proof Luke Cage . . . as a hero for a 'black lives matter moment.'" "On the one hand, the black man who cannot be hurt is an old fantasy of black monstrosity," she writes, and it is the same fantasy "police officer Darren Wilson evoked in 2014 when he described eighteen-year-old Michael Brown as a 'demon' in offering an excuse for shooting him six times. On the other hand, the idea of a strong black man impervious to white supremacy is a resistance fantasy that many people have enjoyed in the past and present, even as it is tied to ideas of racialized masculinity that can be injurious."[12] *Wonder Woman* and *Black Panther* work in a similar vein, promoting both social progressivism and political conservatism within the same text—a notion explored in the rest of this chapter.

Wonder Woman (2017)

Following tepid responses to its first two DCEU movies, Warner Bros. released Patty Jenkins's *Wonder Woman* in 2017, a highly successful film that enjoyed a 93 percent critic score and an 87 percent audience score on Rotten Tomatoes, alongside impressive box-office returns. For many fans and feminists, the success of *Wonder Woman* was particularly sweet. This is because despite being a founding member of the Justice League and first appearing in comics in 1941, Diana Prince never made a big-screen debut until *Batman v. Superman* in 2016 and did not get her own origin film until the following year, highlighting how Hollywood has consistently sidelined female superheroes in favor of their male counterparts. As Tim Hanley explains in his 2014 book, *Wonder Woman*

Unbound, "For the past thirty years, aside from her one sparsely read monthly comic, Wonder Woman has lacked the publication, television, and film presence of her fellow superheroes" and has been "practically nonexistent outside of T-shirts and other memorabilia."[13]

In this respect alone, *Wonder Woman* can be hailed as a socially progressive text, as it not only proved that women can successfully direct big-budget action films but that superhero movies with female leads can prove just as popular with filmgoers, if not more so, as those with male leads. By returning Diana to her Amazonian/Marston roots, Jenkins also helped overcome the more lackluster roles that Wonder Woman has played in the past. As books such as Jill Lepore's *The Secret History of Wonder Woman*, Hanley's *Wonder Woman Unbound*, Noah Berlatsky's *Wonder Woman: Bondage and Feminism in the Marston/Peter Comics*, 1941–1948, and Jacob Held's *Wonder Woman and Philosophy* all demonstrate,[14] Wonder Woman's original creator, William Moulton Marston, used his series to promote female equality, strength, and leadership (as well as his sexual proclivity for bondage). Throughout his series, Marston also argued that women should rule the world given their greater capacity for love, compassion, and honesty. When Marston died in 1947, Wonder Woman became a far more domesticated figure over the next three decades, as she "gave up her powers, left the Justice League (which she had founded), turned into a fashionista, married Steve Trevor (in the alternate history Earth Two), had a kid, and became a housewife."[15] During that same time, however, second-wave feminists adopted Wonder Woman as a feminist icon, with Gloria Steinem famously placing her on the cover of *Ms.* magazine in 1972, highlighting the paradox that "while American women grew from complacent housewives to protesters for women's liberation," Wonder Woman, in her actual comic form, had fallen "backward."[16] While the late 1980s saw a brief resurgence of Wonder Woman's feminist themes under the stewardship of George Perez, that series did not last long, and Wonder Woman was again "thrust back into banality," eventually taking a job at a Mexican fast food restaurant called Taco Whiz, leaving Andrea Zanin to conclude that "the modern era [had] left the heroine without much feminist clout" at all.[17]

Similarly, in Zack Snyder's *Batman v. Superman*, the film's focus is largely on the conflict between two white men, and it is Batman who brings the team together and teaches Wonder Woman how to be a leader. Diana does appear at a crucial moment in the climactic battle against Doomsday (a giant monster created by Lex Luthor) and fights as an equal alongside our pair of male superheroes, but this is her only major contribution to the story, and it is Superman who ultimately defeats Doomsday, sacrificing his own life in the process. While it was a positive step to finally depict Wonder Woman on the silver screen, Snyder's film was a baby step, as he and Warner Bros. chose to follow the script of the original Justice League comics, where Diana ends up as a token female who primarily highlights the greater awesomeness of the men around her. In contrast, Jenkins's *Wonder Woman* features Prince as the unequivocal star, and the plot revolves around her self-appointed mission to save the world by defeating the Greek god Ares, whom Diana believes is the cause of World War I.

Adding to *Wonder Woman*'s progressive credentials is the romantic subplot between Diana and Steve Trevor, which features a charming role reversal, where Diana pursues Steve quite openly while he manifests the uncertainty usually reserved for female characters who are the subjects of male affection. This is especially well drawn out in an early scene where the pair are still on Themyscira, and Diana walks in on Steve while he is naked, showering in a waterfall. While Diana is curious (without being creepy), it is Steve who is shy and embarrassed about his body. Despite the fact that Steve is also an army veteran and an elite spy, he plays second fiddle to Diana for most of the story, thereby reversing the power dynamics of the earlier Justice League comics where Diana was the subject of affection from more powerful superheroes and operated as an adjunct to them rather than as an end in herself.

Finally, *Wonder Woman* can be hailed as a progressive, and even radical, text for the ways it disrupts traditional notions of femininity and bolsters, at least in act I, a more pacifist ideology. The film's story begins on Themyscira, the home to a race of Amazon warriors. Here, we see an eight-year-old Diana longing to be part of the combat training that is part of life for the other older Amazon warriors. Her mother, Hippolyta, tells Diana a story to discourage this desire, explaining that "war is nothing to hope for." She outlines how Zeus created humans in his own image, as beings for the gods to rule over, and that they were "fair and good, strong and passionate" until they were corrupted by Zeus's son Ares, who "poisoned men's hearts with jealousy and suspicion, vengeance and rage." This turned humans against one another and "war ravaged the earth," and so "the gods made us, the Amazons, to influence men's hearts with love and to restore peace to the world." This worked for a time, but Ares eventually turned humans against the Amazons, leading Zeus to create Themyscira as a safe haven. The young Diana accepts this explanation of why conflict, combat, and war are not to be desired and why the Amazons view violence as a last resort in any struggle. Unlike more masculine narratives in the genre, where violence is a first resort or at least openly embraced by the protagonists, the setup in *Wonder Woman* establishes a more feminine, and even feminist, view of violent conflict from the beginning. As Jean Bethke Elshtain argues in *Women and War*, male warriors have long been the "avatars of a nation's sanctioned violence,"[18] protecting the society they defend, while women and children often play the role of those who need protecting. By featuring female warriors who are highly skilled in combat, *Wonder Woman* disrupts this narrative with a race of female protectors rather than females in need of protection. However, as Melanie Johnson-Moxley writes, while "the Amazons have refined their combat skills over centuries, it is their core ethos to seek, whenever possible, non-violent methods of preventing harm or addressing a threat. . . . When these measures fail, or are clearly not an option," only then will the Amazons use violence "in as measured and precise a way as possible to eliminate the threat of more violence. In any event, the end goal is always peace."[19]

Wonder Woman's first act, then, distinguishes itself from its genre's more masculine, pro-war films. By depicting the Amazons as compassionate and peaceful counterparts to men's propensity for violence and aggression, *Wonder Woman* also avoids many of the pitfalls of other "chicks who kick" films. As Frances Early writes in

"The Female Just Warriors Reimagined," too often popular culture's female warriors remain prisoners of male-centered notions about what it means to be a warrior. In other words, they seek to use violence or aggression at every turn, rather than considering alternative methods (such as the Amazons' magic lasso). This trend is dangerous because it echoes Michel Foucault's warning that "marginalized people can be drawn to the power of 'reverse discourse,'" whereby they find themselves seeking legitimacy "in the same vocabulary, using the same categories by which they were disqualified."[20]

Despite these progressive elements, however, *Wonder Woman* was still criticized for not being radical or feminist enough. To cite just one example, Kyle Killian laments the film's heavy emphasis on the heroine's sex appeal, arguing that it should be tertiary, or better yet, not highlighted in the film's dialogue at all. He also notes that while Wonder Woman comes from a decidedly queer background, where she has learned that men "are integral to human reproduction" but not sexual pleasure, the film ultimately rejects a nonheteronormative heroine. Instead, Wonder Woman falls for the first man to land on her island "because that is what happens in the source material from decades ago, and because Hollywood and 90% of audiences expect, no, demand this to happen. Wonder Woman eventually must become as American as red, white and blue, apple pie, and hot dogs in buns."[21]

Wonder Woman is also a politically conservative and revisionist text, especially in its depiction of American and Allied forces. More specifically, the film features our heroine teaming up with a multinational and multiethnic team of sidekicks, including a Scottish sniper, a Moroccan spy, and a Native American smuggler. As Robert Gerwarth and Erez Manela write, World War I is best understood as a conflict between belligerent imperialists who fought with "multi-ethnic armies in colonized spaces," rather than as a war between European nation-states.[22] While the film recognizes the multiethnic nature of the war, *Wonder Woman*'s depiction of an equally integrated unit is a millennial rewriting of history, which makes the Allies, and especially the British military, look far more progressive than they truly were. In reality, while hundreds of thousands of Muslims fought on the British side during World War I, they were primarily colonial subjects from pre-partition India, not North Africa, while the Ottoman empire fought on the side of Germany.[23] Likewise, while over twelve thousand Native Americans fought in the US Army during World War I, the majority were denied US citizenship, which was not formally awarded to most Native Americans until several years after the war. They also died at a rate approximately five times that of other US troops, in part because of their role as scouts, which made them more prominent frontline targets for opposing forces.[24] Finally, the Scottish experience of the First World War involved a disproportionately higher death rate than that experienced by the rest of the United Kingdom and Ireland.[25] This was largely due to the Scots being deemed as more expendable than the English and Irish troops, so they were more commonly used for particularly hazardous missions. By depicting these characters fighting equally alongside Diana, the film conveniently massages history by ignoring how all of these populations were subjugated by the major powers and often deployed as "cannon fodder" during the conflict.

Additionally, in perhaps the most iconic and memorable sequence of the film, Diana and her friends cross no man's land. Using her amulets and shield to deflect the artillery shells and machine-gun fire from the Germans, Diana and her sidekicks reach the German trenches and kill a posse of soldiers before going on to kill more Germans in a nearby town. While a spectacularly thrilling scene for viewers that highlights the superhuman nature of Diana, it nonetheless covers up the grim realities of trench warfare and especially the tactic of sending men "over the top" into a maelstrom of enemy fire and near-certain death. Indeed, none of her sidekicks are even wounded in the crossing, despite their lack of superpowers, and crossing the divide appears relatively quick, taking less than a few minutes. The Battle of the Somme, on the other hand, lasted from July until November 1916, resulted in nearly one million casualties (many of them British), and saw gains of just ten miles of territory for the victorious British and French armies.[26] While the battle was still going on, the British War Office helped produce the film *The Battle of the Somme* as part of its war propaganda effort. The film featured staged sequences that helped minimize the public's awareness of the scale of the deaths and injuries being suffered and maximized their support for such destructive offensives.[27] Just over a century later, *Wonder Woman*, which itself received production assistance from the British Ministry of Defense, recycled the approach of *The Battle of the Somme*, helping cement, albeit through an over-the-top, popular reimagining of the war, the notion that trench warfare wasn't so bad after all.

The film's treatment of chemical warfare also participates in a whitewashing of history. The movie portrays the use of chemical gases in World War I as an exclusively German crime, discovered by Steve at a secret base in Turkey. In reality, the German, French, American, Austrian, and British forces all made use of chemical gas attacks during the war despite them being outlawed and their use constituting a war crime. The French army used tear gas from as early as August 1914, while the German military first made use of it that October, firing shells at British positions at Neuve Chapelle. In April 1915, the Germans used nearly 170 metric tons of chlorine at Ypres, killing over 1,100 people, and the British responded with a large chlorine attack against the Germans in September at the Battle of Loos. As the war went on, the United States established the Chemical Warfare Service to help develop mustard gas weapons, and in June 1918, the Allies started using mustard gas against German troops, including a young Adolf Hitler. By the end of the war, between 90,000 and 100,000 deaths were caused by the use of chemical weapons employed by both sides of the conflict.[28] In this context, *Wonder Woman*'s portrayal of chemical weapons being an act solely deployed by the enemy without once acknowledging that these weapons were used by multiple nations on all sides of World War I (let alone afterward) is a gross revision of history. However, the simplistic depiction of the Germans as the war's clear-cut enemy is in line with how the film treats the group overall.

Throughout the film, the Germans are constantly portrayed as compassionless, disposable enemies from their first appearance on screen, despite the fact that Diana believes *all soldiers* are good people (they are just under the control of Ares). After Steve crash-lands off the coast of Themyscira, a German naval unit appears, having followed him, and he explains to Diana, "I'm one of the good guys, and those are the bad guys. Y'know . . . Germans." The ensuing fight then sees the Germans battle the Amazons, who righteously prevail. This simplistic image of the Germans persists, and Wonder Woman doesn't think twice before crushing dozens of them on her way to find and defeat the god of war. While her dialogue includes numerous references to the insanity of war and how Ares, not humans, is to blame, her actions frequently contradict this philosophy, as she is firmly on the side of the Allied powers and against the Central powers, including Germany. The miscellaneous German soldiers she smashes aside barely speak and have no personality, and their deaths and suffering are ignored almost entirely, while the only two German main characters are the military leader Ludendorff and his chemical warfare specialist Dr. Isabel Maru, also known as Doctor Poison, both of whom are unabashedly evil to the point of being almost inhuman.

This combination of an unrealistically progressive depiction of the British and a grossly simplistic and negative depiction of the Germans fails to use its setting to its fullest potential. According to Delia Harrington, the decision to root *Wonder Woman* in World War I, rather than the more obvious choice of World War II—the time of the character's creation—presented the writers with a unique opportunity. "The West, and America in particular, love World War II because it portrays them in a favorable light" and lends itself to a simple story of good vs. evil with "one very bad man at the center who simply [needs] to be stopped." "World War I, on the other hand, was a far more complex and unfortunate conflict," Harrington writes, and thus was a more appropriate setting to teach Diana about the moral complexities of war.[29] Unlike Harrington, however, we believe *Wonder Woman* fails to highlight those complexities or even the real nature of the Great War. For example, while Diana initially believes the conflict is the full result of Ares's machinations, this belief is eventually complicated when Steve says, "Maybe people aren't just good, Diana . . . I wish I could tell you that there was one 'bad guy' to blame. Maybe we're all to blame." Shortly afterward, Ares echoes this same position, denying that he is responsible for the war and blaming humanity. He tells Diana, "They have always been, and always will be, weak, cruel, selfish, and capable of the greatest horror . . . They start these wars on their own," and even the soundtrack for *Wonder Woman* includes a piece of music titled "We Are All to Blame," which plays during this section of the story. While this perspective challenges, to a degree, a simple good vs. evil narrative, it also means that the only views that *Wonder Woman* offers regarding culpability for World War I are either that a metaphysical entity has been whispering in the ears of humans, driving them toward death and destruction, or that humans simply did it all by themselves and they are all equally guilty. Again, this is cynical historical revisionism that overlooks how World War I was started by aristocratic empires squabbling with each other for territory in Central Europe and that many of the people who signed up to fight weren't doing so because of widespread hatred of the designated enemies or deep flaws in their souls. They did so because they were desperate for employment and/or the coerced subjects of colonial forces.

Likewise, by featuring Steve Trevor as an American do-gooder simply trying to save the world from a German chemical attack, the film also erases America's imperialist objectives for entering the war. As Christopher Capozzola writes, America was deeply invested in securing unfettered access to global markets during the war, especially given its recent opening of the Panama Canal, while Gerwarth and Manela write that President Wilson imagined "a far more ambitious American imperium" during the war. This new empire, composed of an interlocking system of nation-states, was to be organized and "governed by the principles of free trade," with the United States serving "as first among equals," as US economic and military preponderance would sustain Washington's hegemony globally.[30] Even President Wilson himself wrote in 1907 that he viewed the Spanish-American War as necessary:

> Since trade ignores national boundaries and manufacturers insist on having the world as a market, the flag of the nation must follow him and the doors of the nations which are closed against him must be battered down . . . even if the sovereignty of an unwilling nation

> be outraged in the process. Colonies must be obtained or planted in order that no useful corner of the world may be overlooked or left unused.[31]

Wonder Woman, however, pretends that there is almost no American military involvement in World War I beyond our intrepid Steve Trevor, even though the United States deployed roughly two million troops to the French front, despite its original stance of neutrality, in order to achieve its imperialist goals.[32] Indeed, by rebranding World War I as a war of all against all, when in truth it was an entirely unnecessary conflict perpetrated by the richest and most powerful class of people trying to obtain either more territory or more markets, avoids the true responsibility for the forty million deaths and/or injuries that occurred during the war, as well as the suffering and displacement endured by tens of millions more.

Interestingly, earlier versions of the *Wonder Woman* script were far more radical in its war messaging. In 2005, Warner Bros. and Silver Pictures announced that Joss Whedon had been hired to write and direct a *Wonder Woman* film, though Whedon exited the project two years later, unable to produce a satisfactory screenplay. His script leaked online years later, and while it contains many of the same story elements and character relationships as the finished film, it is thematically more radical. Whedon's version begins much the same as the movie, introducing Themyscira before Steve crash-lands on the island, launching Diana's adventure. Rather than being set during World War I, however, Whedon's vision took place in the modern day. Callas, the CEO of a military-industrial megacorporation, Spearhead, worships Ares and has a relationship with his niece Strife, the goddess of chaos. They develop a plan to destroy half of a fictional US city called Gateway, apparently based on New York. In one dialogue between Callas and Strife, it becomes clear that while in the past, "There was a time when the God of War made war," war has now become the de facto result of a military-industrial economy, with Callas outlining, "You want war, you need armies. You need an acceptable level of poverty and ignorance. Despair, rage, religious fervour and above all fear."[33]

Rather than blaming war on Ares's influence, or more generally on flaws in the human soul, Whedon's script identifies specific emotions and socioeconomic conditions that make war easier to provoke. By making the primary antagonist the CEO of a war-profiteering company rather than the more abstract metaphysical entities of Ares or Strife, he also situated responsibility for war in the real world rather than in the mythical realm. Much like earlier drafts of *Hulk*, *Iron Man*, and *Ant-Man*, Whedon's version of *Wonder Woman* was written during the zenith of the Bush administration's War on Terror, at a time when the MIC's influence on foreign policy was becoming more widely recognized. But just like *Hulk* and *Iron Man*, *Wonder Woman* eventually underwent the same political, deradicalization process as the script continued to be rewritten, although the inverted stereotypes in the romance between Steve and Diana, as well as Diana's arc of having to overcome her naivete in order to succeed, made it into the finished film.

Core aspects of Diana's character arc also differ between Whedon's vision and the final shooting script. When Steve crashes on Themyscira, the initial response of the Amazons is that he must be put to death, as no outsider is allowed to know of the island's existence. This leads to a tense standoff between Hippolyta and Diana and to Diana challenging her mother to ritual combat in order to save Steve's life. Diana then defies her mother's wishes to leave the island and travels with Steve to Gateway, where she learns about the corruption, vice, and suffering in the Western world and comes to realize that Spearhead, Callas, and Strife are responsible. After defeating Strife, Ares appears before Diana to declare that the fight has just begun (thus setting up a sequel) and employs similar dialogue to the confrontation between Ares and Diana in the finished film, with some crucial differences:

> ARES: You will suffer for this. You will see this world in ashes.
> DIANA: Will I?
> ARES: You cannot defeat a God.
> DIANA (points to the crowd): They can.
> ARES (laughing): The people? The people of earth, turn their back on me? On war?

DIANA: Someday, maybe.
ARES: I am in mankind. I am in their darkest hearts and their greatest schemes and I am never going away.
DIANA: Neither am I.[34]

This scene then dissolves to Hippolyta's chamber where she and Circe are watching the unfolding drama, with Circe observing, "The fury of Ares is eternal. What Diana has started here will shake the earth." Hippolyta responds, smiling, "That's my girl." In Whedon's script, Diana refuses to accept Ares's claims that the darkness inside the human soul makes war unavoidable, and she predicts that humanity may one day turn away from warfare, asserting that humans are good enough to defeat an evil god. This is then validated by her mother, who had initially opposed any idea of Diana interfering in the world beyond Themyscira.

In the final version of *Wonder Woman*, however, the hope and optimism Diana manifests through the first two acts of the story are broken by her fight with Ares in the final act, and she explains in a closing voice-over, "I used to want to save the world. To end war and bring peace to mankind. But then I glimpsed the darkness that lives within their light. And learned that inside every one of them, there will always be both. A choice each must make for themselves—something no hero will ever defeat. And now I know. Only love can truly save the world." In comparison, Whedon's script situates the responsibility for not only war in the real world but also the solution, concluding with a message of empowerment for the human race to embrace the better angels of their nature. In the released version of the film, Diana abandons her belief in the fundamental goodness of human beings, places the blame for war on abstract entities, and concludes that the only solution is another abstraction, firmly divorcing the story from the real world and thus making it less relevant and radical.[35]

By looking at these different script versions, it becomes clear that female directors will not always champion the more radical creative decisions that are available, just because they come from an outside community (at least in Hollywood). It isn't clear exactly how or why this thematic reversal in the development of *Wonder Woman* took place, but one possibility is the risk-averse nature of major studios who are always concerned with protecting the bottom line. Breaking some of the conventions of the genre and subverting a few of the expectations of audiences is clearly possible, but a consistently anti-war film would have been a risk that could have backfired when it came to securing revenues in a competitive market flooded with superhero movies.

Likewise, Jenkins's conservative approach to the political values of the film helped it win full production support from the British Ministry of Defence (MOD), thereby increasing the film's bottom line. The MOD's directive on support to Non-News Media Projects outlines its criteria for deciding whether to agree to assist a production, including whether the producers "portray [the Ministry of] Defence in a positive manner," "the likely communications effect of participation/non-participation considering the return on investment (including the potential audience reach and the messaging opportunities)," and the "wider consequential relationships with stakeholders, including Other Government Departments and Allies."[36] *Wonder Woman*, a film that portrays a multiethnic but primarily Anglo-American alliance overcoming cardboard cutout villains, set during the Great War and released to a mass audience during the centenary of that war, clearly met these criteria. As such, the filmmakers were allowed to film at RAF Halton, an air force station in Buckinghamshire, where they described the content of the military-supported sequence as "set in a WWI Belgian airfield at the end of 1918," and as "a big action sequence featuring German soldiers attacking the heroes of the film."[37] The producers were also permitted to film at RAF Upper Heyford in Oxfordshire, an air force station that housed US strategic bombers for long periods during the Cold War.[38] The scenes where Diana kills Ludendorff and then defeats Ares were all shot at one of these two British bases. The film then concludes with Diana going back to London, where she is greeted by a crowd in Trafalgar Square waving British and US flags to celebrate her success against the diabolical Germans, a scene that firmly planted the idea that World War I was a noble British victory over evil in the minds of viewers and a trope that would have certainly pleased the MOD (see figure 5.1).

Figure 5.1: The crowd in Trafalgar Square celebrates the Allied victory in World War I in *Wonder Woman*.

In our final analysis, then, *Wonder Woman* is inherently polysemic, subject to praise and criticism from various quarters. The success of a strong female lead in a male-dominated genre certainly helps define *Wonder Woman* as a socially progressive text, as does her romantic dynamic with Steve Trevor. Likewise, the first act of the film is noticeably more feminine, and even feminist, than any prior superhero movie, espousing a more pacifist or at least compassionate approach to conflict. However, in the second and third acts of the film, this tone gives way to a more masculine and pro-war timbre, as Diana's pacifist and potentially feminist approach to war is frequently drawn out in her dialogue, but her actions—which are often violent, compassionless, and even vengeful at times—contradict those words. Other elements of the film also sanitize the image of World War I and maintain the myth that it was a good, noble war that saw the Allied "good guys" overcome the German "bad guys," further highlighting the film's political conservatism and historical whitewashing. Despite, or perhaps because of, the film's polysemic nature, *Wonder Woman* was nonetheless a box-office smash, earning over $821 million in ticket sales and becoming the most successful female-led superhero film at the time (until *Captain Marvel* two years later). It also ranks as the most successful female-directed film ever released and received widespread critical acclaim, with Rotten Tomatoes ranking it as the fourth best superhero film out of its list of seventy-five. Comparable box-office success would be repeated by the MCU just one year later, when it debuted its most racially diverse installment to date in the form of Ryan Coogler's *Black Panther.*

Black Panther (2018)

In numerous interviews, Coogler reveals that *Black Panther* has both personal and political overtones, telling *Rolling Stone* that just before Marvel called to gauge his interest in making the film, he was grappling with his "cultural identity, and what it means to be African." "I'd been wanting to visit Africa," he says. "I had never been, and I felt ashamed that I had never been. So I was like, 'As soon I finish *Creed*, maybe [my wife] Zinzi and I can take that trip.'" Eventually, Coogler visited South Africa, where he discovered that many of his own cultural rituals mirrored those of the Black South Africans he met, which encouraged him to think further about "this concept of us as a people being marooned in this place that we're not from. When people ask me where I'm from, I tell them the Bay Area and there's a sense of pride there. But the truth is, we're really from *that* place. The place that *everybody's* from."[39]

Coogler's personal questions about his cultural identity certainly factored into the creation of his film's antagonist, Erik Killmonger—a royal Wakandan child who is raised in poverty in the Bay Area after his own father is murdered. As a young adult, Killmonger undergoes years of military training to prepare for his return to Wakanda, where he wishes to challenge T'Challa for the throne, in part to exact revenge since it was T'Challa's father, T'Chaka, who murdered Killmonger's father. By seizing control of Wakanda's vibranium to manufacture weapons, Killmonger also aims to empower, through violence, Black people across the globe who have been systemically disenfranchised by white power structures. Such motives place Killmonger among Marvel's newest villains, who, although their means are severe, possess motives that are increasingly compelling.

As Killmonger's description suggests, *Black Panther* is grounded in a historical awareness of white, colonial power, including that held by the comics' original creators—Marvel legends Stan Lee and Jack Kirby.

When interviewed by NPR's David Greene, Coogler noted that both Lee and Kirby were well aware of Africa's exploitation by Western imperial forces. Coogler then reminds listeners that Africa's great reserves of natural resources have led to its "colonization and exploitation," along with the "mental horrors" of that colonization, which include "being told that you're less than, and not worthy of, and losing your language—losing your heritage," as well as the "very scary" cousin of colonization, "which is the theft of bodies, [which] is what happened to my ancestors." Coogler states that when Lee and Kirby created Wakanda, they were fully conscious of this history, asking, "Man, what if that never happened to a place? What if a place had something really cool, had a cool mineral, you know, had a coltan, had a gold, had a diamond, and they never were conquered and they found a way to manipulate it, and stay separate from the world and grow and become great?"[40] The answers to those questions became the foundation for the *Black Panther* series, whose setting appears, through magical forces, as impoverished to outsiders but is in reality a thriving, rich, and technologically advanced society.

Because of this context, *Black Panther* is rich in images and themes of Black cultural identity. Indeed, the film's aural and visual style enhances the theme of African independence, as the writers created a language for Wakandans built on one of the indigenous "clicking" languages of South Africa: Xhosa. The film's costumers also incorporated traditional outfits from varied African regions and blended them with modern shapes and textures to create the film's Afro-futuristic aesthetic. Costumer Ruth Carter specifically explains that Lupita Nyongo's look is based on the traditional clothes and makeup of the Suri tribe, Angela Bassett's headpieces were modeled after those worn by married Zulu women, and the Wakandan warriors' neck rings were based on those worn by the South African Ndebele tribe.[41] Commentators have observed that another "part of the aesthetic pleasure of the blackness in the film" comes from "the number of beautiful dark-skinned women who eschew processed hair," noting that decolonizing Western beauty standards in a Hollywood blockbuster "is no small affair."[42] As Osman Faruqi convincingly writes, through its visual aesthetic, *Black Panther* ultimately presents an image of an indigenous society that didn't have its "culture and traditions eradicated by colonizers, replaced in many instances with European norms of the time."[43]

As explained in chapter 4, *Black Panther* also upsets Western notions of Africa as a scientifically and culturally "dark continent," instead replacing those notions with images of a technologically superior, peaceful, competent, and thriving nation, leading Nicole Gantt to hail the movie as one of the first filmic representations of "black well-being," whose community is "steeped in Black self-love, dignity, power," and discipline.[44] And indeed, *Black Panther* presents a powerful vision of how African nations may have developed if they had been left undisturbed by colonizers, arguing that they would have not only been better off but would have eventually surpassed the economic and technological development of the West if they had been left to independently manage their own natural resources. Importantly, these ideological messages remain constant throughout the film's three acts and thus stand as a progressive message that, as Lewis and Matthews write, gives hope to Black viewers, especially at a time when "it is clear that black and brown lives do not matter" to parts of white culture.[45] But *Black Panther*'s other radical premise—that Blacks are just as entitled as whites to use violence to advance political goals on a global scale—is ultimately withdrawn and compromised by the film's climax, raising questions for some viewers about the MCU's views on racial equality and the progressive nature of the film as a whole.

As mentioned earlier, Killmonger wishes to control Wakandan technology and to use it to wage war against oppressive white forces across the globe. Killmonger despises the fact that T'Challa and his ancestors have chosen to hide Wakandan resources in order to protect its domestic tranquility because that choice meant watching and allowing for its neighbors to be taken into slavery, plundered, and pushed into poverty while doing nothing to prevent these acts. Killmonger's plan, however, is too revolutionary for the conservative MCU, which has championed the use of militarized violence to resolve the majority of conflicts presented in its shared universe but here rejects the concept of Black-led militarized violence. Instead, the film concludes with the defeat of Killmonger and T'Challa coming to more acutely understand the injustices Blacks have suffered, leading him to appear before the United Nations and declare that Wakanda will now use its resources and diplomacy to assist everyone, as if we are "one single tribe." Like all action movies, *Black Panther* culminates in a violent battle, in this case between T'Challa and Killmonger, but when Killmonger is defeated it thereby eradicates his revolutionary cause and leaves the film with no Black leaders who possess both the ability AND the desire to employ violent methods to empower Blacks. At the end of the film, T'Challa and his sister are shown returning to the Bay Area to establish a science foundation/outreach center in Killmonger's hometown. As VanDerWerff writes, the movie's final scene "is a lovely one, but its change is incremental. Wakanda will open its borders, but only a little bit." She continues that while most Black Americans recognize that the government and global systems are broken, in the end the film will not champion a violent revolution. Instead, the movie's answer is synthesis: "Killmonger's aims but T'Challa's methods."[46]

These compromises were not lost on viewers, many of whom championed Killmonger and started a trending hashtag, #teamkillmonger, on social media. As Stephen Thrasher of *Esquire* explains, "Killmonger wants to use Wakanda's weapons to stop the suffering of black people globally, and we, the audience, are manipulated into rooting against this because we live in an ideology in which nonviolence is always expected of black people no matter what."[47] Quoting James Baldwin. who wrote, "The real reason that nonviolence is considered to be a virtue in Negroes . . . is that white men do not want their lives, their self-image, or their property threatened," Thrasher continues that he simply could not bring himself to root against Killmonger. He laments that Coogler asks audiences to cheer when the CIA's Everett Ross, Shuri, and T'Challa stop him from exporting the weapons from Wakanda "*to help Black people*," claiming that the film essentially creates a narrative that suggests "if Black Americans could get access to weapons, they'd be as violent towards the world as white Americans have been," so they should not be allowed to have them. In his article "Why Michael B. Jordan's Killmonger Is the Real Hero of *Black Panther*,"

Faruqi likewise writes that *Black Panther* encourages viewers to root for T'Challa because he wants Wakanda to remain neutral and domestically stable. "We're told that even though [Killmonger's] end goal is worthwhile, it's too violent and risky." However, Faruqi argues that the status quo is also "enormously violent," as remaining neutral has required T'Challa and his ancestors to turn a blind eye to the horrors of slavery, civil war, and police brutality, even as they possess the ability to stop it—something that the film never really explores. "Wakanda, under T'Challa's reign," Faruqi writes, "is just choosing to ignore [these evils]. Killmonger at least wants to do *something* to end the oppression of subjugated people."[48]

Other viewers were less inclined to adopt these readings, however. In our interview with physicist and Marvel film consultant Clifford Johnson, for example, he pushed back against the idea that Killmonger should have triumphed in his goals. "I mean, yes, we could say, we should be allowed to screw up the world as much as others have," but he would like to think "we can be bigger than that and say, 'oh, maybe there is another way, and we can be represented as following that other way for a change.'" Like in *Wonder Woman*, this diversity of perspectives points to the polysemic nature of *Black Panther* and makes a final assessment of the film hard to reach. On the one hand, the MCU does seem to commit an injustice to Killmonger in that it won't ultimately allow him access to large-scale militarized violence to achieve his goals of Black liberation, even though it has afforded—and even championed—the use of such violence to all of its white protagonists/superheroes. On the other hand, as this book has tried to consistently show, the use of militarized violence is often too quickly employed as a short-sighted solution, causing more suffering and destruction in the world than the original suffering it was employed to eradicate. In this way, then, *Black Panther* might be one of *the most* revolutionary films in the MCU, in that T'Challa flat-out rejects solving global problems through a military campaign but instead opts for diplomacy, collaboration, and scientific advancement to help alleviate oppression. The ending of the film also works to challenge centuries-old ideas of the Black body as hyperaggressive and hyperviolent.

The CIA in Black Panther

Given the polysemic nature of the film, the failure of *Black Panther* to address the historical oppression of African nations by the Central Intelligence Agency is probably the clearest indicator of the film's conservative politics. When the CIA replaced S.H.I.E.L.D. as the primary intelligence agency tasked with protecting US and global interests after the events of *Captain America: Civil War* (2016), the agency's place grew more important within the franchise, and Everett Ross (Martin Freeman) provides one of the agency's most benevolent officers seen on screen to date. However, the representation of the CIA in *Black Panther* bears little to no resemblance to its actual history on the continent. Indeed, while Ross debuted in the *Black Panther* comic series in 1998 as an incompetent, bumbling lawyer for the State Department to help bring white readers to the series,[49] his metamorphosis into a benevolent CIA savior functions as an off-key form of historical revisionism in the movie, leading K. Tutashinda to claim that nearly the only flaw in the movie was its depiction of a CIA officer as an African ally.[50]

In order to recognize the historical revisionism in *Black Panther*, one must understand the agency's involvement in Africa, which was most prolific between the 1950s and the late 1970s, when colonial powers lost their control in the region and African nationalist movements emerged. Phillip Agee, a former CIA officer and the author of *Inside the Company*, summarized that these political movements essentially "sought to end five centuries of subjugation, exploitation, and varying forms of tutelage imposed by Western powers." In response, the West strived, "with different degrees of success and failure," to install new regimes and organizations to continue to allow them to extract African resources; to sell consumer products on the continent; to make capital investments in the region; and to continue to use the sea routes involving both the Suez Canal and the Cape.[51]

In the specific case of the CIA, René Lemarchand illustrates how the agency played a direct role in funding, promoting, and establishing several pro-US leaders in the area, including President Mobutu of the

Congo/Zaire, Prime Minister Muhammed Egal of Somalia, and Colonel Richard Ratsimandrava of Madagascar. Lemarchand also shows how the CIA diligently worked to rid its preferred leaders of political opponents and to "dispose" of established leaders who seemed sympathetic to Soviet influence, including the CIA's hiring and training of mercenaries to defeat Gaston Soumialot's Popular Liberation Army during the 1964 Zairian rebellion; the agency's probable financial and technical support to opposition leaders in Burundi during the "pro-Chinese" interlude of 1964; and the CIA's role in the 1967 hijacking of Moïse Tshombe's plane, which led to his surrender to Algerian authorities. In the 1970s, the CIA also participated in the Angolan Civil War by shipping $25 million in arms to pro-Western factions and providing logistical support on the ground in both Zaire and Angola to help ward off communist-backed leaders such as Agostinho Neto.[52]

Agee concludes that US foreign policy during the Cold War inevitably worked to "deny real independence to African countries," as the United States imposed and sustained "client regimes."[53] The destructive legacy of these policies is perhaps best illustrated by the case of the Congo, when Patrice Lumumba was democratically elected as the country's first prime minister alongside President Joseph Kasavubu. However, when the CIA erroneously suspected Lumumba of being a communist sympathizer and Soviet agent,[54] the CIA's area station chief, Larry Devlin, successfully managed a military coup in September 1960, which installed Col. Joseph Mobutu as the nation's new head.[55] Devlin then schemed to assassinate Lumumba through the use of biological toxins, but it was Mobutu's troops who were eventually able to capture Lumumba, with Devlin's help, and transfer him to Katanga, where he was beaten and killed by his political rivals.[56] The CIA's heavy-handed manipulation of the Congolese government[57] ultimately led to Mobutu's corrupt and autocratic rule for more than thirty years and precipitated the Lumumbists' Congo Rebellions, which plunged the country "into the largest postindependence revolutionary uprising anywhere in Africa up to that point," with over a million Congolese losing their lives in the conflict.[58] According to Victoria Brittain, "had Lumumba lived long enough to consolidate the independence of the country, not only would Congo's bloody and undignified history probably have been utterly different but the history of Angola would too, as Lumumba would never have allowed the use of his country by the United States and apartheid South Africa to cripple Angola's independence—as they did."[59]

This history helps illustrate the profound about-face that the CIA enjoys in *Black Panther*. The film begins with Killmonger and Klaue, a white South African mercenary, stealing items made of vibranium from a British museum. Early in the film, viewers learn that Klaue has previously attacked Wakanda in search of the material. As a result, T'Challa seeks to capture Klaue, in order to return him to Wakanda to stand trial. CIA officer Everett Ross is then introduced when he meets T'Challa at a South Korean casino table. Ross is posing as an interested American buyer in order to entrap Klaue for selling stolen vibranium and to punish him for providing the resource in the attack on Sokovia, featured in *Avengers: Age of Ultron*.

It is important to acknowledge in any analysis of Ross that he is constructed as an emasculated character throughout the film. Everett is played by actor Martin Freeman, who is best known for his roles as Bilbo Baggins in the Hobbit trilogy and as the gentle and patient John Watson in the BBC's *Sherlock*. Standing at 5'7, Freeman also appears diminutive in stature, especially when standing next to the chiseled 6'0 Chadwick Boseman. Everett's slight demeanor and social awkwardness work to depict him, and by extension, the CIA, as an unthreatening entity in world affairs. In fact, in the casino scene when Klaue arrives with a large armed entourage, Ross comments on the reinforcements, and Klaue then teases Ross: "You think they're for you? Don't worry, I can do a deal with you all by myself." The message here is clear: the CIA is not a viable threat in the region.

This depiction of the CIA continues throughout most of the film, and it is clear from the CIA's eventual interrogation of Klaue that the United States' most prominent intelligence agency is also in the dark about Wakanda's vibranium. Ross states that he associates Wakanda with "shepherds and textiles" because, for him, Wakanda is little more than an impoverished third-world country—exactly what Wakanda wants him to see. The CIA, as embodied by Ross, then, begins *Black Panther* as an ill-informed entity that poses little threat to Wakandan power. This is a far cry from the real CIA, who employed arrests, assassination attempts, and military coups to ensure the United States would be able to extract African resources and access its markets under sympathetic leadership. While the CIA proves to be underinformed in the movie, Ross's gentler, "friendly neighborhood spy" also works to accent US benevolence on the world stage, especially as he risks sacrificing his life multiple times in the film in order to save Wakanda—another ironic position given the CIA's actual history in the region.

Clearly, then, *Black Panther* repositions the CIA as a benevolent, peaceful force in African affairs. As *Wonder Woman* reveals, such revisionism is not new to the superhero genre. Indeed, similar to how DC rewrote history in *Wonder Woman*, Marvel Studios rewrote World War II history in *Captain America: The First Avenger* to erase America's history of racial segregation and Japanese internment camps during the conflict. During the first half of that film, Steve Rogers is employed by the USO to boost morale by performing for the servicemen stationed in Azzano, Italy, in 1943. Shots of the crowd show Black and white servicemen serving harmoniously alongside one another, while earlier shots in the film depict Black and white Americans sharing recruitment stations and their children happily playing together on the streets. Later in the film, when Captain America forms his elite group of soldiers, known as the Howling Commandos, its members include Private Gabriel "Gabe" Jones, an African American with valuable linguistic skills, and a Japanese American named Private "Jim" Morita, who also served in the army's Nisei Squadron.

As McSweeney writes, these scenes are historically inaccurate: while "nearly a million African-Americans joined the armed forces in World War II in a variety of capacities," they served in segregated units, were trained in separate facilities, and "even had separate blood supplies."[60] Likewise, all Japanese American men who did not join the armed forces during the conflict "were automatically given 4C status as an 'enemy alien,'" and those who did serve were "forbidden from being deployed in the Pacific Theatre, whereas no such restrictions were placed on

Italian-Americans or German-Americans who fought on the Western Front."[61] The *New York Times*'s Charles Blow called the scenes of a fictitious integrated army unsettling, noting that his grandfather was part of the Ninety-Second Infantry Division of "Buffalo Soldiers," who fought in segregated units, under the command of "a known racist" who remained a military segregationist until his death. For Blow, the historical revisionism embodied by *Captain America* "illustrates just how quickly things can fade into the fog of history if not vigilantly and accurately kept alive in the telling," and thus he argues that the history of racial injustice "is not a thing to be toyed with," even in escapist entertainment: "There are too many bodies at the bottom of that swamp to skim across it with such indifference. Attention must be shown. Respect must be paid."[62] The same could be said of *Black Panther* and its depictions of the CIA in Africa, as it too joins the ranks of superhero films that erase or misremember unpalatable aspects of American history, offering "instead another example of the 'mythic massage' that popular media texts are able to perform in their appropriation of cultural memory."[63]

For some viewers, however, *Black Panther*'s CIA mythology did not go uncontested. In a response to an October 21, 2018, CIA tweet about the movie, the author behind the Twitter account, A Flock of Segals, wrote, "If Wakanda was real, you would have assassinated T'Challa by now," a comment to which @obscuria then replied, "Let's give the natives some credit. If Wakanda was real, the CIA wouldn't have been allowed to operate in Africa at all." On the same day, Nicolas Marritz added to the thread by simply writing "Patrice Lumumba" fifteen times in the space provided to make his point that the CIA has a disturbing history in Africa that *Black Panther* works to erase. Or as scholar Ewuare Osayande writes, *Black Panther* is a painful reminder of the failed promise of African independence, writing that because of CIA intervention, Lumumba was unable to carry out his economic reforms, and now, in a reverse picture to that of Wakanda, the Congolese people, with its vast deposits of minerals and metals valued at $24 trillion, remain some of the poorest on the planet.[64]

The CIA, however, was quite pleased with its cinematic depiction, as *Black Panther* works to overturn decades' worth of images of the CIA as obsessed with assassination, as rogue operatives acting without political oversight, as abusing its own officers and assets, as hopelessly ineffective, or as shamelessly immoral.[65] Both Kali Caldwell and Sara Lichterman of the CIA's Public Affairs Office state that the agency did not officially collaborate with Marvel on Coogler's film, with Lichterman suggesting in our March 5, 2019, phone interview that because *Black Panther* is such a fantastical movie, the CIA could provide little with regard to historical insight or technical consultation. Nonetheless, the film depicts Ross as a benevolent and ultimately selfless ally, who risks his life to help save Wakanda from Killmonger.[66] Thus, it is unsurprising that the CIA, which monitors the content of every major movie featuring the agency, live-tweeted the 2019 Oscars show. As part of its #RealvsReel series, where the CIA works to compare fictional representations of the CIA with reality on Twitter, the agency tweeted thirteen times during the ceremony, asserting its understanding and appreciation of Wakandan technology (see chapter 4) and ultimately wishing the filmmakers luck in the Best Picture category. The last time the CIA so publicly tied itself to a film over social media was during the 2013 Academy Awards, when *Argo* was heavily nominated and won Best Picture. That film was based on the real-life CIA success story of Tony Mendez and his role in exfiltrating six Americans out of Iran during the 1970s hostage crisis. The picture was heavily assisted by the agency, who recognized its public relations value and helped get the story turned into a movie in the first place.[67]

In the end, then, *Black Panther* proved to be a widely acclaimed addition to the Marvel Cinematic Universe. Its celebration is largely due to its projection of a refreshing image of African well-being that reverses decades-old colonialist images of Africa as a backward "dark continent" prone to disease, savagery, and corruption. However, the film's radical potential to upend notions of white hegemony and concepts of who is entitled to use military violence are compromised by the film's narrative, which asks viewers to champion the CIA's partnership with T'Challa as they work to prevent Erik Killmonger from using Wakandan technology to launch a war against white oppressors in order to free Black people everywhere. Furthermore, the film works to erase the damaging legacy of the actual CIA in Africa, further contributing to the MCU's legacy of projecting America only as it wants to be seen—as a benevolent force in world affairs. On the other hand, T'Challa's refusal to engage in a militarized campaign against white oppressors can also be seen in a progressive light, as he chooses diplomacy, education, and scientific advancement over warfare, in order to empower both Black and global communities.

Further Thoughts and Questions

While we wish we could argue that the superhero genre's shift toward greater diversity stems from a sincere desire to produce a greater variety of inspirational role models and narratives, studio executives suggest that the shift is primarily motivated by profit. At an October 2014 panel hosted by the Wrap, seven studio executives were asked whether the success of *The Hunger Games* meant that they foresaw more female-led films being made. Mark Weinstock, then president of theatrical marketing for 20th Century Fox, answered affirmatively, arguing that women "are an underserved audience" that they hope to tap into more. Josh Goldstine, then president of Worldwide Marketing at Universal Pictures, also argued that more female-led movies should be made because *Lucy* (2014)—a movie about a woman whose brain is enhanced with superhuman powers—"went on to do over 400 million dollars around the world." Similarly, when asked about the growing popularity of Latin-fronted movies such as the *Fast and Furious* franchise, Weinstock explained that the Latinx demographic is "extremely important" and one that they go after "aggressively," especially once they realized that it made up "a huge portion" of the audiences going to see *Dawn of the Planet of the Apes* (2014) and *X-Men: Days of Future Past* (2014). In short, all of the panelists expressed their hope that there would be more diverse movies coming in the future but mostly because they would help grow profits from underserved markets.[68]

At a roundtable hosted by the *Hollywood Reporter* in early 2020, Disney co-chairman and chief creative officer Alan Horn likewise expressed his studio's pride for producing *Black Panther* and *Captain Marvel* because they "ventured into areas that were not ventured into before." However, he denied that Disney's efforts were politically motivated, stating, "We're not, and we don't wish to be political . . . We're not politicians; it's not what we do. We're not a governmental organization. We're making movies."[69] This perceived need to be apolitical or to at least maintain the status quo in order to be profitable is one of the biggest impediments to how radical filmmakers working within the studio system can be. And perhaps this is why, while *Black Panther* and *Wonder Woman* feature diverse leads, both films embrace politically conservative values that promote the very systems that, in the real world, marginalize and sometimes oppress people like their protagonists.

Comparing these films to the more subversive or anti-establishment films analyzed in chapter 2 then begs a question: is it possible for studios to make a film with both a counter-establishment story *and* diverse lead characters? All of the more diversely led films in the oeuvre have fairly or very conventional story lines that promote the security state, while all of the politically subversive films have highly conventional leads that conform to white, male, straight, and able-bodied identities. It appears that studios will greenlight stories that pose serious questions about the status quo that are fronted by white American males, but a story led by someone from another demographic will often affirm political norms, even while being socially progressive. The tacit studio logic seems to imply that Hollywood can only subvert a few of the conventions in any given film, in order to make the resulting product palatable to the anticipated audience, but is this true? After all, *Black Panther* could have been made without the CIA's Ross playing such a heroic role in the unfolding action, and it could have included T'Challa liberating oppressed people through subterfuge, sabotage, and rescues like the one seen at the opening of the film, without resorting to the paramilitary tactics advocated by Killmonger. *Wonder Woman* could have also accomplished her task of defeating Ares without massacring dozens of characterless Germans en route and included pointed dialogue about the lessons of territorial conquests by greedy and belligerent imperialists. Combining the more radical narrative of a film such as *Iron Man 3* with a demographically unconventional lead is also possible, and the commercial success of both the more diversely led films and those with more subversive narratives suggests that such a film may not be as much of a commercial risk as studio executives think.

As it stands right now, however, the incorporation of a more diverse range of superheroes is caught in the quagmire of exchanging symbolic territory for ideological territory, so the symbols of the system change and evolve, while the underlying values remain the same as before. In some respects this may actually make the situation worse for marginalized people, as their appearance is used to grant legitimacy to a system that frequently ignores or abuses their rights and sidelines them from positions of power and influence. As Cedric Clark wrote in the late 1960s, it is "ironic, if not tragic" when minority groups are employed in "regulatory roles," such as government officials, police officers, and judges (and we would add superheroes), which are dedicated to upholding unfair systems of power. This is because "those who benefit least in society are shown increasingly in roles associated with the protection of that society" and thereby work to legitimize it.[70] Both *Black Panther* and *Wonder Woman* manifest this exchange, as they are symbolically progressive but ideologically conservative, and they do little to challenge the status quo of the security state or the benevolence of Allied forces. But as Wanzo reminds us, even the most racist and imperialist origins and tropes of superhero characters do not always foreclose more progressive political futures. "Binaries of positive and negative or good and bad often have limited analytical value in tracking the complex work of racially problematic representations," she writes, and oftentimes conservative texts do important culturally progressive work in the hands of viewers and fans.[71]

The recent trend of featuring a wider range of protagonists looks set to continue in *Black Widow* and the Black Panther, Aquaman, and Captain Marvel sequels, as well as in *Shang-Chi and the Legend of the Ten Rings*, *Ms. Marvel*, and *Black Adam*, all of which are due for release within three years of the time of this writing. As such, studios and filmmakers will continue to face a choice as to whether they will continue to trade diversity for pro-establishment ideology or instead use the twenty-first century's most popular entertainment genre to offer audiences greater diversity not just in casting but also in stories, settings, values, and power dynamics. Because of the genre demands of cinematic universes, critics have expressed skepticism about these films' potential to disrupt the tropes of American supremacy and its preference for violent conflict resolution, however. For example, while *Black Panther*'s ending suggests that Wakanda, by going public with its vibranium, is positioned to become the new world leader, Gerry Canavan doubts that Marvel Studios feels "genuinely committed to the ongoing depiction of an African superpower that could challenge the West's racist fantasy of its own superiority." Instead, he believes that "Wakanda's true moment of emergence will always be forestalled" because "franchise time demands that the question of Wakandan superiority and its potential challenge to American empire will ultimately just fade into the murky past of the Marvel Cinematic Universe, as the string of sequels introduce new problems, characters, and stories whose own narrative development will also always reset back to one, just in time for the start of the next show, forever."[72] Perhaps this is why *Black Panther* ends with T'Challa *about to* explain Wakanda's reserves of vibranium to the UN but cuts out before he actually makes the announcement and why later installments such as *Captain Marvel* or *Avengers: Endgame* are featured in previous decades or work to reset the MCU by reversing time. Chadwick Boseman's unfortunate death in 2020 also adds extra questions about the future of the Black Panther series and its radical potential, although at this time, some fans are calling for Shuri to take up the helm of the beloved character, placing a black female scientist in charge of the world's most powerful nation. A potential and promising plotline indeed.

CONCLUSION

THE AMERICAN WAY, *THE BOYS*, AND THE WRONG MESSAGE?

According to Jeffrey Johnson's *Super-History*, caped crusaders traditionally reflect contemporary American values, as they are linked to the culture's "hopes, desires, fears, needs, and social norms."[1] Because a society's needs are constantly shifting, superheroes also serve as "social mirrors" and "barometers of the place and time" in which they are created. Likewise, in *Ages of Heroes, Eras of Men*, the editors posit that most superheroes function as ethical role models, committed to "Truth, Justice and the American Way."[2] However, that phrase—the American Way—has always been an ambiguous one, raising questions "of how it is defined and what it means to various sectors of American society" at any given period of time. This book has explored how various elements of society—the US military, Hollywood, scientists, NASA, and others—have each vied to influence the notion of "the American way" in contemporary superhero films. In DOD-assisted productions, the Pentagon works to promote its vision of "the American Way" as one that resolves conflict through unilateral violence, depicts America as a righteous and benevolent force in world affairs, celebrates military service, and depicts its citizens as the innocent victims of foreigners' nefarious plots. As Elisabeth Anker writes, these qualities also mirror the bedrocks of American political discourse since 9/11, which have consistently depicted "the nation-state as a virtuous and innocent victim overwhelmed by villainous action." Such melodramatic discourse has also located "heroism in unilateral state action against dominating forces," depicted state surveillance as a "moral imperative" that will achieve nation-wide freedom, and suggested that the United States "becomes virtuous by the very experience of being injured, as if acts of violence against the nation demonstrate the nation's exceptional virtue."[3]

For other Hollywood players like NASA, the American Way is not defined by military service, violent force, or even moral righteousness.

It is instead defined by concepts of ingenuity, adventure, scientific prowess, intellectual curiosity, and international cooperation, and it too has worked with Hollywood to promote these values. As NASA has become more active in the industry, it has provided filmmakers with new sources of shooting locations, script consultants, and other types of technical expertise, as well as a more optimistic and peaceful vision of humanity's future among the stars. NASA's work serves as an important counterpoint to the US Space Force's argument that the future of space is necessarily a militaristic one. Indeed, Netflix's recent series *Away* (2020–), features a team of international astronauts headed on an inaugural mission to Mars and was a NASA-Hollywood collaboration.[4] At a press conference in the pilot episode, the astronauts are asked why, with only a 50 percent chance of success, the world should spend money on Mars exploration, instead of on social imperatives, such as health services and education, here on Earth. Mission commander Emma Green (Hilary Swank) responds to this common criticism of NASA, arguing that the two endeavors are not mutually exclusive and then challenges America's prioritization of war spending. Green states that the United States alone spends "a trillion dollars each year on military spending," and mostly in case the countries who are represented as partners on their mission, such as Russia and China, "decide to blow each other off the face of the Earth." NASA's internationally cooperative mission "costs a fraction of that," she states, and she also works to repurpose the military's "tools of destruction for discovery." Her comment is then followed by different astronauts explaining the scientific research they are carrying out on the International Space Station to help improve life on Earth, including mining the moon's polar ice caps for new sources of fuel and water. Scenes like this offer an important counterpoint to the DOD's view of space as simply the next theater for militarized combat and help envision the American Way in more peaceful, internationally cooperative, and exploratory terms.

Further helping the superhero genre veer farther away from sheer militaristic narratives is the Science and Entertainment Exchange, which also offers important perspectives on American values.

Admittedly, we have some reservations about the SEEX's work because despite its efforts to promote scientific literacy and diversity, it has also been engaged with the Pentagon since its founding. As such, it often promotes weapons technology and invasive surveillance technology to filmmakers. For example, at one of the exchange's inaugural events, Rodney Brooks, the chairman and CTO of the ironically named Heartland Robotics, presented a talk to Hollywood insiders celebrating his company's robotization of modern warfare and sharing how the military was planning on introducing "tens of thousands of robots into the infantry in the coming years."[5] Similarly, it was an SEEX salon event where the geo-mapping technology firm ESRI talked to the producers of *Covert Affairs* (2010–2014) that led to their technology being featured on the show. Since 2002, ESRI has worked closely with In-Q-Tel, the US intelligence community's venture capital firm in the tech industry, which was founded by the CIA in 1999. In 2012, ESRI bought GeoIQ, a company that has received funding from In-Q-Tel since 2007 and that works closely with the National Geospatial Intelligence Agency.[6] That ESRI, an NGA/CIA-affiliated company, and its surveillance technology appeared on a CIA-supported TV spy drama courtesy of a SEEX event, further emphasizes how the exchange helps promote and normalize the technocratic surveillance state, presenting it as mere "cool tech" used by glamorous secret agents to keep its citizens safe from threats.

Our reservations about the SEEX do not seem to have significantly affected the superhero genre at this time, however. By teaming up its writers, directors, and producers with a network of scientific advisors who are largely employed by universities rather than the security state, the SEEX has been able to create inspiring images of science, science-based resolutions to conflict, and images of diverse scientists to increase American participation in STEM careers. In fact, NASA may do well to adopt some of the SEEX's practices by offering up its own experts to filmmakers through a hotline and fun, salon-styled events, in order to help the agency advance its vision of science and technology as resting at the heart of America's future (without the somewhat militarized agenda of the exchange).

Although it is obvious, superhero filmmakers also play a key role in defining "the American Way" in popular culture. Some of their efforts have worked to promote traditional and exceptionalist values. For example, Jeremy Latcham told us that he valued Marvel movies for the way they help "export our equality, values, democracy, freedom, and liberty" and provide "optimism for the world." As the world has grown more cynical, he stated, Americans have started to question their value, "but to me we have this great thing to share. I mean almost no other country in the world is as free as America . . . I think we have an awesome society and culture, and I want to be able to share that with other cultures." Other writers and critics have taken a far less "exceptionalist" view of the United States. James Schamus, the writer of Ang Lee's *Hulk*, suggested in our interview that American foreign policy is too often dictated by its military-industrial complex—"a revolving door of generals-lobbyists-contractors"—who produce their own "blowback" to generate more demand for its endlessly proliferating production of destruction. Schamus more cynically suggests, then, that too often "the American Way" revolves around a quest for profit and power more than a pursuit for truth and justice. Likewise, Stephen McFeely and Christopher Markus, the writers of *Captain America: Winter Soldier*, explained that they believe the values that govern the United States have grown far more "grey" since the 1940s. Steve Rogers, they note, is like "this Gary Cooper figure" who wants to be back in the black-and-white world of the Second World War.[7] He "once represented America," but due to the passage of time, he has grown "alien" to its values and thought systems, which are now more nuanced. As a result, they purposely paired him with Natasha Romanoff (Black Widow) to help him navigate contemporary America in *Winter Soldier*, as she "is a lot more flexible in terms of loyalties" if it helps her get a job done. "We didn't pick her out of thin air," the writers state. "She best represented the century and that grey morality" that now governs so much activity in American and global life. In the United States, the writers suggest, the ends now often justify the means.

As chapter 2 explains, these more nuanced and even critical views of American values have been explored in superhero films like *The Incredible Hulk*, *Captain America: The Winter Soldier*, *Captain America: Civil War*, *Iron*

Man 3, and others. While these films may be seen as more cynical, they explore important ideologies, especially since the genre continues to seek to function as relevant social critique. And indeed, post-9/11 superhero films have been important sites for problematizing the concepts of American righteousness and benevolence, especially as the War on Terror progressed, and policies such as rendition, drone strikes, the Patriot Act, and enhanced interrogation techniques (i.e., torture) became more prevalent. These movies, almost all of which operated in the absence of DOD support, took greater freedoms to explore counter-establishment narratives and moved beyond the exceptionalist tendencies presented in the earlier films. Most of these later films were more lucrative than their predecessors too, demonstrating that the genre can thrive with both establishment and counter-establishment themes guiding their plots.

Finally, the casting choices made in superhero films have also contributed to concepts of the American Way and who, precisely, embodies it. As Chambliss, Svitavsky, and Donaldson note, superheroes have often promoted the best and most progressive philosophies of the United States, but in their efforts to uphold "the American Way," they have also perpetuated "conservative values" and the more "offensive" elements of the status quo, which have marginalized women, people of color, the LGBTQ+ community, and others.[8] Indeed, for most of their history, superheroes have been white, straight, male, and able-bodied, but the genre has increasingly embraced more diverse leads in recent years. This trend seems predominantly motivated by profit, as it helps bring in audiences to which classic superhero stories do not always appeal. While such images broaden our conceptions of American heroism, greater inclusivity does not always lead to narratives that challenge the political status quo. As chapter 5 demonstrates, films like *Black Panther* and *Wonder Woman* largely championed establishment narratives, while the most counter-establishment narratives in the genre have continued to be fronted by white men. This suggests that filmmakers are ready to include diverse characters in texts so long as they uphold conservative concepts of the United States and are only willing to challenge those concepts with heroes who are so embedded in the image of traditional American heroism. It is perhaps a way for the studios to hedge their bets, refusing to produce any one text that threatens several aspects of the American status quo in fear of losing audiences. Things may be shifting even here, though. The recent Netflix film *Project Power* (2020) features a Black lead in a counter-establishment story about a mysterious drug distributor offering free pills of "Power" to the residents of New Orleans. "Power" grants its users various superpowers for five minutes but has also led to overdoses, sudden deaths, and heightened crime rates in the city. The drug, it turns out, is developed by Teleios, a private defense contractor, looking to increase its profits, but when the drug proves unstable, they flood it into the streets of New Orleans to use its residents as test subjects to figure out how to stabilize it. The film's main superhero then fights against the government-backed Teleios in order to protect his family and stop a dangerous drug experiment that uses poor, mostly Black citizens as little more than guinea pigs. The film has obvious references to the real-life opioid epidemic that hit New Orleans particularly hard. While not a theatrically released superhero movie with the same reach as those produced by Marvel or Warner Bros., *Project Power* does hint at a future for the genre that offers audiences more, both in terms of representation and the issues, narratives, and identities it addresses.

The Wrong Message?

When superhero movies embrace establishment and exceptionalist narratives, they work to bolster one of America's most beloved self-images—the idea that it is "the greatest nation in the world." But despite politicians' constant repetition of this slogan, as Jeff Daniels famously reminded us in the pilot episode of *The Newsroom* (2012–2014), the United States does not serve as the world leader in most important categories. For example, in 2020, the United States ranks as only the thirty-fifth healthiest country in the world, according to the Bloomberg Global Health Index.[9] The CIA also ranks the United States as forty-third in the world for life expectancy at birth[10] and puts the United

States at 170th for infant mortality rates, which means that countries such as New Caledonia, Latvia, Greece, Cuba, Belarus, and Bermuda all have lower infant mortality rates than the United States.[11] Additionally, the United States ranks as twenty-fourth in the 2020 Environmental Performance Index published by Yale and Columbia University,[12] and while the World Bank positions the United States as the twelfth richest nation in the world using gross national income (GNI) and eleventh by using gross domestic product (GDP),[13] it also ranks the country first among developed nations for its gap in income disparity. Even in the category of how educated its populace is, the United States is still not the world leader. The United States ranked sixth on the Organization for Economic Co-operation and Development's list, behind countries such as Canada and Japan, with 45.7 percent of American adults having completed some kind of tertiary education in the form of a two-year degree, four-year degree, or vocational program.[14] Political partisanship, protests, and the dissolution of trust in its media, government, and even health officials increasingly plague the country as well.

One of the few categories in which the United States does rank first in the world, however, is the amount it devotes to war spending. The 2019 SIPRI Index demonstrates that the United States currently outspends China (the second-largest investor in military spending) by almost three to one and that the United States spends more on its military than even the next thirteen countries combined (see figure 6.1).[15] Such expenditures come at the cost of other national projects, including education, health care, environmental quality, and infrastructure—areas where the United States often lags behind. By continuing to create stories about exceptional individuals who work alongside the American military to save the world through weaponized violence, the establishment narratives of the superhero genre work to justify such disproportionate war spending. They reinforce the country's self-image, not only as the world's police but as "the best in the world" because these texts define "best" in terms of who has the greatest weaponry. While such stories may serve as needed wish fulfillments, as Stacy Takacs reminds us, Americans cannot begin to improve their society or even reckon with its realities, "at least in part, because we do not represent them honestly to ourselves."[16]

Furthermore, by featuring superpowered individuals as national and even global saviors, these stories may prime viewers in harmful ways. As author and journalist Mark Bowden writes, contemporary superheroes trade in an "exaggerated Cult of Self." These heroes are uniquely and supremely powerful, but they often derive their talents by accident, scientific mishap, or governmental experimentation gone awry. "The old American ideal of succeeding through cleverness, virtue and grit is absent, as is the notion of ordinary folk banding together to overcome a threat." These solutions used to permeate films such as *It's a Wonderful Life* or the original *The Magnificent Seven*, but instead of encouraging social change through persistent, collective action, today's superhero films often encourage average people to either wait on an exceptional individual or engage in vigilante justice that fails to respect the law or community's institutions.[17] To repeat Bill Maher's words quoted earlier in this book, one of the problems with superhero movies may be that they "imprint this mindset that we are not masters of our own destiny, and the best we can do is sit back and wait for Star-Lord and a f—ing raccoon to sweep in and save our sorry asses. Forget hard work, government institutions, diplomacy, [or] investment."

The Boys and the Future of the Genre?

One recent superhero product that offers a consistently different approach to the genre is *The Boys* (2019–), an Amazon series based on the comics of Garth Ennis.[18] The show is a fairly authentic adaptation of Ennis's comics and depicts what our world might look like if superhumans actually existed and were employed as crime fighters by private corporations and/or government agencies. The counterconventional approach of the original comics is key to the tone, style, and content of the TV version, with showrunner Eric Kripke describing how his team tries to "make this not just the most realistic superhero show ever made, but . . . to make it a commentary on the up-to-the-minute world

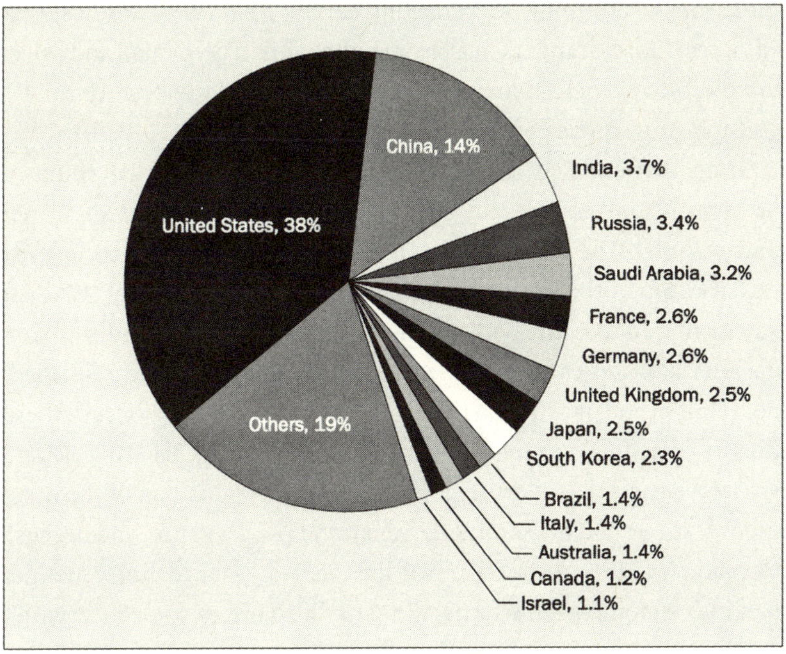

Figure 6.1: The share of world military expenditure of the fifteen countries with the highest spending in 2019. Source: SIPRI Military Expenditure Database, April 2020.

we live in," elaborating that "the three triangles of the show" are strong characters, madness, and discussions about contemporary issues.[19]

For Kripke, *The Boys* tries to reverse the superhero genre's cult of self. He told the *Hollywood Reporter*,

> It's a little dangerous to train an entire generation to wait for someone strong to come in and save you. That's I think how you end up with people like Trump and populists who say, "I'm the only one who can come in, it's going to be me." . . . So I think it's nice to have a corrective, at least a small one in us, to say, "They're not coming to save you. Hold your family together and save yourselves."[20]

But how exactly does *The Boys* suggest this happens? And is its message any less dangerous than the narrative of the superpowered savior? After all, as TV scholar Kristen Warner told the *Chicago Tribune*, in many ways, narratives that tell us to wait on a savior may not be as dangerous as we think; they may simply be "reflecting certain realities back to us: that we do feel like bystanders in a larger fight, while a very small and select group of people determine our fate."[21] Sometimes the best we can do is simply hope those people are good people.

Given that *The Boys* represents one of the most pivotal shifts in the genre's tone in recent decades, this book concludes with a brief examination of the series, evaluating its themes and characters against the backdrop of the tropes explored in the previous chapters. While it may seem odd to end a book about superhero films with a discussion of a television series, in late 2020 when this book was being finished, most Hollywood productions were put on hold and the major superhero films expected as summer blockbusters—including *Black Widow* and *Wonder Woman 1984*—were delayed. *The Boys*, then, is one of the most recent texts we had to examine current trends in the genre, and because television is able to respond to real-life events in a more timely manner than major studio productions, the series also offers some interesting clues into the issues and tone that future texts may explore, including the rise of white supremacism and a renewed emphasis on ordinary people banding together to resist overwhelming threats.

For readers unfamiliar with the show, *The Boys* centers around a giant corporation named Vought that secretly creates superheroes—known as "supes"—using a mysterious chemical called Compound V. Vought hires the supes out to major US cities to deal with their crime problems, but it also profits from its supes by producing movies and video games starring its heroes, along with the usual spin-off merchandise such as clothing and action figures. Their flagship product is the Seven—a team of elite superheroes based on the Justice League. The story begins when Hughie, a mild-mannered young man, sees his girlfriend Robin killed by A-Train, the world's fastest man and a member of the Seven, when he runs through Robin while on a mission to smuggle Compound V. This leads to Hughie being recruited by Billy Butcher, a former CIA contractor on a quest for vengeance against Vought, the Seven, and superheroes in general. Butcher and Hughie team up with two of Butcher's former colleagues, M.M. and Frenchie, to form the Boys, a renegade vigilante group dedicated to taking down Vought and exposing the truth that the supes are reckless and violent celebrities protected by a corrupt corporation. Through this setup, *The Boys* departs from many of the traditional conventions of the superhero genre, presenting a much darker but also more realistic vision of a world with superheroes than even DC-based films have explored. Indeed, while numerous films have featured superpowered villains, they have only done so in narratives where they are thwarted by equally powerful superheroes. In *The Boys*, however, the gang that tries to reveal the truth about the supes are a ragtag group of misfits with no special powers. The dynamic helps the show mirror the emotions of average citizens disgusted with and frustrated by corporate and political policies but who lack equal clout in order to incite change.

Adding to the complexity of the narrative is the fact that while the supes are shown occasionally fighting crime and otherwise doing benevolent things, they are nonetheless a group of psychologically broken people who engage in or tolerate violence against innocent civilians, the mass destruction of property, and the exploitation of people's fear and anger. The Seven are led by Homelander—*The Boys*' equivalent of Superman—who is a neurotic and sadistic megalomaniac. As actor Anthony Starr, who plays Homelander, described it: "The strongest man, physically, on the show is also the weakest emotionally."[22] Indeed, Homelander's response to realizing he is the most powerful person on the planet is not to use his strength to protect the weak, as in the original Superman films, nor is it to be ambivalent and tortured, struggling to make sense of his role in the world, as Superman is portrayed in the DCEU. Instead he holds the rest of humanity in utter contempt, including the lesser-powered supes in the Seven, who live in fear of him. He joyously and flippantly kills humans, which causes, among other things, PR problems for Vought, as they must consistently cover up for the collateral damage he causes.

No More Heroes? Satirizing American Exceptionalism

A consistent theme in *The Boys* is its critical and often sardonic view of the myth of American exceptionalism. In the show, this exceptionalism is not real but is upheld through highly deceptive PR and propaganda operations. In one key sequence, Homelander and Queen Maeve (the Seven's equivalent of Wonder Woman) are sent to intercept a hijacked passenger plane headed for the United States. They arrive and kill the stock Arabs in the passenger cabin, but when they reach the cockpit, the remaining terrorist shoots the pilot, so Homelander uses his laser eyes to kill the terrorist, destroying the flight controls in the process. Realizing his mistake, Homelander immediately opts to leave the plane and let the passengers die, despite Maeve begging him to take some of the passengers with them. In Homelander's sociopathic, approval ratings–driven mindset, any survivors would be witnesses to his screwup, so for PR purposes, it is undoubtedly better to simply let them all die when the plane crashes into the ocean. Rather than being shown as an exceptional individual capable of policing the world, Homelander is careless and inept, accidentally sentencing dozens of innocent civilians to their deaths in order to cover up for his mistake.

If, as implied by his name, we interpret Homelander as a metaphor for the various parts of the state that claim to be the only ones who can protect us, this is a damning indictment of the state's reckless indifference to human life, its willingness to lie when its incompetence results in large-scale death, and its willingness to trade lives for positive press images and profits. Because Starr has mentioned that he uses Donald Trump as an inspiration when devising his performance as Homelander, the character's behavior can also be interpreted as a commentary on the Trump presidency, which was characterized by narcissism, an obsession with approval, and a refusal to admit to mistakes and incompetence. As such, this sequence typifies how *The Boys* both criticizes and satirizes the US security state, its foreign policies, and the White House. It also exemplifies the show's premise that abuses of power and the violation of human rights are not viewed as problematic by the state in and of themselves, so much as they are seen as public relations problems that may prevent a group's continued exercise of power. These values function in sharp contrast to DOD-supported superhero products such as *Iron Man*, *Man of Steel*, and *Captain Marvel*, all of which sanitize the US military's image and promote its missions as the benevolent, successful, and necessary acts of an exceptional nation-state.

Government Power and the War on Terror

The Boys not only works to challenge the concept of American exceptionalism; it also presents an uncompromised image of a system where people have vastly different amounts of power and capacities for violence. Unlike the sanitized depictions of militaristic combat in the majority of superhero products, *The Boys* graphically depicts the gory consequences of superpowered humans acting with near-total authority and no accountability, and in doing so presents a more realistic image of the suffering caused by real-life militaristic power centers such as the DOD and MOD. The DC and Marvel films often feature large-scale violence, but there is very little blood or crippling body horror, and just a few deaths are shown on screen even during city-scale destruction. The requirements of the MPAA's certification process mean that the MCU and DCEU do not depict the physical or emotional consequences of violence, that is, gore and suffering, in order to obtain lower age certificates and thus maximize their potential audiences and revenues. *The Boys*, distributed via Amazon's Prime streaming platform, grants its producers far greater freedom to include such horrors, with Kripke stating that Amazon "gave us as much latitude as we could possibly ask for."[23] The result is a product that more accurately depicts how violence affects the people it is directed at and thus does not truly endorse violence as a primary means of resolving conflict, although it recognizes that sometimes it is the only option. Indeed, while the series contains a plethora of violent acts, they rarely resolve anything and usually further entrench the cycles of revenge that help drive the plot forward and motivate the characters. This critique of violence is also emphasized by the fact that the Boys do not have the same capacity for ultraviolence as the Seven, since they do not possess superpowers. While some might argue that depicting ultraviolence in all its gory glory helps desensitize audiences to violence in the real world, the disgusting nature of much of the action in *The Boys*, as well as the underlying dramatic dynamics that make our sympathies lie with the less powerful characters, ensure that the audience does not come away with the message that violence is cool, or that we don't need to concern ourselves with its consequences. In fact, as M.M. tells Hughie when he admits he felt a positive rush as he committed murder, there is a heavy psychological toll to be paid for each act of violence. As such, *The Boys* serves as the cultural antidote to the Pentagon's "clean wars," which work to visually minimize or hide death, injury, and gore in order to make war more palatable to viewers and potential recruits.

Additionally, *The Boys* suggests that the government is often incapable of stopping powerful, well-coordinated threats—in this case the threat posed by the supes and Vought. In the series, both the DOD and CIA are portrayed in a very critical fashion, with its officials expressing their reservations about the growing dominion of Vought but doing little to try to stop it despite their positions of power. A major plotline in the first season is that Vought is trying to persuade the DOD to hire its supes to become part of the national defense establishment, using tactics ranging from lobbying to secret surveillance and blackmail. Homelander also begins a scheme to create batches of supe-terrorists who can overpower US armed forces, necessitating that the DOD hire Vought's supes to counter the supe-terrorist threat and fight a Super War on Super Terror. In short, the DOD are portrayed as weak and ineffective both in the face of the manufactured threat from the supe-terrorists and in response to Vought's aggressive pursuits to get their supes into the military, so the company can reap the profits of enormous military contracts.

This problem of being depicted as lesser than superpowered beings or subservient to superhero organizations caused the DOD's Hollywood office to withdraw from cooperating on *The Avengers* and to rewrite the closing scenes of *Man of Steel* to make themselves appear to be on at least an equal footing to superheroes. *The Boys*, however, makes these underlying ideas central to the plot of its first season, and as such, *The Boys* is more critical of the War on Terror than even the anti-establishment narratives covered in chapter 2. While the first Iron Man film depicted a military-industrialist selling weapons to Afghan militants, he is one bad apple pursuing short-term profits, with no wider scheme to perpetuate or intensify the war for his own gain. Homelander's scheme, in contrast, is a deliberate and willful attempt not merely to keep the War on Terror going so that Vought can increase its profits but to expand and augment the war to force Congress to make a permanent change in how the US military operates. While Homelander's scheme is similar to Killian's plot to use the Mandarin in *Iron Man 3* to generate fear to increase his profits, in *The Boys* the conspiracy extends well beyond one insane, rogue scientist whom Iron Man easily defeats (with a little help from Pepper Potts and Rhodey). Instead, *The Boys* features a vast corporation that is creating a small army of superhumans and is almost impossible to overcome. Though people may differ on the plausibility of the military-industrial complex conspiring to create terrorists in order to profit from being hired to fight those same terrorists, *The Boys* is a more critical view of the relationship between capitalism and foreign policy than has previously been explored in the genre.

Even the mighty CIA, who, it is revealed, originally created the Boys as a special unit with a mission to take down Homelander and Vought, are repeatedly shown to be cowardly in the face of the supe-terrorist threat. In season 1, the Boys manage to obtain a sample of Compound V and map out how Vought is covertly distributing the drug to hospitals in order to dose babies and create the next generation of supes. Butcher makes a deal with the CIA to hand over all the evidence they have collected in exchange for the agency protecting them and their families from Vought. The CIA enjoy a momentarily positive depiction here, as one of their officers confronts Vought's vice president and demands that she give up her efforts to get supes into the military, or the CIA will expose the truth about Compound V, leading the company to be destroyed by civil suits and criminal prosecutions. However, the agency is then shown as gutless and amoral, as it reneges on the deal after finding out that supe-terrorists exist. In *Black Panther* the CIA character is courageous and self-sacrificing, but in *The Boys* the agency is shown to be spineless, deceitful, manipulative, and deferential to corporate power and the demands of US foreign policy, even when this means turning a blind eye to rampant criminality and its responsibility to protect its own assets. While they are the only part of the government who try to stand up to Vought and the supes, the CIA's deputy director for operations admits that even she is "terrified" of Homelander and ultimately backs out of taking action against the Vought corporation, again placing the government in an ineffectual position and depicting the CIA as cowardly overall. The show's message here is clear: you can't rely on an exceptional individual NOR can you rely on the government to save you in the face of overwhelming threat. They are too invested in their own reelections or maintaining their institutional status to make tough choices that may ultimately benefit society.

White Supremacism

To date, superhero films in the DCEU and the MCU have not really addressed the threat of radical, white supremacists outside of Hydra, even though their ideas were met with public acceptance and even encouragement by the Trump administration.[24] As such, *The Boys* is tackling new ideological ground in the genre, as season 2 takes a darker turn to explore how white supremacy has rebranded itself, through the Seven's newest member, Stormfront. Vought, now trying to capitalize on having three women in the Seven, creates a new PR campaign to champion their image as a diverse and inclusive group. However, Stormfront—a young, sassy, sardonic woman, skilled in promotion on social media platforms—is later revealed as a hundred-year-old white supremacist who was created by the Nazi scientist turned corporate founder, Frank Vought. Vought, the corporation, has a secret mission to create a million supes to fight nonwhite races. While this is somewhat similar to the Hydra plot in *The Winter Soldier*, the treatment of the secret Nazi infiltration of the United States in *The Boys* is more realistic. Hydra simply existed for decades without anyone realizing it, but *The Boys* illustrates how white supremacism has quietly lingered in Western society before being remarketed for the digital age. Indeed, Stormfront initially appears as a forward-thinking, social-media-savvy feminist but quickly reveals herself to be a hateful racist who takes pleasure in killing nonwhite people, before recruiting Homelander to lead Vought's fascist army. As Kripke outlines, this arc was written to reflect how the contemporary alt-right and associated movements fashion themselves as new and alternative, while ultimately advancing a profoundly regressive agenda. He explains that Stormfront, a male character from the comics, was gender-flipped in the show to accentuate the social media savvy of the character. "What's different about today," he states, "is that a lot of people who have really hateful notions really wrap themselves in a pretty attractive social media package. They come across as disruptors who just wanna be free-thinkers, but then you ask them what their free thoughts are, it's the same hateful shit that people have been talking about for thousands of years, and we wanted to reflect that."[25] Kripke acknowledges that changing Stormfront's gender from the comic's male figure upset some fans. However, by making the change, and casting a petite, Jewish woman (Aya Cash) as a Nazi superwoman, the show's producers created a powerful plot twist that demonstrates how easily audiences can be beguiled by charismatic people with vile beliefs, how a sole emphasis on diverse representations does not always equate to progressive thinking, and how appearances are not always what they seem.

Indeed, as season 2 progresses, Stormfront makes adept use of social media memes to get her racially antagonistic messages across, and she begins publicly conflating supe-terrorists with immigrants, reflecting how the Trump administration increasingly turned immigration into a national security issue (think of Trump's rhetoric regarding MS-13 or his emphasis on building the wall between Mexico and the United States). It also reflects how the US-led War on Terror has become more inward-looking and focused on domestic, rather than foreign, extremist movements and organizations. Meanwhile, Stormfront's racist violence, along with her excuses of "white genocide," present an uncompromising image of white supremacist terrorism, which has been on the increase since Anders Breivik launched a Mumbai-style attack in Norway in 2011. Other attacks followed in Sweden, the United Kingdom, New Zealand, and elsewhere, while the problem of white supremacist violence has become so prominent in the United States that one study found that racially motivated terror attacks killed around nine times as many Americans in recent years as Islamist extremist attacks.[26] Even the Department of Homeland Security, which has arguably been much more vocal about arresting the leaders of left-wing groups such as Antifa and Black Lives Matter, conceded in a leaked report that white supremacists "pose the most persistent and lethal threat" to the nation's security.[27] As such, *The Boys* shows how diversity can be commodified and weaponized to put a millennial-friendly gloss on oppressive, militaristic, and racist ideas and mentalities. In doing so, the show demonstrates how there are things that are much more serious than representation, because even a secret Nazi corporation can use diverse representation to promote itself. The show also draws attention to the fascist undercurrents in Western society that have become more vocal, more violent, and more widely recognized in recent years.

A Better Solution?

Given the threats now posed by both domestic and foreign groups, what does *The Boys* suggest concerned citizens do? Do they blow up Vought? Race into its headquarters with guns ablaze? Because of the nature of television, which must prolong conflict over several seasons, *The Boys* will likely not destroy Vought until the series finale, and it is difficult to say how, or even if, they will succeed. Perhaps the most profound difference between *The Boys* and the more conventional products offered in the MCU and DCEU, however, is that our sympathies lie not with the superhumans but with the ordinary humans battling against them. Butcher and the others are far less powerful than Vought and the Seven, so they cannot win through using superior force, unlike Superman, Iron Man, or Thor. Instead we see them using subterfuge, asset recruitment, espionage, science, media attention, and other tactics to try to expose and defeat Vought. This is perhaps most prominently depicted in season 2 when Hughie recruits Starlight to work as a double agent inside the Seven, culminating in her obtaining a sample of Compound V and leaking it to the media, leading to widespread outrage and to Vought's stock price crashing. Here, the show suggests that one way to fight dangerous powers in a capitalist society is for average people to either band together to economically wound a company, often through mass boycotts or negative media publicity, or for company whistleblowers to step forward and bring attention to a company's problematic practices. Later on in season 2, Starlight and Hughie obtain a dossier of photographs and other evidence of Stormfront's Nazi origins, and they likewise leak it to the news media to unmask her past and her true agenda. Similarly, the season climaxes with an arc of redemption for Queen Maeve, who threatens Homelander, saying she'll go public with a video of his actions on board the hijacked flight in season 1, thus preventing him from killing Butcher and Homelander's superpowered child, Ryan.

Likewise, when the Boys directly fight the supes, they have to use ingenious tactics, which are often backed by scientific understanding. For instance, in season 1, Hughie realizes that because Translucent has impenetrable skin made out of a "carbon metamaterial," he will be highly susceptible to electricity. The group then uses high-voltage electrical currents to successfully incapacitate the supe, while Frenchie, after watching a nature documentary, realizes that Translucent's insides are as fragile as those of regular humans and thus inserts a plastic explosive through the supe's anus in order kill him. Similarly, when the Boys wish to gather information about A-Train, they decide to search his supe girlfriend's apartment. Rather than try to fight their way in, however, Hughie, who works as a video equipment specialist, realizes that they can just tap into her device's cameras, so they pose as tech geeks working to upgrade the complex's Wi-Fi speeds, in order to log into her server and surveil her place. Such creativity is also echoed in season 2 during a fight between Black Noir and Butcher, M.M., and Hughie. Unable to overpower or even meaningfully strike at Black Noir, Butcher tells Noir that he has photos of Homelander's son and threatens to expose Vought's dirty secret if Noir doesn't let them go. Vought CEO Stan Edgar, who is monitoring the fight remotely, calls off Noir, before Butcher reveals to Hughie and M.M. that no such photos exist and that it was simply a clever deception in order to save their lives. The use of bluffs, the threat of exposure, surveillance, and the acquisition of valuable information (like the fact that Homelander even has a son) are all nonviolent but powerful means of thwarting public and powerful figures.

Additionally, in the first episode of *The Boys*, Butcher, shortly after introducing himself, explains to Hughie that Robin's death was not an anomaly, and "supes lose hundreds of people each year to collateral damage." Hughie can't understand why this isn't on the news or causing widespread outrage, and Butcher responds,

> Ain't it obvious? Movie tickets, merchandising, theme parks, video games. A multi-billion-dollar global industry supported by corporate lobbyists and politicians on both sides. But the main reason you won't hear about it is because the public don't want to know about it. People love that cozy feeling that supes give them. Some golden cunt to swoop out of the sky and save the day, so you don't gotta do it yourself.

Rather than paint Vought or capitalism as simple, cartoonish villains, dialogue such as this draws attention to the complicity of politicians in colluding with a harmful state of affairs so long as it keeps them in profits and power. It also points to the apathy of the general public who could use their sheer numbers to resist the status quo or even change it but choose not to. While Butcher is a highly trained former government contractor, the rest of the Boys are fairly ordinary people who team up to fight against a common enemy using their wits more than their fists. So while *The Boys* does indict ordinary people for their apathy on important issues here, it also sends a message that everyday people can make a difference, that resistance and change are possible, without endorsing the very violent methods sometimes employed by our band of renegade protagonists. But to start to achieve anything, the show reminds us that people have to care.

Overall, the underlying values of the show are diametrically opposed to conventional superhero narratives, in that the Boys aren't exceptional individuals swooping out of the sky to save the day, but need to function as a team in order to win battles in their war against

Vought. Instead of the individualism and exceptionalism inherent in many superhero stories, *The Boys* is a tale of a group of disparate, damaged people learning to work together for mutual gain. Karl Urban, who plays Butcher, was asked about the Boys' greatest strength, and he responded that it is "their compassion for each other." Kripke added, "Ultimately the strength of the Boys is their humanity and vulnerability; generally the more vulnerable you are in this show, the stronger you are, and the stronger you pretend to be the weaker you really are." While in conventional superhero narratives vengeance and violence against the enemy is heralded and rewarded as the righteous acts of exceptional individuals, *The Boys* employs the opposite emotional dynamic. The show's message is not that the public should seek to ape the often lawless, vigilante justice of the Boys, which results in them suffering major physical and psychological scars and often fails to accomplish their aims. Rather, as Kripke explained, "A lot of the [first] season was phrased in this way of humanity and vulnerability versus vengeance. . . . One of the huge themes of the show is that vengeance does as much damage on the person seeking it as it does on the person on the receiving end."[28] While the supes are unambiguously corrupt or even evil, the alternative of the Boys is no more alluring or desirable. As Kripke summarized,

> I actually have no specific problem with either DC or Marvel. My issue more is they are training the public to wait for a strongman to come in to save them. They are teaching the wrong lesson ultimately, because we all have to save ourselves and work together, and it's slow and it's small and it's boring, and that's how the world gets better. But we're not being trained to feel that way, we're being trained for these big grand gestures and these powerful people, and that's why certain politicians can say "I'm the only one who can save you" and have people listen to that.[29]

Conclusion

Ultimately, *The Boys* acts as a cultural opposite to the MCU and DCEU, both satirizing the superhero genre and eschewing the militarism and stereotyping that have dominated the genre for decades. This approach has proven extremely successful, with the first season becoming one of Amazon's most-watched series within just two weeks of its release and gaining an 84 percent critics' score and 92 percent audience score on Rotten Tomatoes.[30] The second season, which was commissioned before the first season was released, suffered from review-bombing, so while its critics' score went up to 96 percent, the audience score on Rotten Tomatoes dropped to 77 percent, despite an 89 percent increase in the overall audience size compared to season 1.[31] A third season is now in development, and a spin-off show set at a superhero college is being fast-tracked by Amazon. The combination of explicit violence, deep character exploration, and a subversive approach to both the superhero genre and the themes explored in the show have offered audiences a dramatically different product, and audiences have responded very positively in kind.

One possible future for the superhero genre, then, is that it takes its lead from *The Boys* and incorporates more real-world subjects and issues, offering an increasingly skeptical view of government policies, corporate practices, and wider societal phenomena. Indeed, the series does not depict Vought or the supes as crazed, exotic villains operating alone. The show offers even its most brutal and cruel characters a small degree of understanding, or at least an explanation for how they have become the brutes that they are. For example, despite his psychotic behavior, even Homelander is portrayed somewhat empathetically in the series, as it emerges that Homelander grew up in a Vought laboratory with no parents or friends, again somewhat reminiscent of Trump's elite and isolated childhood. This upbringing caused Homelander to become very lonely, starved for human connection, but also incapable of building trusting and affectionate relationships, leading both to self-hatred and enmity toward lesser-powered or nonpowered humans. While in conventional superhero narratives, the combination of superpowers, worldwide fame, and enormous wealth is depicted as the enviable and deserved status of exceptional individuals, in *The Boys* this is inverted, and supes have to bear the pain of their isolation, commodification, and moral indifference while the rest of the world suffers the consequences of their excess of power. The show, in other words, features no traditional superhero villains who, like the Joker, Lex Luthor, or Hydra, simply want to subjugate and control people or cause destruction and chaos. Even Stormfront, the clearest-cut villain in the show, is revealed to simply be a tool for Vought to expand use of Compound V, their primary product and the basis for their stock price. Indeed, the real villain of the piece is corporate America, embodied in Vought, who only care about their profits and their share value and are willing to do anything to enhance their position. As Kripke commented, "The true monster of this show is Vought."[32] Instead of presenting a simple heroes-versus-villains conflict, therefore, *The Boys* presents a worldview where every individual is flawed, and corrupt institutions and established centers of power exploit those flaws for their own ends, causing widespread damage and suffering in the process. Its approach is far more realistic than its generic predecessors.

While it would be rather depressing if the entire genre adopted the grisly tone of *The Boys*, the enormous popularity of the series may encourage superhero producers—especially during a production slowdown—to rethink their next steps. This may be especially true now that most of the first generation of MCU protagonists have reached the end of their story arcs, so new heroes are being introduced in Phase Four, while the DCEU has largely abandoned the restrictions of a shared universe and is developing more stand-alone projects, again necessitating the introduction of new characters, settings, and stories. The combination of the need for renewal in both in the MCU and DCEU, a highly popular show satirizing not only the genre but its relationship with the real world and many of its underlying tropes and ideological tendencies, and the growth of less militaristic or nonmilitaristic entertainment liaison offices make it unlikely that the next decade of superhero-themed screen entertainment will mirror the last decade.

Despite the COVID-related disruption to production and release schedules, two major Marvel TV series were released in the early months of 2021: *WandaVision*, a surreal psychological thriller, and *The Falcon and the Winter Soldier*, a more typical action-comedy adventure.

Both productions deserve praise for departing from established norms of narrative and for focusing on unconventional protagonists—indeed, Sam Wilson/Falcon's arc throughout the latter series revolves around whether he, as a Black man, can take on the mantle of becoming the new Captain America. However, it should be noted that both series had support from the DOD and feature violent climaxes in order to resolve their central conflicts, including the deaths of main characters. Likewise, in March 2019 the DOD "began a conversation with Warner Brothers Studios exploring possible DoD support" on the sequel to *Suicide Squad*, before reviewing the script and providing notes.[33]

Hopefully, Marvel and DC will resist future overtures from the Pentagon and audiences will get to see a more diverse range of heroes in a wider scope of settings, exhibiting a greater variety of powers and virtues. Rather than the militarism and dependence on glorified violence that has remained prominent even as the genre has evolved, there is both room and appetite for stories about the importance of discovery and innovation, diplomacy and negotiation, creativity, intelligence, teamwork, and compassion. Superheroes are icons, and superhero movies turn them into role models for entire peoples and nations. As America, and indeed the whole world, faces an increasingly uncertain future, the superhero genre has a unique opportunity to reflect the best of humankind back at itself, in the hope of inspiring us to view our future in more optimistic terms, and to make our societies less violent, angry, and fearful places to live.

APPENDIX

UNIVERSAL CITY STUDIOS, INC. AN MCA INC. COMPANY

April 14, 1975

Mr. Donald E. Baruch
Chief, Audio-Visual Production Branch
Directorate for Defense Information
Office of Asst. Secretary of Defense
Washington, D. C. 20301

Dear Don:

John Horton has forwarded your good wishes to me and I am delighted to receive them. You have been most helpful to us, not only on THE SIX MILLION DOLLAR MAN, but on many of my other projects as well, and I am most appreciative.

Speaking for the creative staff of the program, we are indeed receptive to any input the Services might give us for potential stories. We look forward to hearing from you in that regard.

Here's hoping THE SIX MILLION DOLLAR MAN is on for many seasons to come. I look forward to our continuing relationship.

Very truly yours,

Harve Bennett
Harve Bennett
Executive Producer
THE SIX MILLION DOLLAR MAN

HB:sr

100 UNIVERSAL CITY PLAZA · UNIVERSAL CITY, CALIFORNIA 91608 · 985-4321

Document 1: Memo from Harve Bennett, producer of *The Six Million Dollar Man*, to Don Baruch asking for story line suggestions from the military services, April 14, 1975.

July 26, 1977

MEMORANDUM FOR PRODUCTION SERVICES DIVISION, CHINFO
Department of the Navy
Attention: Mr. Manning

SUBJECT: Warner Bros. TV Production "Trouble in Paradise" for Wonder Woman Series

As discussed by phone, after reviewing subject screenplay, no objections are interposed to Navy assisting by making available the bridge of a destroyer for filming sequences providing the following script changes or deletions are accomplished:

1. Page 2 - delete the jokes during transmission between aircraft and show facility, i.e. "Tell Sparks I said to stop drinking on the job. Unless I happen to be there."

2. Page 3 - delete reference to that was just a cover. Also delete reference to neutron, suggest "nuclear" instead.

3. Page 4 - delete or rewrite exchange with Southern, Diana and Atkinson to drop references to neutron bomb and its awesomeness but necessary to maintain our country's defense.

4. Page 60 - delete "neutron" in Atkinson's speech.

Assistance should be arranged on a non-interference, no additional cost to the government with the Studio carrying insurance to hold the government/Navy harmless in case of accident or loss of property. Request an after action resume, including any charges, after assistance has been rendered.

DONALD E. BARUCH
Chief, Production Branch
Audiovisual Division
Directorate for Defense Information

BARUCH/ng/7-26-77/PA/2E773/74596

NOTE: Advised, by phone, Richard Vane, location manager, Warner Bros.; he saw no problem and would get changes made.

Document 2: Memo from Don Baruch to the US Navy regarding script changes on the *Wonder Woman* TV episode "Trouble in Paradise," July 26, 1977.

(b)(6) I'm very apprehensive about sending these notes to you. For one thing, they're incomplete, (b)(6) won't have (b)(6) input until later, perhaps as early as today (Monday). But the main reason for my hesitancy is that in the past we've usually been able to offer suggestions within the context of existing plot and characters. These, however, are pretty radical. I hope they don't have the effect of aggravating everyone, because we certainly aren't trying to intrude on the creative process. It's just that I see no other practical, straightforward way of communicating our concerns.

(b)(6)

DoD "Hulk" Notes of Sunday, Feb 3.

Overall: The primary purpose of these notes is civilianize the desert lab and the direct action against the Hulk, leaving only one actual deadly military strike, against the Absorbing Man at the end. All the other military operations would be nonlethal and other unconventional attempts to contain, distract, or subdue the Hulk, or to provide reconnaissance information regarding him. There are also some technical suggestions.

Pg 1, Sc 1 and elsewhere, INT. DESERT BASE: This would be a commercial entity (Talbot's later "Atheon"?), as a company under contract to the Defense Advanced Research Projects Agency - even though there wasn't one per se in 1965. If the physical look of the place is military, it would be good to make it clear that it's no longer an active military installation, using signage and/or superimposed titles to make the distinction.

Pg 1, Sc 2: To keep General Ross as an active-duty general in the present day, he'd have to be younger and more junior in 1965, probably a major. Technically, after 30 years of commissioned service, officers face mandatory retirement, though there have been exceptions (Admiral Rickover, the submariner, for one). As a young major, Ross could be an important program manager in an emerging mission area - unconventional defenses. In this encounter with Banner, then, he'd be with his civilian "employees," perhaps, his "I" and "I've" would be "We" and "We've," emphasizing the nature of the relationship between program manager and contractor.

Would Talbot be here, too? As a lieutenant or captain? We would prefer that Talbot left the military and assumed Ross's role as director of the lab in the present day. We would like Ross to be at a distance organizationally from the lab, and unaware of all that's going on there. This is so that he does not give orders that would exceed his military authority and also so that he is credible as a general officer now in charge of overall unconventional defenses for the entire DoD.

Document 3: First pages of a DOD memo from Phil Strub to producer Larry Franco regarding the script for Hulk, February 3, 2002.

Pg 2, Sc 8, ROSS'S OFFICE: Would be better if Ross was in company with his civilian counterparts.

Pg 4, Sc 14, INT. DESERT BASE, 1973: Now Lieutenant Colonel Ross not be directly in charge of the lab, and would not have the authority to fire Banner, that would have to be a civilian contractor. It would be best if there were no uniforms at all in this scene, so that later the audience doesn't think that the military was responsible (through its proxy, the lab) for what later took happened to Banner senior and junior. This would fit with the story point revealed later, that the senior Banner would likely have been incarcerated for murdering his wife/dangerous mental illness.

Pg 11, Sc 32, INT LAWRENCE BERKELEY LAB: Talbot's conversation with Betty should reflect that he's in charge of the lab, which is still doing contract work for DoD. He no longer be working closely with Ross, Ross would be too senior for that, and Ross's scope long broadened beyond one lab and one project. But Talbot could perhaps refer to the "good old days."

Pg 15, Sc 38, EXT DESERT BASE, PLAYGROUND: In Betty's flashback, there would be civilian lab security officers, not military police.

Pg16, Sc A38, REDWOOD CABIN: Betty would use the civilian name for the former base.

Pg 20, Sc A52, EXT DESERT BASE, NIGHT, and elsewhere: Since the "desert base" is a civilian contract lab and that Talbot or someone else instead of Ross is in charge of it, we suggest that Ross's office be in a different place, like the Pentagon or Treasure Island. Treasure Island is no longer considered an active installation, but could be the site of Ross's fictional unconventional defenses command. Ross would be annoyed that Talbot was coming to him directly, instead of "through proper channels." We don't know what "Op-Comm" is.

Pg 33, Sc 67, TREASURE ISLAND/OFFICERS CLUB: Talbot wouldn't be in any position to ask Ross to do anything, and making inquiries implies that Ross would have the authority, inclination, and ability to spy on Krenzler. It would be better if Ross was just reacting to things that Talbot told him, knowing that Ross is an overly-protective father, and hoping to manipulate him by playing on this fault.

Pg 36 and elsewhere, Sc 71, BANNER'S HOUSE: It would be local law enforcement, not Ross or military MPs who would come to see Banner and ask Betty to wait outside. Ross could be waiting outside to talk to her. But he wouldn't have the authority to close the lab himself, he would only be an advisor to the justice department or whomever would be taking the action in the name of national security.

FEB 11 1999 11:26 FR SAF-PAHE 310 235 7500 TO 913105503125 P.10/12
04/11/2007 09:57 3105503?'5 PAGE 10/13

U.S. DEPARTMENT OF DEFENSE
MOTION PICTURE AND TELEVISION
PRODUCTION ASSISTANCE AGREEMENT
- ~~U.S. Air Force~~ License Number SAPA-LA 002-2007
DoD (EPR)

Attachment 1: DoD Resources Required in Support of Production

1. Film at Edwards AFB for two days in and around the Marine Aircraft Group 46, Detachment B hangars and Edwards' flightline and tarmac.
2. Film in and around a static C-17 at Edwards AFB.
3. Approximately 150 extras at Edwards AFB to play military member from various services and Afghan nationals during days of filming.
4. Facilitate the acquisition of the new Airman Battle Uniform fabric for a costume house to produce approximately 100 uniforms.
5. Film opportune take-offs, landings and taxiing of Edwards AFB aircraft.
6. Mission allowing, an F-22 Raptor from a unit to be determined for directed photography at a base or location to be determined – the billable rate or an F-22 is approximately $26,000 an hour.
7. Mission allowing, directed photography of two HH-60 helicopters from Nellis AFB at a set near Lone Pine, Calif. – the billable rate for an HH-60 is approximately $5400 per hour.
8. Production Company agrees to immediately deposit a check into the Edwards Air Force Base Account #C07MAN00 ("JON Account") the amount of $15,000 for incidentals expenses occurred during filming. Should this amount be exceeded during filming, Production Company agrees to supplement the account upon request of the DoD project officer. Any unused funds will be refunded to the production company upon completion of production.

____ DoD ____ Production Company

Page 1 of 1

Document 4: Attachment to the DOD Production Assistance Agreement for *Iron Man* detailing the military resources required to support the film, April 11, 2007.

OCPA-West Weekly Report, 25 APR 2011

discussed with producers sliding target window to MAR-APR. Working with FORSCOM PAO to support. **ASSESSMENT**: National viewership estimated in the 12-14 million range over two day airing. Supports Building Resiliency. (b) (6)

Major Motion Pictures

(FOUO) INDEPENDENT FILM, 'WHITE RABBIT' (FOUO) (SAPA-CRD) UPDATE: Based on treatment OCPA-LA declining to provide support. OCPA-LA contacted by independent filmmaker for support of story about female Army veteran returning to college. The treatment includes PTSD issues. The script is still in development, however, agreed to provide filmmaker input and insight on Army character, for purposes of guiding the portrayal. The character is a Signal Corps officer (mostly in plain clothes - but she often wears a Signal Corps T-shirt). **ASSESSMENT:** Supports Building Resiliency. (b) (6)

(FOUO) INDEPENDENT FILM, 'WAR BRIDE' (FOUO) (SAPA-CRD) OCPA-LA contacted by an independent filmmaker for support of his low-budget film. The story involves an American soldier falling in love with an Arab woman and how their love story represents peace in the world despite religious and cultural differences. The film is loosely based on the experience of an U.S. Army Iraq veteran the filmmaker interviewed. The filmmaker would like to film a kidnapping scene at Fort Irwin. Directed the filmmaker to OSD(PA) for approval. **ASSESSMENT:** Supports Building Resiliency. (b) (6)

(FOUO) FEATURE FILM, 'THE AVENGERS' (FOUO) (SAPA-CRD) OSD(PA) agreed to support feature film, 'The Avengers'. The film is an American superhero story being produced by Marvel Studios and being distributed by Walt Disney Pictures in 2012. OCPA-LA has read initial draft screenplay and rewrites. The Army is represented well in the character of Captain America, a former WWII GI brought back to life in contemporary America. Following feedback to producers – including strengthening connection of legacy Army to today's Soldiers - OCPA-LA has agreed to requests for support; access to White Sands Missile Range and a company of Soldiers for the climactic battle scene. Filming of the final battle scene will take place in Cleveland, OH, in AUG. Coordinating with USAR for support. **ASSESSMENT**: Film being designed as a blockbuster release; U.S. and worldwide audiences expected to be sizable. Supports Maintaining Our Combat Edge. (b) (6)

(FOUO) "SUPERMAN: MAN OF STEEL", WARNER BROS. (FOUO) (SAPA-CRD) UPDATE: OCPA-LA and the USAF Office reviewed the updated script 20 APR 11; writer incorporated many of the script changes requested by DOD. OCPA-LA Director, Mr. (b) (6) is working with Warner Brothers Studios on shaping the U.S. Army portrayal in the upcoming "Superman" feature film now in development. Mr. (b) (6) met with the studio, read the latest version of the script, and is discussing the military portrayals with the film's producers and writers. This latest version of the 'Superman' saga will focus on the character's origin story and the early days of the character. **ASSESSMENT**: Warner Bros. has budgeted $175 million for production and is aiming this film as a 2012 summer blockbuster. Supports Building Resiliency. (b) (6)

Entertainment – Documentaries

(FOUO) SOLDIERS OF PEACE: A GLOBAL DOCUMENTARY ABOUT THE POWER OF PEACE (FOUO) (SAPA-CRD) A documentary story about growing up on opposite corners of

OCPA-LA, 'Telling the Army story millions of viewers per showing.'

Page | 6

FOIA FA-15-0157 Page 658 of 1379

Document 5: Excerpt from US Army entertainment liaison office report mentioning script review and input on *The Avengers and Man of Steel*, April 25, 2011.

(b) (6) A CIV USARMY HQDA OCPA (US)

From: (b) (6) OSD PA (b) (6) @osd.mil>
Sent: Friday, May 27, 2011 11:29 AM
To: Hamm, Francisco G LtCol USAF SAF SAF/PAYL; A Mr CIV USA
Subject: Autumn Frost - DoD Notes - 5-27-2011.doc
Attachments: Autumn Frost - DoD Notes - 5-27-2011.doc

Gents,

Here's the attachment pasted into this email:

We recognize and appreciate the many changes that have already been made, but we need to fully resolve the concerns below before going ahead with finalizing equipment and locations, and also providing input for realistic radio-transmission dialogue, tactical orders, military ranks, etc,

Pg 32, INT. NORTHCOM SCIENCE STATION – Morrow must identify himself as being affiliated with a legitimate military command, as Hamilton now does, he would have no reason to conceal it. And that command should probably be "the U.S. Northern Command." Lois can still challenge him later about the NSA, though we don't know why she'd think they'd be from a DoD agency that focuses on electronic and signals intelligence gathering.
Note for Paco: I think that NSAT as an acronym is just as suggestive of being fake and as spoken is too long.
Note for Paco: I think we can give them the actual name of the NORAD/NORTHCOM ops center with our other more technical input later, if they make these changes.

Pg 63, DAILY PLANET – There must be no "Tier 1 Operatives" or any other special operators/SWAT police, etc. Only a few (no "army of") FBI agents in suits. And they must not be "storming through the cubicles" as if they're conducting a drug bust in a thuggish way. The Planet staff are hardly posing a security threat, and there would be no reason to be heavy-handed at all. Morrow has no authority at all, and shouldn't cite any. Please change his line to Perry to something like "I'm Colonel John Morrow, as Ms. Lane knows. I've been tasked by the national command authority to accompany her to Northern Command headquarters."

- Also, in response to Perry's line to Morrow about the limits of his authority, an FBI agent, not Morrow, must reply with something like "You're right, Sir. But we can. FBI." He should hold out his badge,no one must produce handcuffs. Lois isn't showing any signs of needing to be restrained.

Pg 67, SWANWICK'S OFFICE – Swanwick, Hamilton, and Morrow's clumsy and ineffective attempts at intimidation must be sigificantly reduced. They have no authority and no training in interrogation, and wouldn't be doing anything of the kind. Also, there need be no other people in that office, certainly no "quartet of AIRMEN," since Lois is not posing any security threat. We recognize that in direction they can be more earnestly frustrated with her than threatening. To further support that portrayal:

- Please change Morrow's line to "The FBI has your hard drive ...." And "You might as well explain things to us."

- Please give Swanwick Hamilton's questions, and give Hamilton Swanwick's line about treason. Lois can accuse the group, rather than singling out Swanwick in her response.

Note to Paco: We negotiated the following line down from the original, which was an order to drop the big one.

GENERAL SWANWICK
Only the unthinkable one. Code words have already been issued.

Note to Paco: I think we can ask what's CGI and what's not later on if they make these changes.

1

Document 6: Department of Defense email from Phil Strub to USAF entertainment liaison office director Francisco "Paco" Hamm on the script for *Autumn Frost* (*Man of Steel*), May 27, 2011.

Pg 102, Sc 193 – NORTHCOM OPS CENTER – EXT AIRFIELD: Please give Swanwick Hamilton's line about the "singularity." We don't want Hamilton to be the only one with some knowledge of astrophysics.

Pg 106, Sc 202 and elsewhere – DOWNTOWN METROPOLIS: We assume that the point of this and Sc 235 on Pg 118 is to portray (via CGI) the heroic sacrifices of fighter pilots to divert the Kryptonians from the C-17, because the destructive capability of the Kryptonians has already amply been demonstrated. If so, these must all be Air Force fighter aircraft, F-35 or otherwise.

Pg 126, Sc 255 – EXT NORTHCOM OPS CENTER – AIRFIELD. While we're not thrilled with the portrayal of the U.S military relentlessly spying on Superman, we can live with this scene, provided that:

- Superman describes the drone as "one of your spy camera drones," to make it clear that it is not armed;

- Superman left it somewhere in the U.S., not the Maldives, to maintain the "violating U.S. airspace" concept;

- The whole general's hat business is replaced by something that doesn't appear to trivialize him. While the following alternative is admittedly a corny cliché, it would show more of a meeting of minds and the beginning of a relationship if Superman concluded his comment "...you hadn't earned my respect. You have now," by extending his hand to offer a handshake, and the General, after a pause, takes it warmly and says something grudgingly, like "OK, that's good enough for now."

- Major Herrera teasing the General about his hat would of course be obviated if the hat gag routine was replaced. Perhaps the two could merely exchange resigned or rueful or bemused looks.

I'd like to be able to email this with your revisions to Lisa NLT COB Tuesday.

Hope you have a great weekend!

Best,

(b) (6)

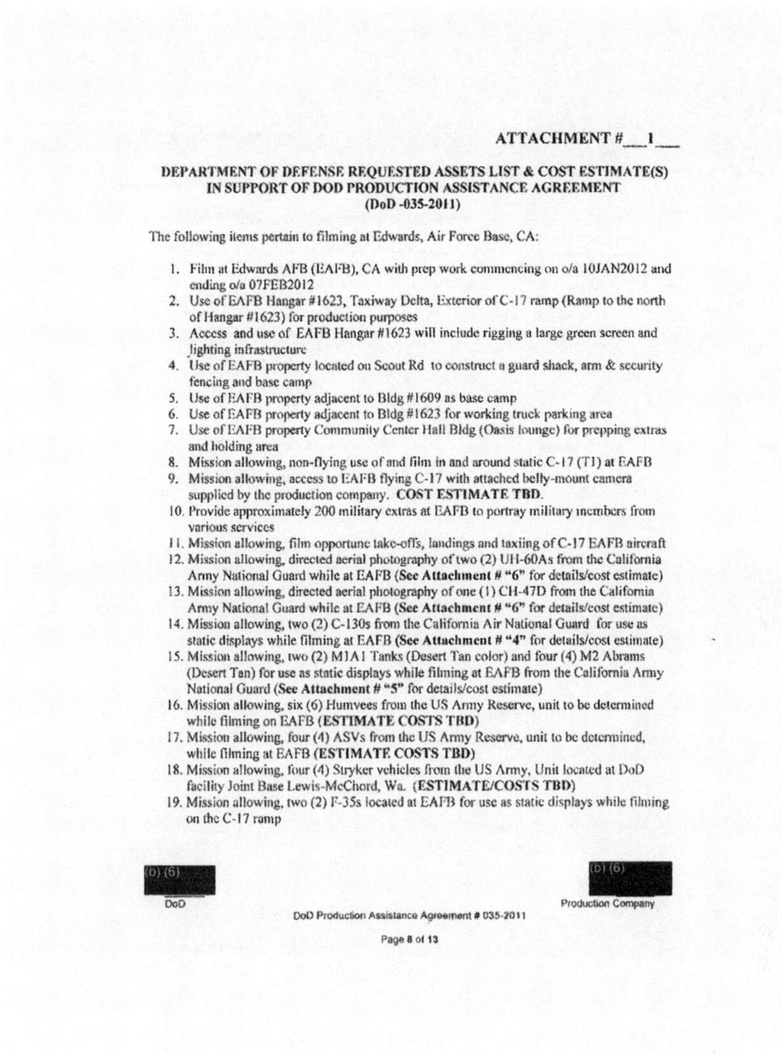

ATTACHMENT #__1__

DEPARTMENT OF DEFENSE REQUESTED ASSETS LIST & COST ESTIMATE(S) IN SUPPORT OF DOD PRODUCTION ASSISTANCE AGREEMENT (DoD -035-2011)

The following items pertain to filming at Edwards, Air Force Base, CA:

1. Film at Edwards AFB (EAFB), CA with prep work commencing on o/a 10JAN2012 and ending o/a 07FEB2012
2. Use of EAFB Hangar #1623, Taxiway Delta, Exterior of C-17 ramp (Ramp to the north of Hangar #1623) for production purposes
3. Access and use of EAFB Hangar #1623 will include rigging a large green screen and lighting infrastructure
4. Use of EAFB property located on Scout Rd to construct a guard shack, arm & security fencing and base camp
5. Use of EAFB property adjacent to Bldg #1609 as base camp
6. Use of EAFB property adjacent to Bldg #1623 for working truck parking area
7. Use of EAFB property Community Center Hall Bldg (Oasis lounge) for prepping extras and holding area
8. Mission allowing, non-flying use of and film in and around static C-17 (T1) at EAFB
9. Mission allowing, access to EAFB flying C-17 with attached belly-mount camera supplied by the production company. **COST ESTIMATE TBD.**
10. Provide approximately 200 military extras at EAFB to portray military members from various services
11. Mission allowing, film opportune take-offs, landings and taxiing of C-17 EAFB aircraft
12. Mission allowing, directed aerial photography of two (2) UH-60As from the California Army National Guard while at EAFB (**See Attachment # "6"** for details/cost estimate)
13. Mission allowing, directed aerial photography of one (1) CH-47D from the California Army National Guard while at EAFB (**See Attachment # "6"** for details/cost estimate)
14. Mission allowing, two (2) C-130s from the California Air National Guard for use as static displays while filming at EAFB (**See Attachment # "4"** for details/cost estimate)
15. Mission allowing, two (2) M1A1 Tanks (Desert Tan color) and four (4) M2 Abrams (Desert Tan) for use as static displays while filming at EAFB from the California Army National Guard (**See Attachment # "5"** for details/cost estimate)
16. Mission allowing, six (6) Humvees from the US Army Reserve, unit to be determined while filming on EAFB (**ESTIMATE COSTS TBD**)
17. Mission allowing, four (4) ASVs from the US Army Reserve, unit to be determined, while filming at EAFB (**ESTIMATE COSTS TBD**)
18. Mission allowing, four (4) Stryker vehicles from the US Army, Unit located at DoD facility Joint Base Lewis-McChord, Wa. (**ESTIMATE/COSTS TBD**)
19. Mission allowing, two (2) F-35s located at EAFB for use as static displays while filming on the C-17 ramp

(b) (6) (b) (6)

DoD Production Company

DoD Production Assistance Agreement # 035-2011

Page 8 of 13

Document 7: Attachment to the DOD Production Assistance Agreement for *Man of Steel* detailing military resources required to support the film, January 12, 2012.

ATTACHMENT #___2___

20. Allow EAFB access for the following privately owned aircraft: Hughes 500 "Little Bird" helicopter; Camera ship helicopter (AStar) and Lear jet. This will include landing/taking off from EAFB
21. Mission allowing, provide four (4) EAFB emergency vehicles (TBD) for static display during filming
22. Provide heavy duty fork lifts upon request. Operators will be EAFB personnel
23. Provide one (1) K-loader; Operators will be EAFB personnel
24. Provide one (1) EAFB fuel truck for use as static display
25. Production company agrees to immediately deposit a check into the EAFB Account #CZZSUP00 ("JON" Account") in the amount of $50,000 for incidentals and expenses incurred during filming. (See **Attachment # "3"** for details/cost estimate)
    a. The check should be made payable to the order of:
        i. US TREASURY
           POPSON AVE BLDG 2750
           EDWARDS AFB CA, 93524
           ATTN: (b) (6)
           (b)
26. Production company agrees to coordinate payment for California Air (CIANG) and Army National Guard (CAANG) Assets directly with the CAANG Budget Analyst in accordance with **ATTACHMENT "6."** Attachment "6" is an estimate of time and costs. Production company is not required to use as many flying hours indicated in Attachment "6."

(b) (6) (b) (6)

DoD Production Company

ATTACHMENT #_3___

The following items pertain to Edwards, Air Force Base, CA :

Cost estimate for filming at EAFB is:

- C-17 Maintenance engineering and related expense to include a dedicated C-17 flight (if necessary): (b) (4)
- Overtime EAFB civilian costs (Comp/Credit hours): (b) (4)
- General base wide assets such as fire stand by for filming: (b)
- Damage deposits: (b) (4)
- K loader and crews (b) (4)
- Civil engineering, Environmental and other staff studies and staff work: (b) (4)

(b) (6) DoD

(b) (6) Production Company

**FULLY REIMBURSABLE SPACE ACT AGREEMENT
BETWEEN THE NATIONAL AERONAUTICS AND SPACE ADMINISTRATION
AND
MARVEL STUDIOS**

ARTICLE 1 - SCOPE AND AUTHORITY

This Fully Reimbursable Space Act Agreement ("Agreement"), in accordance with The National Aeronautics and Space Act of 1958, as amended (51 U.S.C. § 20113 (c), formerly 42 U.S.C. § 2473 (c)), is made and entered into by the National Aeronautics and Space Administration (hereinafter "NASA") and MARVEL EASTERN PRODUCTIONS, LLC (hereinafter, "COMPANY"). NASA and COMPANY may be individually referred to as a "Party" and collectively referred to as the "Parties."

ARTICLE 2 – PURPOSE AND RESPONSIBILITIES

1. The purpose of this Agreement is to address the Parties collaboration on the feature film currently titled "MARVEL STUDIOS' THE AVENGERS" (the "Film"). This Agreement expresses the terms and conditions under which COMPANY may conduct filming at the NASA Glenn Research Center ("NASA GRC") at NASA GRC's Plum Brook Station location, which is located at 6100 Columbus Avenue Sandusky, Ohio 44870 (the "Plum Brook Site") and under which NASA will assist COMPANY regarding production of the Film. This Agreement also expresses the terms and conditions under which NASA will permit the use by COMPANY of the NASA name, initials and emblems ("NASA Symbols") as defined in Article 3 of this Agreement.

2. COMPANY's Responsibilities. COMPANY shall use reasonable efforts to undertake the following:

a. Report damage to Government property or injury to or death of any individual during the performance of this Agreement. COMPANY shall immediately notify the NASA GRC Security Office of such an incident. Further, COMPANY shall coordinate any news releases relating to an incident with the NASA Communications Contact identified in Article 16. If the NASA GRC Safety and Mission Assurance Directorate, at its discretion, perform an investigation of the mishap, COMPANY will fully cooperate and provide assistance to the conduct of the investigation.

b. Provide projections of any activities within the scope of this Agreement including the anticipated NASA GRC support requirements for the Film.

c. Coordinate with the NASA GRC Technical Point of Contact identified in Article 16 for access to and use of NASA GRC facilities and services.

d. Reimburse NASA for use of Government property and services pursuant to Article 5 Financial Obligations.

1

Document 8: Opening pages of NASA Space Act Agreement with Marvel Studios for *The Avengers*, July 28, 2011.

e. Submit to NASA, through the NASA Communications Contact, a draft of relevant portions of the script of the Film in advance of filming. NASA, through the NASA Communications Contact, will read the draft script provided by COMPANY and will either (a) approve the script as it pertains to the portrayal of NASA, its scientific programs and research, and NASA employees (including astronauts) ("NASA Portrayal") or (b) provide written comments in accordance with NASA Responsibility 3.j. NASA acknowledges receipt by e-mail of COMPANY's draft script on March 27, 2011, and revisions to COMPANY's draft script on April 5, 2011, and acknowledges approval of COMPANY's draft script as it pertains to NASA Portrayal on April 18, 2011 ("Approved Script").

f. Submit to NASA, care of the NASA Communications Contact, any changes to the Approved Script ("Subsequent Script Revisions"), which substantively change NASA Portrayal in the Film ("Material NASA Portrayal Changes"). Subsequent Script Revisions that contain Material NASA Portrayal Changes must be approved by NASA in accordance with NASA Responsibility 3.j. Pursuant thereto, the Parties acknowledge that once principal photography of the Film has commenced, NASA, through the NASA Communications Contact, may give (and COMPANY may rely upon) verbal approval of Subsequent Script Revisions ("Approved Subsequent Script Revisions"). To ensure clear understanding, any such verbal approval shall thereafter be confirmed in writing by COMPANY (written confirmation delivered by email is satisfactory) and such confirmation will be acknowledged by the NASA Communications Contact and a copy will be provided to COMPANY (written acknowledgement delivered by email is satisfactory).

g. Submit requests for use of the NASA Symbols in the Film (on various sets, costumes, and similar uses) and in promotional and advertising materials generated by COMPANY for the Film for approval by NASA through the NASA Communications Contact in accordance with NASA Responsibility 3.i. NASA must approve such requests in writing ("Approved Usages"), provided however, that once principal photography of the Film has commenced, NASA, through the NASA Communications Contact may give (and COMPANY may rely upon) verbal approval. Any such verbal approval shall thereafter be confirmed in writing by COMPANY (written confirmation delivered by email is satisfactory) and such confirmation will be acknowledged by the NASA Communications Contact and a copy will be provided to COMPANY. NASA shall not withhold approval for use by Company of NASA Symbols in the Film so long as such uses are in accordance with the Approved Script (and/or Approved Subsequent Script Revisions). The Approved Script, Approved Subsequent Script Revisions, and Approved Usages shall hereafter collectively be referred to as the "Approved Materials."

h. If during editing of those portions of the Film that include NASA Portrayal, COMPANY makes Material NASA Portrayal Changes that portray NASA in any manner that will degrade or diminish the goodwill associated with the NASA Symbols (e.g., portrays NASA as an evil or corrupt agency), NASA shall not be deemed to have given COMPANY approval for use of the NASA Symbols in the Film. If the parties disagree about whether there have been such Material NASA Portrayal Changes, the terms of Paragraph 17, DISPUTE RESOLUTION shall apply. NASA acknowledges that the Approved Script does not degrade or diminish the goodwill associated with the NASA Symbols.

INITIAL APPLICATION TO FILM OR PHOTOGRAPH AT A MOD LOCATION

This document is not legally binding and is subject to contract. It does not create rights or obligations enforceable in law, whether of partnership, agency or otherwise and shall not be construed as implying any present or future commitment and no reliance shall be placed on any of its content when completed.

Details of Facility/Location required:
RAF Halton,
Halton Camp,
Aylesbury,
Buckinghamshire HP22 5PG

Please state whether military personnel and/or equipment will also be required: **NO**

Working Title of Production:	Please circle as appropriate:	Will MOD assets be altered in any way? YES	Date of Application:
NIGHTINGALE	**Feature Film**	If YES, please give brief details: Please see attached intentions document	**8/12/15**

Dates & Times Facility/Location required (including for set up / cleardown and details of any proposed filming/photography at night):	Estimated No. of Cast & Crew involved:
Prep from 7/1/16 to 27/1/16 **Shoot 28/1/16** **Hold 29/1/16** **Prep 8/2/16 to 19/2/16** **Shoot 22/2/16 to 27/2/16** **Strike 29/2/16 to 5/3/16**	**200 crew** **150+ cast**

Description of all proposed Activity on this Facility/Location:	Estimated No. of Essential Vehicles involved:
Please see attached Filming Intentions	**28 technical trucks** **25 Facility vehicles**

Please provide a brief synopsis of the storyline and indicate if there is any military content regardless of era, including the possible depiction of any existing MOD establishments.
The scene is set in a WW1 Belgian airfield at the end of 1918. This will be a big action sequence featuring german soldiers attacking the heroes of the film

Name of Location Manager:	
CHARLES SOMERS	■

Production Company Address:	
SLOANE SQUARE FILMS **WARNER BROS STUDIOS LEAVESDEN** **WARNER DRIVE** **LEAVESDEN** **HERT WD25 7LS**	Email: **as above** Tel No. Mobile: FAX:

PUBLIC LIABILITY INSURANCE FOR A MINIMUM OF ■ WILL BE REQUIRED FOR EACH EVENT DEPENDANT UPON LEVEL OF RISK FOR FILMING AT HALTON HOUSE THE FIGURE IS ■

Document 9: Application from the producers of *Nightingale* (*Wonder Woman*) to film at a MOD location, December 8, 2015.

Exemption (b)(4)

- Latest News: NSTR.

Outreach and Miscellaneous *(Brief description new contact made w/industry prodcos, etc. and misc)*

Maj Underwood has meeting scheduled at Warner Brothers 25 May with Barry Ziehl, SVP, Public Affairs and Strategic Initiatives, Michael Walbrecht, VP, Public Affairs, and Karla Sayles, Manager, Public Affairs.

Major Underwood has tentative meeting 24 Apr with Rick Loverd. Program Dir at the National Academy of Sciences & Entertainment Exchange. Mr. Loverd was key to the massive entertainment industry interest in the Alaska CLT.

Leslie met with Tony Lund, Senior Creative Director of Ample Entertainment, 21 Apr, which currently has three documentary-style shows airing on TV. Mr. Lund attended the Alaska CLT. He stated the trip made him realize that, "… the Air Force cares about storytellers," and he wants to schedule a meeting in the coming weeks to discuss Air Force storylines that PAYL is interested highlighting.

Major Underwood met with David Shapiro of the Creative Directory, 19 Apr, about the possibility of placing the AF in Creative Directory. Need to discuss with SAF/PA.

Leslie and Lt Schirner are in contact with Mike Pierson, Space Command PA, regarding the possibility of a CLT. Mr. Pierson offered an exciting range of options to include, but not limited to NORTHCOM, MAFF (firefighting) C-130 sq and TACPs at Fort Carson. Nellis AFB was initially under consideration, but staff agreed that Space Command may have more to offer.

Major Underwood, Capt Abbott and Lt Schriner screened video produced by OL-H for PAYL. Will re-screen video next week, gather input and coordinate with OL-H to complete video.

Lt Schirner will provide an outline next week of small picture book (softback) that would be given to directors and producers to provide a visual sample of what the AF offers the filmmaking community. Project inspired by what film commissioners from other states and countries offered at the AFCI (Assoc of Film Commissioner Int'l) Global Locations Show the staff recently attended.

Personnel Items *(Reports due, projected leave, out of office, office work events)* Exemption (b)(6)

Maj Underwood:

Ms. Watson:

Capt Abbott:

Ms. Finstein:

6

Document 10: Extract from USAF entertainment liaison office report attributing the success of the USAF tour to Alaska to Rick Loverd of the SEEX, April 21, 2017.

AIR FORCE ENTERTAINMENT LIAISON OFFICE
INDUSTRY LEADER TOUR AGENDA
COLORADO – JULY 2017

HOLLYWOOD

MISSION & OBJECTIVE

SAF/PAYL MISSION
To project and protect the image of the United States Air Force within the global entertainment environment.

OVERVIEW
Three day, two night trip to Colorado Springs, Colorado to showcase the vital role Space Command plays in our nation's defense. Attendees will visit Cheyenne Mountain, Schriever AFB, Peterson AFB, Fort Carson, and the beautiful Air Force Academy campus. The trip aims to inspire realistic storytelling of Air Force people, missions, and assets in the entertainment industry.

PERSONNEL

SAF/PAYL HOST
Maj. Hamilton Underwood, Director, USAFELO

SAF/PAYL STAFF
*1st Lt Travis Schirner, Project Officer; [redacted]
*Ms. Leslie Finstein, Project Officer; [redacted] Exemption B-6
*MSgt Valda Wilson, Superintendent; [redacted]
SSgt Corban Lundborg, Photographer

* = your primary trip contacts

FELLOW ATTENDEES

	FIRST NAME	LAST NAME	JOB TITLE	COMPANY	NOTABLE PROJECTS
1	Samuel (Sam)	Ameen	Director of Photography	Int'l Guild of Cinematographers	Blackish, Supernatural, Betas, The New Normal
2	Jonathan (Jon)	Amiel	President	Quickstep Pictures	The Tudors, Halt and Catch Fire, Marco Polo
3	Leo	Amiel	Producer	Quickstep Pictures	The Flood (2018)
4	Anna	Boden	Director	Marvel Studios	Half Nelson, Sugar, Captain Marvel (2019)
5	Rebecca (Becky)	Brake	Supv. Location Mgr/Producer	Various	Men In Black, Star Trek Beyond, Tomorrowland
6	Wendolyn (Wendy)	Calhoun	Writer/EP	Edgewood Place Entertainment	Hell's Kitchen, Justified, Revenge, Empire
7	James	Coyne	Screenwriter	HHD	Tekken (Film), Avengelyne (2018/19)
8	Adam	Cozad	Screenwriter	Harry the Tenth	Jack Ryan: Shadow Recruit, Suicide Squad 2 (2019)

1

Document 11: List of Hollywood production bigwigs who attended the USAF-hosted tour of Space Command in July 2017, including Rick Loverd of the SEEX and the codirectors and two producers of *Captain Marvel*, undated.

9	Naia	Cucukov	SVP, Development and Production	Walden Media	Limitless, The Giver
10	Michael (Mike)	Dowling	Actor/Associate Producer	Allentown Productions	NCIS, Patriot's Day
11	William (Bill)	Doyle	Producer	Netflix	Mindhunter, The Social Network
12	Douglas (Doug)	Dresser	Supervising Location Manager	Freelance	Kill Bill, Hunger Games, Baby Driver
13	Debrah	Farentino	Actor/Producer/ Journalist	Abilene Pictures	NYPD Blue, Eureka
14	Ryan	Fleck	Director	Marvel Studios	30 for 30, Half Nelson, Captain Marvel (2019)
15	Adam	Fratto	SVP, Series	ReelOne Entertainment	Greek, Cleverman, Swimfan
16	Allison	Friedman	Director of Development	Color Force	The People v O.J. Simpson
17	Louis G.	Friedman	Line Producer	Production Logistics	Return of the Jedi, Titanic, Lone Survivor
18	Mark	Goffman	Writer/EP	Mark Goffman Productions	The West Wing, Studio 60, Law & Order: SVU
19	Marc	Guggenheim	Writer	Warner Bros.	Law & Order, Daredevil (TV), Arrow
20	Illtyd (Ilt)	Jones	Supervising Location Manager	Marvel Studios	Pulp Fiction, Transformers, Inception
21	Stewart	Kaye	Screenwriter	Netflix – Medal of Honor Series	Various shorts
22	Mary	Livanos	Associate Producer	Marvel Studios	Captain Marvel (2019)
23	Richard (Rick)	Loverd	Program Director	National Academy of Sciences	N/A
24	Kent	Matsuoka	Line Producer	Freelance	Hawaii Five-0, War for the Planet of the Apes (2017)
25	Lewis	Morphew	Editor	Freelance	Ace of Cakes, Little People, Big World
26	Steven (Steve)	Natt	Producer/Direct or	Hurdler Productions	Rizzoli & Isles
27	Adam	North	Senior Manager	Activision Blizzard Studios	Call of Duty (Films)
28	Jaime	Paglia	Writer/Producer	Two Joes Entertainment	Eureka, The Flash (TV), Scream (TV)
29	Michael	Parets	Production Executive	Free Association	Magic Mike, Logan Lucky (2017)
30	Aaron	Rapke	Writer/Producer	Netflix – Medal of Honor Series	Various upcoming

AIR FORCE ENTERTAINMENT LIAISON OFFICE
INDUSTRY LEADER TOUR AGENDA
COLORADO – JULY 2017

31	William (Will)	Russell-Shapiro	Vice President	Aversano Films	Team America: World Police, Failure to Launch
32	Jonathan	Schwartz	Executive Producer	Marvel Studios	Captain America, Guardians of the Galaxy, Captain Marvel (2019)
33	Jon	Silk	Executive VP, Production	Studio 8	Annapolis, Gangster Squad, It (2017)
34	Jonathan (Jon)	Spaihts	Screenwriter	Freelance	Doctor Strange, Prometheus
35	John (Will)	Staples	Writer	Freelance	Call of Duty (Game); Need for Speed (Game)
36	Janet (JT)	Tamaro	Writer/EP/ Showrunner	Hurdler Productions	Lost, CSI: NY, Bones, Rizzoli & Isles
37	Daniel (Dan)	Wilson	President	Hutch Parker Entertainment	Patriots Day, Boston Strong (2018/19)

WEATHER

Riverside, CA |------------------------ *Colorado Springs, Colorado* -------------------------|

ATTIRE

Dress in casual clothes and comfortable shoes for the entirety of the tour with two exceptions. Smart casual attire is recommended for our group dinner on Monday, July 17th. Comfortable field attire is recommended for the Academy's Expeditionary, Survival, and Evasion Training on Wednesday, July 19th. Breathable and comfortable pants and trail running or hiking boots (similar to hiking attire) are recommended. If you do not have trail running or hiking boots, normal running shoes are a sufficient backup option. Ensure that the clothing you wear on Wednesday can get dirty and is comfortable while still protective. Given the forecast above, please ensure that you have water-repellent outerwear. Our optional social in Riverside on Sunday, July 16th is informal and casual wear is recommended.

U.S. Air Force Entertainment Liaison Office – 310.235.7511 – afelohollywood@gmail.com

Captain Marvel – USAF Support Summary

NOTICE: This report contains information on the development and progress of TV programs, feature films, and other entertainment-oriented media projects. This information is shared with the Air Force for the purpose of determining whether the project qualifies for Dept of the AF and DoD support. It is pre-decisional information for our chain of command. The information contained in this report, if publicly disclosed, could be financially and professionally detrimental to the entertainment media production entity or individual filmmaker(s) providing the information, and would deter these companies and individuals from seeking AF assistance. IT IS NOT INTENDED FOR PUBLIC DISSEMINATION

Overview

Capt. Carol Danvers is a young Air Force pilot in the late 1980s. After graduating from the Air Force Academy, she excels in pilot training, flies the F-15 and moves quickly to the exciting world of test flight. A flight test incident leaves Carol infused with alien DNA. As a result, she gains extraordinary powers and becomes Captain Marvel. As an integral part of Marvel Comics, she is poised to lead the next chapter of the Marvel Cinematic Universe.

"**Captain Marvel embodies the barrier-breaking spirit of Airmen**, and her story attests to the power of service and sacrifice. The U.S. Air Force is proud to be a part of Captain Marvel's story and to continue our creative partnership with Marvel storytellers." **Brig. Gen. Edward Thomas, Director, Air Force Public Affairs**

"You're going to get the **most powerful superhero** that we've ever introduced with, I think, one of the **most unique and inspiring origin stories**." **Kevin Feige, head of Marvel Studios**

Timeline

July 2017
(b) (6) attend PAYL Industry Leader Tour to Colorado Springs

August- Sept 2017
Production support request received. Location scouts at Edwards AFB

December 2017
Marvel presents formal support request to SAF/PAYL & OSD for access to Edwards AFB

January – February 2018
Preparations for base filming; Historical research – period correct uniforms, equipment and technology; planning for potential flying operations; immersion in flying ops and pilot culture

March 2018
Filming starts in Los Angeles Brig. Gen. Jeannie Leavitt and Thunderbirds #4 and #6 appear in 1980s flashback scenes

April 2018
Filming takes place at Edwards AFB, Calif. 490 cast/crew and 37 trucks come to base for 21 days of set-up, filming and tear down

May – June 2018
Provided on-set tech advising for lead actors; started post production prep with producers

July 2018 – March 2019
PAYL actively engages with Disney and Marvel marketing teams to create impactful engagements, highlighting Air Force involvement in the film, to include STEM outreach events, Air Force-wide messaging & recruiting opportunities

By the Numbers

- **Edwards Air Force Base, 412 Test Wing**
  - 3 On-Base Locations: Housing, Hangar 1600, Flightline and Runways
  - 51 Airmen Cast as Extras
  - Aircraft Provided: B-1, B-2, 4 F-16s, F-22, F-35, NASA Global Hawk
  - Production Value: $1.9 Billion / Cost to Production: $56,000
  - Cost to Taxpayer: $0

- **144 Fighter Wing, Fresno CA, California Air National Guard**
  - Provided 4 F-15s to Edwards AFB
  - 22 Airmen Cast as Extras
  - Production Value: $120 Million / Cost to Production: $17,000
  - Cost to Taxpayer: $0

Document 12: US Air Force Summary of Support to *Captain Marvel*, undated.

U.S. Air Force Entertainment Liaison Office – 310.235.7511 – afelohollywood@gmail.com

Captain Marvel – USAF Support Summary

NOTICE: This report contains information on the development and progress of TV programs, feature films, and other entertainment-oriented media projects. This information is shared with the Air Force for the purpose of determining whether the project qualifies for Dept of the AF and DoD support. It is pre-decisional information for our chain of command. The information contained in this report, if publicly disclosed, could be financially and professionally detrimental to the entertainment media production entity or individual filmmaker(s) providing the information, and would deter these companies and individuals from seeking AF assistance. IT IS NOT INTENDED FOR PUBLIC DISSEMINATION

Air Force Immersions

- In December 2017, Lead actress Brie Larson, directors Anna Boden and Ryan Fleck, along with Producer Jonathan Schwartz visited Nellis Air Force Base. The Marvel team spent one-on-one time with Brig. Gen. Jeannie Leavitt, 57th Wing Commander and the military's first female fighter pilot. Additional engagement aggressor pilot Capt. Dani "Kazi" Kanga, the Thunderbirds, and other Air Force personnel positively impacted character development and storylines.

- ***March 26, 2018*** **Marvel announces production underway for Captain Marvel** with this photo of Brig. Gen. Jeannie Leavitt and Brie Larson together on an F-15 at Nellis AFB. **Retweeted 4.7K times!**
- Lead actress Brie Larson and director Anna Boden flew in F-16s at Nellis AFB in Dec. 2017. Co-star Lashana Lynch flew in an F-16 at Luke AFB in April 2018 with Lt. Col. Kristen "Mother" Hubbard

Air Force Screen Time

- **Brig Gen. Jeannie Leavitt** - Commander, AFRS; **Maj. Stephen "Cajun" Del Bagno** - Thunderbird #4 and **Maj. Matt "Spider" Kimmel** - Thunderbird #6 **appear as featured extras in key 1989 flashback scenes**

History & Technical Expertise

- Air Force historians were critical to an accurate Air Force depiction. Materials collected from Airman Magazine Archives and consultations with AFMC, Edwards Air Force Base, and U.S. Air Force Academy historians resulted in period-correct 80s and 90s hardware, uniforms and details appearing on screen.
- 5 Pilot Tech Advisors assisted actors in "flying" aircraft on screen
- 6 Pilot Tech Advisors taught actors about off-duty pilot culture
    - ZERO Added Cost to Taxpayer

Themes & Messages

Innovation

- The Air Force and Captain Marvel share common goals "Higher, Further, and Faster."

Breaking Barriers

- As the first female character to headline a Marvel franchise, Capt. Carol Danvers exemplifies the barrier-breaking spirit found in every generation of Airmen going back to 1947.
- Captain Marvel may be fiction but her story represents generations of real women who broke through barriers to serve their nation in air, space, and cyberspace.

Air Force Support to Entertainment

- Access to Airmen, aircraft, and equipment provides unbeatable production value and authenticity to productions targeting key recruiting demographics.
- Stories like Captain Marvel exemplify our fighting spirit and allow audiences everywhere to understand Air Force core values.

ENTERTAINMENT MEDIA Weekly – March 8, 2019

FEATURE MOTION PICTURES

- "Captain Marvel" – Air Force hosted the film's co-directors at the Pentagon on Thursday, March 7. During their visit they attended office calls and had lunch with Air Force leaders. They also participated in a professional development session for Air Force and OATSD(PA) PAOs in the PBR. Disney further arranged for two screenings at the National Air & Space Museum on Thursday, March 7 at 5:00 and 7:30 p.m.
    - Twenty OATSD(PA) staff and guests attended the 5:00 pm screening and 29 attended the 7:30 pm screening.
- "Island Plaza" (working title) (aka "Top Gun: Maverick") – Paramount has resumed active production at NAS Lemoore. Current production calendar has DoD/Navy support continuing until early April. Lawyers from Paramount and Navy Trademark & Licensing are actively discussing edits of the addendum covering marketing, trademarks, licenses and fees, copyrights and publicity rights. Pressing for a mid-March resolution.
- Upcoming releases
    - Captain Marvel – March 8, 2019
        - DC screening Thursday, March 7.
    - Midway – November 8, 2019
    - Greyhound – May 8, 2020
    - Top Gun: Maverick – June 26, 2020

EPISODIC TELEVISION

- Script review for proposed HBO episodic series, "We Are What We Are" is complete. Series is set in Italy and features U.S. Army dependents from U.S. Army installation, Camp Darby. Numerous problems exst with the current drafts of scripts including underage drinking and instances of physical abuse without repercusions. Army has provided producers/writers with copious notes.
- "SEAL Team," "NCIS," "NCIS New Orleans," and "Hawaii 5-0" production teams continue to forward scripts for review as well as finished DVDs of each

NON-SCRIPTED/DOCUMENTARY

- Reviewed and approved three requests for production support.

Document 13: Department of Defense entertainment liaison office report detailing promotional efforts on *Captain Marvel*, March 8, 2019.

NOTES

INTRODUCTION. HOLY BOX OFFICE, BATMAN

1. "Top Lifetime Grosses," Box Office Mojo, last accessed March 29, 2021, https://www.boxofficemojo.com/chart/top_lifetime_gross/?area=XWW; Travis Clark, "'Joker' Will Cross $1 Billion at the Box Office Today, Becoming the First R-rated Movie in History to Do So," *Business Insider*, November 15, 2019, https://www.businessinsider.com/joker-first-r-rated-movie-to-make-billion-box-office-2019-11.

2. Yvonne Tasker, *The Hollywood Action Adventure Film* (New York: Wiley-Blackwell, 2015), 181.

3. Ryan Lambie, "How Marvel Went from Bankruptcy to Billions," Den of Geek, April 17, 2018, https://www.denofgeek.com/movies/how-marvel-went-from-bankruptcy-to-billions/.

4. Sean Howe, "Avengers Assemble!," Slate, September 28, 2012, https://slate.com/business/2012/09/marvel-comics-and-the-movies-the-business-story-behind-the-avengers.html.

5. Matthew McEniry, Robert Moses Peaslee, and Robert Wiener, "Introduction," in *Marvel Comics into Film: Essays on Adaptations since the 1940s*, ed. Matthew McEniry, Robert Moses Peaslee, and Robert Wiener (Jefferson, NC: McFarland, 2016), 3.

6. McEniry et al., 1.

7. Claudia Eller and Ben Fritz, "DC Comics Gets Redrawn by Warner," *Los Angeles Times*, September 10, 2009, https://www.latimes.com/archives/la-xpm 2009-sep-10-fi-ct-warner10-story.html.

8. "15 Summer Box Office Disasters from the Last 20 Years," *Rolling Stone*, last accessed May 26, 2020, https://www.rollingstone.com/movies/movie-lists/15-summer-box-office-disasters-from-the-last-20-years-17494/12-cat woman-2004-128390/.

9. Eller and Fritz, "DC Comics Gets Redrawn by Warner."

10. Terence McSweeney, *Avengers Assemble: Critical Perspectives on the Marvel Cinematic Universe* (New York: Wallflower Press, 2018), 19.

11. John Shelton Lawrence and Robert Jewett, *The Myth of the American Superhero* (Grand Rapids, MI: Wm. B. Eerdmans, 2002), 116.

12. McSweeney, *Avengers Assemble*, 8.

13. Philip Smith and Michael Goodrum, "We Have Experienced a Tragedy

Which Words Cannot Properly Describe: Representations of Trauma in Post-9/11 Superhero Comics," *Literature Compass* 8, no. 8 (2011): 488.

14. Quoted in Robert Eberwein, *The Hollywood War Film* (New York: Wiley-Blackwell, 2010), 52.

15. McSweeney, *Avengers Assemble*, 23.

16. Donald Pease, *The New American Exceptionalism* (Minneapolis: University of Minnesota Press, 2009), 158.

17. Anthony Spanakos, "Exceptional Recognition: The US Global Dilemma in *The Incredible Hulk*, *Iron Man*, and *Avatar*," in *The 21st Century Superhero: Essays on Gender, Genre and Globalization*, ed. Richard Gray II and Betty Kaklamanidou (Jefferson, NC: McFarland, 2011), 15–28.

18. Peter Bruno, *Infinity Wars: Post 9/11 Superhero Films and American Empire* (master's thesis, City University of New York, 2019), 25.

19. McSweeney, *Avengers Assemble*, 26, 27.

20. See, for instance, James Chapman, *License to Thrill: A Cultural History of the James Bond Films* (New York: Columbia University Press, 1999); Janet Woollacott and Tony Bennett, *Bond and Beyond: The Political Career of a Popular Hero* (London: Macmillan, 1987).

21. Tim Gruenewald, "Superhero Films after 9/11: Mitigating Collateral Damage in the Marvel Cinematic Universe," in *Imperial Benevolence: U.S. Foreign Policy and American Popular Culture since 9/11*, ed. Scott Laderman and Tim Gruenewald (Los Angeles: University of California Press, 2018), 144.

22. Rebecca Davis, "How the Avengers Became Such a Marvel in China," *Variety*, April 25, 2019, https://variety.com/2019/film/news/avengers-endgame-marvel-universe-china-box-office-1203197686/.

23. Tanner Mirrlees, "The Economics, Geopolitics and Ideology of an Imperial Film Commodity," *Cineaction* 92 (2014): 9, 10.

24. Matthew Alford, "The Political Impact of the Department of Defense on Hollywood Cinema," *Quarterly Review of Film and Video* 33, no. 4 (2016): 332.

25. Abraham Reisman, "Bombing Out Hollywood," Vice, March 22, 2012, https://www.vice.com/gr/article/jmvjv3/the-military-hollywood-complex-is-booming.

26. Donald Baruch, "Memorandum for Broadcast/Pictorial Division, SAFOI," January 10, 1978, 190/31/13/05, box 32, National Archives, Washington, DC.

27. Roger Williams, Colonel USAF, "Memorandum for Chief, Audiovisual Production Branch," December 23, 1975, 190/31/13/02, box 14, National Archives, Washington, DC.

28. Marshall Green to Donald Baruch, June 10, 1975, 190/31/13/02, box 14, National Archives, Washington, DC.

29. The relationship between the DOD and Harve Bennett, *The Six Million Dollar Man*'s executive producer, was so positive that Bennett wrote to Baruch thanking him for his continued support of the series and made the unusual invitation on behalf of "the creative staff of the program" to submit "any input the Services might give us for potential stories." In April 1975, Baruch wrote to each of his armed forces public affairs offices, noting that *The Six Million Dollar Man* had been renewed for another season, and that the studio welcomed any ideas for episodes featuring their service, which Baruch argued would be a positive "opportunity to obtain television exposure," although it is unclear what story lines, if any, emerged from this invitation.

30. Richard Vane to Lt. Col. Cunningham, "Letter," July 20, 1977, 190/31/13/05, box 32, National Archives, Washington, DC.

31. Donald Baruch, "Memorandum for Production Services Division," July 26, 1977, 190/31/13/05, box 32, National Archives, Washington, DC. The neutron bomb was a controversial, specialized type of nuclear weapon that produced a smaller but much more lethal blast radius. It was proposed for tactical use in the 1970s, but as the antinuclear movement gained strength throughout the decade, Ronald Reagan was forced to shut down the program in the 1980s. The idea that the navy was secretly developing neutron bombs behind the public's back did not sit well with the branch and was requested to be struck from the script.

32. "The Bionic Woman Script by Kenneth Johnson," October 21, 1975, 190/31/13/02, box 14, National Archives, Washington, DC.

33. Roger Williams, Colonel USAF, "Memorandum for Chief, Audiovisual Production Branch," November 20, 1975, 190/31/13/02, box 14, National Archives, Washington, DC.

34. Tricia Jenkins, "How the Central Intelligence Agency Works with Hollywood: An Interview with Paul Barry, the CIA's New Entertainment Industry Liaison," *Media Culture and Society* 31, no. 3 (2009): 491.

35. David Robb, *Operation Hollywood: How the Pentagon Shapes and Censors the Movies* (Amherst, NY: Prometheus Books, 2004), 182.

36. See Michelle Pautz, "*Argo* and *Zero Dark Thirty*: Film, Government, and Audiences," *PS: Political Science and Politics* 48, no. 1 (2015): 120–121.

37. This is a standard clause in the LAPD's Trademark License Agreements, as evidenced by the agreement for the TV series *Modern Marvels*, signed June 5, 2015, on file with the authors.

38. Megan Telles and Chris Wolfe, "LAPD Faces Growing Criticism for Excessive Force and Poor Tactics during Protests," *Los Angeles Times* / KTLA.com, June 6, 2020, https://ktla.com/news/local-news/lapd-faces-growing-criticism-for-excessive-force-and-poor-tactics-during-protests/.

39. Jeff Cohen, "The Agency on CBS: Right Time but Wrong Show," FAIR, October 8, 2001, https://fair.org/article/quotthe-agencyquot-on-cbs/.

40. Bert Ulrich, phone interview with Tricia Jenkins, October 27, 2019.

41. David Kirby, *Lab Coats in Hollywood: Science, Scientists and Cinema* (Cambridge, MA: MIT Press, 2011), 51.

42. Robb, *Operation Hollywood*, 183.

43. Rick Loverd et al., "The Story of the Science and Entertainment Exchange, a Program of the National Academy of Sciences," *Integrative and Comparative Biology* 58, no. 6 (2018): 1307.

44. Tricia Jenkins, *The CIA in Hollywood: How the Agency Shapes Film and Television* (Austin: University of Texas Press, 2016), 94.

45. Robb, *Operation Hollywood*, 42.

46. Turley quoted in Robb, 21.

47. Liam Burke, "'A Bigger Universe': Marvel Studios and Transmedia Storytelling," in *Assembling the Marvel Cinematic Universe*, ed. Julian Chambliss et al. (Jefferson, NC: McFarland, 2018), 33, 35, 36, 34.

48. Sinai Diaz, "Marvel vs. DC: How a Core Difference between Two Franchises Mirrors Modern Society," Texas Christian University, unpublished student paper, 2019.

49. Alford, "Political Impact," 343.

50. Secker's website, Spy Culture, can be found at www.spyculture.com.

51. FOIA Request DON-NAVY-2016-004870 and responses submitted by Tom Secker to the US Department of the Navy, March 28, 2016.

52. David Welch, "Introduction: Propaganda in Historical Perspective," in *Propaganda and Mass Persuasion: A Historical Encyclopedia, 1500 to the Present*, ed. Nicholas John Cull, David Holbrook Culbert, and David Welch (Santa Barbara: ABC-CLIO, 2002), xix.

53. Culbert quoted in Jenkins, *CIA In Hollywood*, 180.

54. Turley quoted in Robb, *Operation Hollywood*, 17, 14.

Chapter One. "If You Get Killed, Walk It Off"

1. Matthew Alford and Tom Secker, *National Security Cinema* (N.p.: Drum Roll Books, 2017), 1.

2. Robb, *Operation Hollywood*, 26.

3. Alford and Secker, *National Security Cinema*, 1.

4. Department of Defense, Principal Deputy Assistant Secretary, "DOD Assistance to Non-Government, Entertainment-Oriented Motion Picture, Television, and Video Productions," January 26, 1988, 2, available at https://biotech.law.lsu.edu/blaw/dodd/corres/pdf/i541016_012688/i541016p.pdf.

5. Matthew Alford, *Reel Power: Hollywood Cinema and American Supremacy* (New York: Pluto Press, 2010), 3.

6. Roger Stahl, *Militainment, Inc.: War, Media and Popular Culture* (New York: Routledge, 2009), 25, 26.

7. On the entertainment liaison offices and sexual assault, see Tom Secker, "Documents Reveal Hollywood Cover-up of Pentagon's Sex Crime Problem," Insurge Intelligence, May 31, 2019, https://www.spyculture.com/documents-reveal-hollywood-cover-up-of-pentagons-sex-crime-problem/. On military mental illness and suicide, see Tom Secker, "Documents Reveal Pentagon Censorship of Military Suicides, Trauma in Hollywood," Insurge Intelligence, June 19, 2018, https://www.spyculture.com/documents-reveal-pentagon-censorship-of-suicide-in-hollywood/. On alcohol, see Tom Secker, "How the Pentagon Uses Hollywood to Cover Up Its Alcohol Problem," SpyCulture, September 7, 2018, https://www.spyculture.com/how-the-pentagon-uses-hollywood-to-cover-up-its-alcohol-problem/. On drug use, see Tricia Jenkins, "Remembering the American Experience in Vietnam: A Look at the Film Industry's Relationship to the Department of Defense," *Journal of American Culture* 42, no. 2 (2019): 99–111.

8. Tanner Mirrlees, *Hearts and Mines: The U.S. Empire's Culture Industry* (Vancouver: UBC Press, 2016), 7.

9. All Schamus quotes are from his email interview with Tricia Jenkins on July 22, 2020.

10. Phil Strub to Larry Franco, "DoD Hulk Notes of Sunday, Feb 3," February 3, 2002, 1, on file with the authors.

11. Strub to Franco, 1–2.

12. Strub to Franco, 4.

13. "Original Hulk Script," n.d., 71, on file with the authors.

14. Strub to Franco, 1, 4, 5.

15. Project on Defense Alternatives, "New Study Finds: 11,000 to 15,000 Killed in Iraq War; 30 Percent are Non-combatants; Death Toll Hurts Post-war Stability Efforts, Damages US Image Abroad," October 28, 2003, available at https://reliefweb.int/report/iraq/new-study-finds-11000-15000-killed-iraq-war.

16. "A Dossier of Civilian Casualties 2003–2005," Iraq Body Count Project, November 24, 2006, last accessed July 20, 2020, http://reports.iraqbodycount.org/a_dossier_of_civilian_casualties_2003-2005.pdf.

17. Andrew Cohen, "The Torture Memos, 10 Years Later," *Atlantic*, February 6, 2012, https://www.theatlantic.com/national/archive/2012/02/the-torture-memos-10-years-later/252439/.

18. Alette Smeulers and Sander van Niekirk, "Abu Ghraib and the War on Terror: A Case against Donald Rumsfeld?" *Crime, Law and Social Change* 51, no. 3 (2009): 328. Distancing the military from its more inhumane operations may also be one reason why Strub successfully petitioned for the movie name of the operation to contain the Hulk be switched from Ranch Hand to Angry Man, as Ranch Hand was the name of an actual Vietnam-era military campaign that involved spraying herbicides, such as Agent Orange, to defoliate the rural areas of South Vietnam in order to deprive the Viet Cong of food and cover. In more than a decade of spraying, nearly five million acres of forest and a half million acres of crops were destroyed, while the effects of Agent Orange left millions of Vietnamese and/or many American and Australian soldiers with long-lasting health problems or birth defects among their children. A similar change was made on *Red Dawn* (1984) to remove a reference to Yellow Rain, a hotly disputed chemical weapons attack during the Vietnam War.

19. Stahl, *Militainment, Inc.*, 26.

20. Vesta Anderson, "9/11: 14 Years Later," Wounded Warrior Project, last accessed July 21, 2020, https://www.woundedwarriorproject.org/featured-campaign/911-14-years-later.

21. Jeffrey Ewing, "The Superhero Challenge to State Sovereignty," in *Iron Man vs. Captain America and Philosophy: Give Me Liberty or Keep Me Safe*, ed. Nicolas Michaud and Jessica Watkins (Chicago: Open Court, 2018), 201, 203, 204.

22. Stacy Takacs, "Exceptional Soldiers: Imagining the Privatized Military on U.S. Television," in Laderman and Gruenewald, *Imperial Benevolence*, 98.

23. A. O. Scott, "Tall and Green, but No Ho, Ho, Ho," *New York Times*, June 20, 2003, https://www.nytimes.com/2003/06/20/movies/film-review-tall-and-green-but-no-ho-ho-ho.html.

24. See the US Air Force Entertainment Liaison Office website, https://www.airforcehollywood.af.mil/. The current version of this site does not include these details, but older snapshots are available via the Wayback Machine, e.g., https://web.archive.org/web/20110215095847/http://www.airforcehollywood.af.mil/portfolio/index.asp, last accessed November 23, 2019.

25. US Air Force Entertainment Liaison Office website; US Department of

Defense, "Production Assistance Agreement for *Iron Man*," April 11, 2007, on file with the authors.

26. US DOD, "Production Assistance Agreement."

27. Nick Turse, *The Complex: How the Military Invades Our Everyday Lives* (New York: Metropolitan Books, 2008), 112.

28. Mirrlees, "Economics, Geopolitics and Ideology," 9.

29. "Unofficial Live Commentary for *Iron Man* by Jon Favreau and Robert Downey Jr.," recorded September 6, 2008, at the Aero Theater, https://soundcloud.com/user-236443084/iron-man-live-commentary.

30. "US Army Comments on Required Changes to Script of *Clear and Present Danger*," July 15, 1993, in DOD Film Office file on *Clear and Present Danger*, available at https://www.spyculture.com/black-hawk-down-the-la-riots-and-clear-and-present-danger/.

31. Mirrlees, "Economics, Geopolitics and Ideology," 10.

32. "Future Warrior Concept," Wikipedia, last accessed July 20, 2020, https://en.wikipedia.org/wiki/Future_Force_Warrior.

33. Jared Keller, "SOCOM's Iron Man Suit Is Officially Dead," Task and Purpose, February 15, 2019, https://taskandpurpose.com/military-tech/talos-iron-man-suit-dead.

34. "Unofficial Live Commentary."

35. Respectively, Garth Franklin, "Review: *Iron Man*," Dark Horizons, May 2, 2008, www.darkhorizons.com/reviews/423/Iron-Man; "Downey Steels the Show as Irrepressible 'Iron Man,'" *Chicago Sun Times*, May 1, 2008, 33; Carrie Rickey, "Superhero Genre Welded into a New Form," *Philadelphia Inquirer*, May 2, 2008, W8; Peter Bradshaw, "Scrap Metal: Robert Downey Jr's Iron Man Is a Cheerfully Unpretentious Addition to the Superhero Pantheon," *Guardian*, May 2, 2008, Film and Music section, 7; Des Partridge, "Hardcore Hero," *Daily Telegraph* (Australia), May 1, 2008, 43.

36. Mirrlees, "Economics, Geopolitics and Ideology," 11.

37. "Draft Screenplay for *Iron Man* by Alfred Gough and Miles Millar, Revisions by David Hayter," October 21, 2004, last accessed July 20, 2020, http://www.pdfscreenplays.net/pdfscripts/screenplays/Iron%20Man.pdf.

38. "Draft Screenplay," 90.

39. "Draft Screenplay," 90.

40. "Unofficial Live Commentary."

41. Similar moments occur in other DOD-sponsored films including *Goldeneye*, *Apollo 13*, *The Sum of All Fears*, and *Jurassic Park III*, which are undoubtedly positive PR for the Pentagon because they show the military in a nonfighting

capacity. Indeed, the DOD supported the nonmilitary film *Deep Impact* precisely because, according to their Film Office file, it "offer[ed] the Army several opportunities to demonstrate its role in disaster preparedness and disaster assistance," and they even made changes to the script to help emphasize this "multifaceted" depiction.

42. "Unofficial Live Commentary."

43. The DOD Film Office file on *Behind Enemy Lines* reveals that one of the Pentagon's major concerns with that film was that it showed Admiral Reigart calling a journalist to leak information to them. On file with the authors.

44. Iron Man Salmon #2 draft, scene 72, on file with the authors.

45. "2,100 Civilians Killed in Afghanistan in 2008: UN," Australian Broadcasting Corporation, February 3, 2009, https://www.abc.net.au/news/2009-02-04/2100-civilians-killed-in-afghanistan-in-2008-un/282520.

46. Neta Crawford, "Update on the Human Costs of War for Afghanistan and Pakistan, 2001 to mid-2016," Watson Institute, August 2016, https://watson.brown.edu/costsofwar/files/cow/imce/papers/2016/War%20in%20Afghanistan%20and%20Pakistan%20UPDATE_FINAL_corrected%20date.pdf.

47. "U.S. Department of Defense Motion Picture and Television Productions Assistance Agreement," US Department of Defense, March 30, 2009, available at Tom Secker, "Pentagon Production Assistance Agreements for Iron Man 1 and 2," Spy Culture, last accessed November 5, 2019, https://www.spyculture.com/pentagon-production-assistance-agreements-iron-man-12/.

48. Department of Defense and Hollywood Database, last accessed November 5, 2019, http://www.mediafire.com/file/7rpoqocxvevsoh8/DOD-Hollywood-Database.pdf.

49. "USMC Television and Motion Picture Liaison Office, Los Angeles Weekly Reports 2008–2015," United States Marine Corps, on file with the authors.

50. All Latcham quotes are from Jeremey Latcham, phone interview with Tricia Jenkins, June 15, 2020.

51. Stephen Losey, "Race and the Air Force: The Truth about How Minorities Get Promoted," *Air Force Times*, March 1, 2016, https://www.airforcetimes.com/news/your-air-force/2016/03/01/race-and-the-air-force-the-truth-about-how-minorities-get-promoted/.

52. Stephen Losey, "Air Force Punished Black Airmen More, Report Says—and Covered It Up," *Air Force Times*, May 27, 2020, https://www.airforcetimes

.com/news/your-air-force/2020/05/27/air-force-punished-black-airmen-more-report-says-and-covered-it-up/.

53. For example, see William O'Brien, "Iron Man Visits Edwards," US Airforce, May 27, 2009, https://www.af.mil/News/Article-Display/Article/120211/ironman-visits-edwards/.

54. Daniel Malloy, "TM and © Stark Industries: Iron Man and Property Rights," in *Iron Man and Philosophy*, ed. Mark White (Hoboken: John Wiley & Sons, 2010), 116, 117.

55. Malloy, 125.

56. Malloy, 125.

57. "OCPA-WEST Weekly Report, 12–18 April 2011," US Army Entertainment Liaison Office, April 2011, on file with the authors.

58. Takacs, "Exceptional Soldiers," 99–100.

59. Emily Todd VanDerWerff, "With Great Power Comes Great Uncertainty: Marvel's Slowly Evolving Politics," Vox, February 26, 2018, https://www.vox.com/culture/2018/2/26/17029572/black-panther-marvel-politics.

Chapter Two. "I Told You, I Don't Want to Join Your Super-Secret Boy Band"

1. Marc Di Paolo, *War, Politics, and Superheroes: Ethics and Propaganda in Comics and Film* (Jefferson, NC: McFarland, 2011), 12–13.

2. Dirs. Anthony and Joe Russo, Commentary Feature on *Captain America: Civil War*, DVD (Burbank, CA: Buena Vista Home Entertainment, 2016).

3. Bruno, *Infinity Wars*, 26.

4. Allan Austin, "An Age of (Super)Heroes? Hollywood and the 'Global War on Terror,'" Vault of Culture, September 3, 2019, https://www.vaultofculture.com/vault/feature/austin/ageofsuperheroes.

5. Michael Curley, "'The Incredible Hulk' Is the Black Sheep of the Marvel Cinematic Universe," Pop Matters, August 9, 2018, https://www.popmatters.com/the-incredible-hulk-louis-leterrier-2584392033.html.

6. Curley, "'The Incredible Hulk.'"

7. Lori Maguire, "The American Military in *The Incredible Hulk* during the Vietnam War," in *The Ages of the Incredible Hulk: Essays on the Green Goliath in Changing Times*, ed. Joseph J. Darowski (Jefferson, NC: McFarland, 2016), 49, 50.

8. Robert Genter, "'With Great Power Comes Great Responsibility': Cold War Culture and the Birth of Marvel Comics," *Journal of Popular Culture* 40, no. 6 (2007): 960.

9. Ewing, "Superhero Challenge to State Sovereignty," 197.

10. "OCPA-WEST Weekly Report," US Army Entertainment Liaison Office, November 16–22, 2010, on file with the authors.

11. Joanna Robinson, "Joss Whedon on the Original Avengers Script: 'Pretend This Draft Never Happened,'" *Vanity Fair*, July 21, 2014, https://www.vanityfair.com/hollywood/2014/07/joss-whedon-first-avengers-script-disaster.

12. "OCPA-WEST Weekly Report," US Army Entertainment Liaison Office, April 4, 2011, on file with the authors.

13. "OCPA-WEST Weekly Report," US Army Entertainment Liaison Office, August 30, 2011, on file with the authors.

14. Joss Whedon Director's Commentary, *The Avengers*, DVD (Burbank, CA: Buena Vista Home Entertainment, 2012).

15. Spencer Ackerman, "Pentagon Quit *The Avengers* Because of Its 'Unreality,'" *Wired*, May 7, 2012, https://www.wired.com/2012/05/avengers-military/.

16. In his *Wired* interview, Strub tried to deflect from this, saying the planes were not provided by the military but were "digitally inserted" by the studio and thus not a sign of them initially granting full support to *The Avengers* before the falling-out over the script. This is a moment of extreme hairsplitting, because the F-22s seen fighting the Decepticons in the Transformers movies and the F-35s shown battling General Zod's forces in *Man of Steel* were all CGI, not actual footage of real military planes, but both of those movies were granted full DOD support.

17. Whedon, DVD commentary on *The Avengers*.

18. Chris Bell, "White House Down: How Roland Emmerich Was Snubbed by the Pentagon," *Telegraph*, September 12, 2013, https://www.telegraph.co.uk/culture/film/10277220/White-House-Down-how-Roland-Emmerich-was-snubbed-by-the-Pentagon.html.

19. Ackerman, "Pentagon Quit."

20. DOD Film Office files on *Independence Day* and *Clear and Present Danger*, on file with the authors.

21. Jeremy Latcham, phone interview with Tricia Jenkins, June 15, 2020.

22. "The Pentagon's 'Hollywood Liaison,'" *Kojo Nnamdi Show*, July 19, 2012, https://thekojonnamdishow.org/shows/2012-07-19/pentagons-hollywood-liaison.

23. This is very similar to a scene in the original *Superman* movie (1978) where Superman catches a nuclear missile midair, leading Whedon to mention on the DVD commentary that he hoped audiences "hadn't seen Superman" and wouldn't notice his dubious homage.

24. Samantha Quigley, "To Tap into the Military's Arsenal, Hollywood Needs the Pentagon's Blessing," USO, December 18, 2015, https://www.uso.org/stories/105-to-tap-into-the-military-s-arsenal-hollywood-needs-the-pentagon-s-blessing.

25. Jennifer Beckett, "Acting with Limited Oversight: S.H.I.E.L.D. and the Role of Intelligence and Intervention in the Marvel Cinematic Universe," in *Assembling the Marvel Cinematic Universe: Essays on the Social, Cultural and Geopolitical Domains*, ed. Julian Chambliss et al. (Jefferson, NC: McFarland, 2018), 209, 210.

26. "USMC Television and Motion Picture Liaison Office Weekly Report," February 6, 2012, US Marine Corps Entertainment Liaison Office, February 2012, on file with the authors.

27. McSweeney, *Avengers Assemble*, 132.

28. When *Iron Man* went into production, it was affected by the 2007–2008 Hollywood writers' strike, leaving them without a completed script or an on-set writer to handle last-minute changes. This led to the actors improvising many lines during filming, which proved problematic for the DOD. In one scene where Rhodey tells his general he is going back to Afghanistan to search for Stark, the general responds, "Any one of these guys would kill for your career," referring to Rhodey's cushy position as a liaison to the weapons industry, and asks if he's willing to walk away from that to look for his friend. As the script developed and the actors improvised, the general's line became that people would "kill themselves for the opportunities [Rhodey] has," which led to an argument between Strub and Favreau. As Strub recalls it in a 2015 interview, "Now we're on the flight lines at Edwards Air Force Base (California), and there's 200 people, and [the director] and I are having an argument about this. He's getting redder and redder in the face and I'm getting just as annoyed. It was pretty awkward and then he said, angrily, 'Well how about 'they'd walk over hot coals?' I said 'fine.' He was so surprised it was that easy." Quoted in Quigley, "To Tap into the Military's Arsenal." In the end, this scene was cut from the final film, but this argument is merely one example of the long-term concern for the Pentagon's public affairs offices that is the portrayal of military mental illness and suicide. This has been a particular issue for the DOD since the Vietnam War, both in PR terms and in reality, as Vietnam veterans have the highest suicide rates of any group in the United States. As a result, the Pentagon rejected films like *Coming Home* (1978) and *Home of the Brave* (2006) due to their depiction of military mental illness and suicide; they deleted a military character's suicide from both *The Presidio* (1988) and an episode of

NCIS (2003–); and they toned down the depictions of PTSD in *Rules of Engagement* (2007–2013) and *Hawaii Five-0* (2010–), among many other similar script edits. It is another example of the "clean war" approach to military PR, and it seems even an ironic and metaphorical reference to military suicide such as the one in *Iron Man* is deemed unacceptable. In the deleted scene version on the *Iron Man* DVD, the general says, "Any one of these guys would walk through fire to have your career," reversing the "kill themselves" joke to emphasize just how tough the men of the US military really are.

29. Travis Langley, "Does *Iron Man 3*'s Hero Suffer Posttraumatic Stress Disorder?" *Psychology Today*, May 4, 2013, https://www.psychologytoday.com/us/blog/beyond-heroes-and-villains/201305/does-iron-man-3s-hero-suffer-posttraumatic-stress-disorder.

30. Andrea Letamendi, "'Iron Man 3': Does Tony Stark Have PTSD?" The Hollywood Reporter, May 10, 2013, https://www.hollywoodreporter.com/movies/movie-news/iron-man-3-does-tony-520868/.

31. "Unofficial Live Commentary."

32. Bruno, *Infinity Wars*, 40.

33. Zbigniew Brzezinski, "Terrorized by 'War on Terror,'" *Washington Post*, March 25, 2007, https://www.washingtonpost.com/wp-dyn/content/article/2007/03/23/AR2007032301613.html.

34. Michael Curley, "'Captain America: The Winter Soldier': A Black and White Morality in a Politically Grey Time," Pop Matters, April 16, 2019, https://www.popmatters.com/captain-america-the-winter-soldier-2633776064.html.

35. Owen Gleiberman, "Captain America: The Winter Soldier Movie," *Entertainment Weekly*, April 18, 2014, https://ew.com/article/2014/04/18/captain-america-winter-soldier-movie/.

36. Darren Franich, "The Real, Subversive Politics of 'Captain America: The Winter Soldier,'" *Entertainment Weekly*, April 6, 2014, https://ew.com/article/2014/04/06/captain-america-the-winter-soldier-hydra-shield-paranoia/.

37. Russo quoted in Asawin Suebsaeng, "'Captain America: The Winter Soldier' Is About Obama's Terror-Suspect Kill List, Say the Film's Directors," *Mother Jones*, April 4, 2014, https://www.motherjones.com/politics/2014/04/captain-america-winter-soldier-obama-kill-list-politics-drones-nsa/.

38. Russo quoted in Suebsaeng, "Captain America."

39. DOD Hollywood database entry on *Captain America: The Winter Soldier*, on file with the authors.

40. Peter Bergen, "Drone Wars: The Constitutional and Counterterrorism

Implications of Targeted Killing," testimony presented before the US Senate Committee on the Judiciary, Subcommittee on the Constitution, Civil Rights and Human Rights, April 23, 2013, 2, 4–5, 10, available at https://www.judiciary.senate.gov/imo/media/doc/04-23-13BergenTestimony.pdf.

41. Scott Shane, "The Lessons of Anwar Al-Awlaki," *New York Times Magazine*, August 27, 2015, https://www.nytimes.com/2015/08/30/magazine/the-lessons-of-anwar-al-awlaki.html.

42. Russo quoted in Suebsaeng, "Captain America."

43. Bruno, *Infinity Wars*, 17–18.

44. Matt Goldberg, "'Captain America: Civil War' Screenwriters Explain How This Is Not an 'Avengers' Movie," Collider, March 8, 2016, https://collider.com/captain-america-civil-war-screenwriters-interview/.

45. Nathan Bosma and Adam Barkman, "Iron Kant or Captain Kant," in Michaud and Watkins, *Iron Man vs. Captain America and Philosophy*, 152, 153.

46. Bosma and Barkman, 207.

47. William Wan, "'Iron Man 3' Is Latest Hollywood Movie to Court Chinese Censors," *Washington Post*, May 6, 2013, https://www.washingtonpost.com/world/asia_pacific/iron-man-takes-heroic-efforts-to-satisfy-chinas-state-censors/2013/05/06/62d11e08-b62e-11e2-92f3-f291801936b8_story.html.

48. Marlow Stern, "Bill Maher Blames Hollywood for Ruining America and Giving Us President Trump," Daily Beast, May 22, 2017, https://www.thedailybeast.com/bill-maher-how-hollywood-ruined-america-by-helping-deliver-president-trump.

49. Austin, "Age of (Super)Heroes?"

Chapter Three. "Hi. I'm from the Military. Space Is the Next Frontier"

1. All Latcham quotes are from Jeremy Latcham, phone interview with Tricia Jenkins, June 15, 2020.

2. Henry Lambright, *Why Mars: NASA and the Politics of Space Exploration* (Baltimore: Johns Hopkins University Press, 2014).

3. Howard McCurdy, "Fiction and Imagination: How They Affect Public Administration," *Public Administration Review* 55, no. 6 (1995): 502.

4. The other five are the US Army, Air Force, Marines, Navy, and Coast Guard.

5. NASA, "Mission Statement," last accessed April 15, 2020, https://govinfo.library.unt.edu/npr/library/status/mission/mnasa.htm.

6. *United States Space Force*, February 2019, https://media.defense.gov/2019/Mar/01/2002095012/-1/-1/1/UNITED-STATES-SPACE-FORCE-STRATEGIC-OVERVIEW.PDF.

7. Alex Hern, "Elon Musk: The Real-Life Iron Man," *Guardian*, February 8, 2018, https://www.theguardian.com/technology/2018/feb/09/elon-musk-the-real-life-iron-man.

8. All quotes from Bert Ulrich are from his phone interview with Tricia Jenkins on October 27, 2019.

9. NASA Multimedia Liaison Office annual summaries, 2006 to 2019, on file with the authors.

10. "NASA Space Act Agreement for *The Avengers*," Spy Culture, last accessed April 15, 2020, https://www.spyculture.com/nasa-production-agreement-avengers/.

11. Jenkins, "How the Central Intelligence Agency Works with Hollywood," 492.

12. Joss Whedon Director's Commentary, *Avengers*, DVD, dir. Joss Whedon (Burbank, CA: Buena Vista Home Entertainment, 2012).

13. Michael Sangiacomo, "Avengers Filming Wrapping Up at NASA Facility in Sandusky," *Cleveland Plain Dealer*, August 11, 2011, https://www.cleveland.com/avengers/2011/08/avengers_filming_wrapping_up_a.html.

14. "Plum Brook Station Goes Hollywood for Avengers Filming," NASA (website), May 23, 2012, https://www.nasa.gov/centers/glenn/technology/avengers.html.

15. This is a notable departure from the film's depiction of the Pentagon, which is shown as S.H.I.E.L.D.'s junior in *The Avengers* (see chapter 2).

16. Sangiacomo, "Avengers Filming Wrapping Up."

17. Dan Leone, "NASA IG Scrutinizes Seldom-Used Plum Brook Test Facilities," *Space News*, April 24, 2015, https://spacenews.com/nasa-ig-scrutinizes-seldom-used-plum-brook-test-facilities/.

18. Vivian Sobchack, "Sci-Why: On the Decline of a Film Genre in an Age of Technological Wizardry," *Science Fiction Studies* 41, no. 2 (2014): 293.

19. See, for instance, Tom Pollard, *Hollywood 9/11: Superheroes, Supervillains, and Super Disasters* (New York: Paradigm, 2011); Cathy Schlund-Vials, "Crisis of Memory: Memorializing 9/11 in the Comic Book Universe," *Modern Language Studies* 41, no. 1 (2011): 12–25.

20. Pamela McClintock, "Box Office Report: 'Avengers' Even Bigger with $207.4 Million Opening," *Hollywood Reporter*, May 7, 2012, https://www.hollywoodreporter.com/news/avengers-box-office-joss-whedon-320876.

21. "Marvel's 'The Avengers' to Screen for Crew of International Space Station," CBR (website), May 31, 2012, https://www.cbr.com/marvels-the-avengers-to-screen-for-crew-of-international-space-station/.

22. Robert Pearlman, "Groot & Rocket from 'Guardians of the Galaxy' Soar as Space Science Symbols," Space (website), May 5, 2017, https://www.space.com/36737-rocket-raccoon-groot-space-station-science.html.

23. "NASA Helps Marvel's Avengers Exhibit Bring the Science," NASA (website), June 3, 2014, https://www.jpl.nasa.gov/news/news.php?feature=4166.

24. Omari Daniels, "Marvel Studios Thanks NASA for Assistance in Helping Locate Tony Stark," Heroic Hollywood, December 20, 2018, https://heroichollywood.com/marvel-studios-nasa-avengers-tony-stark/.

25. In fact, Ulrich, who also works with merchandisers wishing to use the NASA logo on clothing, notes that before 2017, his office would get one or two requests for merchandising permissions per week. Then Coach, the high-end designer best known for its purses, decided to create a line of clothing and accessories that were NASA-related and employed the old 1970s worm logo that "caught the whole design industry by storm quite frankly," he stated. "And what became merchandising requests coming in once or twice a week, became multiple times a day to the point that we get like twenty requests a day now, and not only from mom-and-pop stores, but also major brands—higher-end brands, lower-end brands, Walmart, Target, Coach. And the logo is free. It's considered a public good so we don't license it out. There's no way to accept that money."

26. Jennifer Vineyard, "How to Reboot the Superman Movie Franchise—Comic Writers Chime In," MTV News, August 11, 2008, http://www.mtv.com/news/2592674/how-to-reboot-the-superman-movie-franchise-comic-writers-chime-in/.

27. Geoff Boucher, "Christopher Nolan Takes Flight with Superman: 'We Have a Fantastic Story,'" *Los Angeles Times*, March 10, 2010, https://tinderboxpictures.typepad.com/smallvilletalk/2010/03/christopher-nolan-takes-flight-with-superman-we-have-a-fantastic-story-updated-hero-complex-los-angeles-times-small.html.

28. Adam Chitwood, "'Man of Steel' Writer David S. Goyer Explains Why Superman Kills Zod, Reveals an Alternate Ending," Collider, July 25, 2020, https://collider.com/man-of-steel-ending-explained-why-superman-kills-zod-david-s-goyer/.

29. The producers of the original Superman films approached the Pentagon looking for missile launch footage to help depict Lex Luthor's dastardly

plot to nuke the San Andreas fault line and cause the US West Coast to fall into the ocean. The script shows Lex and his bumbling sidekick Otis stealing the nuclear warheads from a US military convey, who are utterly incompetent. They tried to convince the entertainment liaison office that such scenes were "intended to be humorous and in no way derogatory," but the Pentagon saw through that. While the air force was willing to consider limited support, Strategic Air Command refused point blank to provide any help, so Don Baruch referred the filmmakers to NASA to obtain film of rockets taking off. Thus, the original Superman films show the military as bumbling incompetents, but *Man of Steel* (after heavy rewrites) shows them to be noble, self-sacrificing, and protecting humans from a profound and grave threat. The originals are superhero movies where the military are mostly irrelevant, but *Man of Steel* is an alien invasion movie where Superman teams up with the military to stave off the threat.

30. Justin Change and Peter Debruge, "Does *Man of Steel* Exploit Disasters Like 9/11?" *Variety*, June 17, 2013, https://variety.com/2013/film/columns/does-man-of-steel-exploit-disasters-like-911-1200497860/.

31. "Studio A Interview with Phil Strub," George Mason University, YouTube, April 14, 2015, https://www.youtube.com/watch?v=SZAJiVf1U-E.

32. These script negotiations went on for months, with the army's entertainment liaison office reports first noting their involvement with the film in early February 2011, at which point the director of their LA office was "working with Warner Brothers Studios on shaping the U.S. Army portrayal in the upcoming 'Superman' feature film now in development." The army felt they would end up assisting on the film as it "Supports Building Resiliency." Nearly two months later, another army report says, "OCPA-LA and the USAF Office will review the script on 30 MAR 11 and recommend script revisions and alternative dialog [*sic*] for the military scenes." By the end of April, another update recorded reads, "OCPA-LA and the USAF Office reviewed the updated script 20 APR 11; writer incorporated many of the script changes requested by DOD." It took until August that year before they were "in the final phase of approving support" and had even helped scout locations in Plano, Illinois, where a major fight sequence would take place, with Plano doubling for Smallville—Clark Kent's childhood hometown.

33. "DOD Script Notes on Autumn Frost a.k.a. Man of Steel," May 27, 2011, on file with the authors.

34. "DOD Script Notes on Autumn Frost."

35. The FBI denied having any records of their input on *Man of Steel*, so it

appears the DOD made this change on their behalf, to protect the image of the FBI even though the bureau has its own entertainment liaison office to handle that. While it is unusual for the DOD to take on the role of policing images of the entire US government, this is not the first time they have done so. The Pentagon rejected *Attack of the Killer Tomatoes* because it mocked the president and the White House, insisted the makers of *Clear and Present Danger* alter the script so the president is not party to the evil conspiracy being run by his national security advisor, and insisted that a scene in *Air Force One* depicting an NSA listening post not include a corpulent, lazy-looking NSA technician.

36. "DOD Production Assistance Agreement for Autumn Frost a.k.a. Man of Steel," January 11, 2012, on file with the authors.

37. "US Air Force Entertainment Liaison Office Report, June 21, 2013," on file with the authors.

38. See Chang and Debruge, "Does *Man of Steel* Exploit Disasters?"; Kyle Buchanan, "Is It Possible to Make a Hollywood Blockbuster without Evoking 9/11?" Vulture, June 13, 2020, https://www.vulture.com/2013/06/hollywood-blockbusters-cant-stop-evoking-911.html.

39. Ryan Pumroy, "Recruiting Soldiers of Steel: The Cross-Promotion of *Man of Steel* and the National Guard," *Journal of Popular Culture* 48, no. 4 (2015): 762.

40. National Guard, "Soldier of Steel Theater Spot 1," YouTube, last accessed August 10, 2020, https://www.youtube.com/watch?v=agWOW5uy3TA.

41. Pumroy, "Recruiting Soldiers of Steel," 765, 766, 767.

42. Lisa Lambert, "Trump Directs Establishment of U.S. Force to Dominate Space," Reuters, June 18, 2018, https://www.reuters.com/article/us-space-moon-trump/trump-directs-establishment-of-u-s-force-to-dominate-space-idUSKBN1JE28D.

43. Luke Dormehi, "Space Force Needs to Prepare for a New Cold War in Earth's Orbit," Digital Trends, March 14, 2020, https://www.digitaltrends.com/cool-tech/space-force-cold-war-space-chris-bogdan/.

44. "US Air Force Entertainment Liaison Office File on the 2016 Entertainment Industry Leader Tour to Alaska," 2016, on file with the authors. This air force outreach effort helped the branch make important network connections, with one report from April 2017 citing the Alaska tour as a big success. The report argues that as a result of that tour, air force project officer Leslie Finstein "met with Tony Lund, Senior Creative Director of Ample Entertainment, 21 Apr, which currently has three documentary-style shows airing on TV. Mr Lund . . . stated the trip made him realize that ' . . . the Air Force cares

about storytellers' and he wants to schedule a meeting in the coming weeks to discuss Air Force storylines that PAYL is interested [in] highlighting." "US Air Force Entertainment Liaison Office Report," April 21, 2017, on file with the authors.

45. "US Air Force Entertainment Liaison Office Report," April 21, 2017.

46. "US Air Force Entertainment Liaison Office file on the 2017 Entertainment Industry Leader Tour to Space Command," 2017, on file with the authors.

47. Gen. John Hyten, "Space Mission Force: Developing Space Warfighters for Tomorrow," Air Force Space Command (website), June 29, 2016, https://www.afspc.af.mil/Portals/3/documents/White%20Paper%20-%20Space%20Mission%20Force/AFSPC%20SMF%20White%20Paper%20-%20FINAL%20-%20AFSPC%20CC%20Approved%20on%20June%2029.pdf?ver=2016-07-19-095254-887.

48. "President Donald J. Trump Is Building the United States Space Force for a 21st Century Military," Global Public Affairs, US Department of State (website), August 9, 2018, https://2017-2021-translations.state.gov/2018/08/09/president-donald-j-trump-is-building-the-united-states-space-force-for-a-21st-century-military/index.html.

49. "US Air Force Summary of Support to Captain Marvel," undated, on file with the authors.

50. Sonaiya Kelley, "Building 'Captain Marvel': How Brie Larson Trained to Be a Superhero," *Los Angeles Times*, January 10, 2019, https://www.latimes.com/entertainment/movies/la-ca-mn-captain-marvel-training-brie-larson-20190110-story.html.

51. James Barber, "How Brigadier General Jeannie Leavitt Inspired 'Captain Marvel,'" Military.com, June 11, 2019, https://www.military.com/daily-news/2019/06/11/how-brigadier-general-jeannie-leavitt-inspired-captain-marvel.html.

52. "Brie Larson Flew with the Air Force for Captain Marvel Training," *Entertainment Tonight*, available on YouTube, last accessed April 20, 2020, https://www.youtube.com/watch?v=QPAVd1W8Lm8.

53. "US Air Force Entertainment Liaison Office Report," August 3, 2018, on file with the authors.

54. "Department of Defense Entertainment Media Weekly," March 8, 2019, on file with authors.

55. "Red Carpet Interview with Brig Gen Jeannie Leavitt," YouTube, last accessed April 20, 2020, https://www.youtube.com/watch?v=YAi1E6kLR-k.

56. "Captain Marvel F-15 Flyover at the Disneyland Resort," YouTube, March 3, 2019, https://www.youtube.com/watch?v=osqXrVoup3M.

57. Jeremy Fuster, "Air Force's Use of 'Captain Marvel' to Recruit Women Ignores a Grim Record on Sexual Assault," The Wrap, March 8, 2019, https://www.thewrap.com/air-force-captain-marvel-recruit-women-sexual-assaults-martha-mcsally/.

58. "US Army Entertainment Liaison Office Report," February 22–28, 2012, on file with the authors.

59. Stephen Losey, "Captain Marvel Pays Tribute to Air Force History—and a Fallen Thunderbird," *Air Force Times*, March 5, 2019, https://www.airforcetimes.com/news/your-air-force/2019/03/05/captain-marvel-pays-tribute-to-air-force-history-and-a-fallen-thunderbird/.

60. Starr Bowenbank, "*Captain Marvel* Is the First Female Superhero Movie to Gross $1 Billion Worldwide," *Elle*, April 4, 2019, https://www.elle.com/culture/celebrities/a27041715/captain-marvel-one-billion-box-office-record/.

61. Oriana Pawlyk, "Captain Marvel Effect? Air Force Academy Sees Most Female Applicants in 5 Years," Military.com, January 5, 2020, https://www.military.com/daily-news/2020/01/05/captain-marvel-effect-air-force-academy-sees-most-female-applicants-5-years.html.

62. "US Air Force Biography of Jeannie Leavitt," US Air Force (website), last accessed April 20, 2020, https://www.af.mil/About-Us/Biographies/Display/Article/1952656/major-general-jeannie-m-leavitt/.

63. Sobchack, "Sci-Why," 285.

64. Geoff King, *Spectacular Narratives: Hollywood in the Age of the Blockbuster* (London: IB Tauris, 2000), 1–2.

65. Arthur Asa Berger, *Popular Culture Genres: Theories and Texts* (Thousand Oaks, CA: Sage, 1992), 139.

Chapter Four. You Can't Just Fall Off a Planet

1. Benjamin Radford, "Superhero Science," *Skeptical Inquirer* 31, no. 4 (July/August 2007): 35–36.

2. Radford, 36.

3. Jason Bainbridge, "You Were the World's First Superhero," in *Assembling the Marvel Cinematic Universe: Essays in the Social, Cultural and Geopolitical Domains*, ed. Julian Chambliss, William Svitavsky, and Daniel Fandino (Jefferson, NC: McFarland, 2018), 161.

4. Scott Frank, "Reel Reality: Science Consultants in Hollywood," *Science as Culture* 12, no. 4 (June 2010): 448.

5. Kirby, *Lab Coats*, 9.

6. All Latcham quotes are from his phone interview with Tricia Jenkins on June 15, 2020.

7. Kirby, *Lab Coats*, 9.

8. Frank, "Reel Reality," 430, 432.

9. Kevin Hand, phone interview with Tricia Jenkins, June 12, 2020.

10. Sean Carroll, phone interview with Tricia Jenkins, June 8, 2020. All Carroll quotations are from this interview.

11. Kirby, *Lab Coats*, 9.

12. Clifford Johnson, phone interview with Tricia Jenkins, July 24, 2020.

13. Kirby, *Lab Coats*, 9.

14. One can watch these at "The Science of Zero Matter—Marvel's Agent Carter," YouTube, February 4, 2016, https://www.youtube.com/watch?v=34ARvvZHHQw; "The Science of Intangibility—Marvel's Agent Carter," YouTube, February 2, 2016, https://www.youtube.com/watch?v=XNsKtYqz6oo.

15. This video can be watched at "Science of Watchmen," YouTube, February 24, 2009, https://www.youtube.com/watch?v=zmj1rpzDRZo.

16. Quoted in Kevin Grazier and Stephen Cass, *Hollyweird Science: The Next Generation, from Spaceships to Microchips* (New York: Springer Nature, 2017), vii.

17. According to its website, this interactive experience allows visitors "to delve into the history, science, engineering, genetics, technology and profiles of Captain America, Hulk, Thor and Iron Man" to assemble files on each character and "become a qualified member of the Avengers S.T.A.T.I.O.N."

18. Loverd et al., "Story of the Science and Entertainment Exchange," 1305.

19. Susan Carol Losh, "Stereotypes about Scientists over Time among US Adults: 1983 and 2001," *Public Understanding of Science* 19, no. 3 (2010): 373–374.

20. Christopher Frayling, *Mad, Bad and Dangerous? The Scientist and the Cinema* (London: Reaktion Books), 41.

21. Eva Flicker, "Between Brains and Breasts—Women Scientists in Fiction Film: On the Marginalization and Sexualization of Scientific Competence," *Public Understanding of Science* 12, no. 3 (2010): 309.

22. Losh, "Stereotypes about Scientists," 373–374.

23. J. Burris, "Testimony Offered to the Research Subcommittee of the Committee on Science of the US House of Representatives Hearing on 'Undergraduate Science, Math & Engineering Education: What's Working?,'" March

15, 2006, https://www.govinfo.gov/content/pkg/CHRG-109hhrg26481/html/CHRG-109hhrg26481.htm, and Bill and Melinda Gates Foundation, "High Schools for the New Millennium: Imagine the Possibilities," Gates Foundation, last accessed September 6, 2008, https://docs.gatesfoundation.org/Documents/edwhitepaper.pdf.

24. "The Science & Entertainment Exchange," YouTube, February 24, 2015, https://www.youtube.com/watch?v=1e1x4v1M8yI, last accessed July 2, 2020.

25. "Science & Entertainment Exchange."

26. Johnson, phone interview.

27. Johnson in Eric Kohn, "Meet the Physicist Who Is Changing Movie Science, from 'Avengers' to 'Palm Springs,'" IndieWire, July 9, 2020, https://www.indiewire.com/2020/07/movie-science-avengers-palm-springs-1234572211/.

28. "Hollywood's Newest Stars: Black Holes & More / Kevin Hickerson at Mindshare LA," YouTube, August 28, 2015, https://www.youtube.com/watch?v=lIFYpzPnnQI.

29. "Hollywood's Newest Stars."

30. Cassidy Ward, "Science Behind the Fiction: Making Thor's Infinity War Hammer with a Neutron Star," SYFY (website), May 1, 2018, https://www.syfy.com/syfywire/science-behind-the-fiction-making-thors-infinity-war-hammer-with-a-neutron-star.

31. For one example, see "How to Forge Thor's Infinity War Weapon," YouTube, May 10, 2018, https://www.youtube.com/watch?v=bOLOBJSJLoI&list=LLY9fGcfnSVGscOeh8XN1rQg&index=715.

32. William Svitavsky, "Your Ancestors Called It Magic," in Chambliss et al., *Assembling the Marvel Cinematic Universe*, 81.

33. M. F. Fox, "Organizational Environments and Doctoral Degrees Awarded to Women in Science and Engineering Departments," *Women's Studies Quarterly* 28 (Spring/Summer 2000): 47–61.

34. See, for example, Margaret Eisenhart and Elizabeth Finkel, *Women's Science: Learning and Succeeding from the Margins* (Chicago: University of Chicago Press, 1998); H. Etzkowitz et al., "Athena Unbound: Barriers to Women in Academic Science and Engineering," *Science and Public Policy* 19, no. 3 (1992): 157–179; Sandra Harding, *Whose Science? Whose Knowledge? Thinking from Women's Lives* (Ithaca, NY: Cornell University Press, 1991).

35. Jouhaneau quoted in Frayling, *Mad, Bad and Dangerous*, 41.

36. "Science & Entertainment Exchange."

37. Matthew Nisbet et al., "Knowledge, Reservations, or Promise? A Media

Effects Model for Public Perceptions of Science and Technology," *Communication Research* 29, no. 5 (October 2002): 586–587.

38. This scene was originally expanded, showing Thor and Selvig stumbling down the street singing native ballads before Selvig passes out from drunken excess. These sections did not make the final cut, however.

39. Kirby, *Lab Coats*, 73.

40. Todd McCarthy, "*Ant-Man*: Film Review," *Hollywood Reporter*, July 8, 2015, https://www.hollywoodreporter.com/review/ant-man-film-review-807018; Kenneth Turan, "Review: Marvel Comes Up Big with Playful 'Ant-Man,'" *Los Angeles Times*, July 15, 2015, https://www.latimes.com/entertainment/movies/la-et-mn-ant-man-review-20150716-column.html.

41. "Ant Man DVD Commentary with Director Peyton Reed and Scott Rudd," *Ant-Man*, DVD, dir. Peyton Reed (Burbank, CA: Buena Vista Home Entertainment, 2015).

42. "Honest Reactions: Ant-Man and the Wasp Director Reacts to Honest Trailers," YouTube, last accessed June 21, 2020, https://www.youtube.com/watch?v=x-GqbjzrKrU.

43. Rocco Gangle, "The Technological Subversion of Technology: Tony Stark, Heidegger, and the Subject of Resistance," in *Iron Man and Philosophy*, ed. Mark White (Hoboken, NJ: Wiley & Sons, 2010), 29.

44. Katy Macek, "Military Vets Museum Tank Makes Appearance in 'Ant-Man,'" *Oshkosh Northwestern*, July 20, 2015, https://www.thenorthwestern.com/story/entertainment/movies/2015/07/17/military-vets-museum-tank-makes-appearance-ant-man/30316613/.

45. David Kirby, "Science and Technology in Film: Themes and Representations," in *Routledge Handbook of Public Communication of Science and Technology*, 2nd ed., ed. M. Bucchi and B. Trench (New York: Routledge, 2014), 107.

46. Stephen Kutcher, Skype interview with Tom Secker, June 10, 2020. *Spider-Man* was made during the early days of CGI, so for the scene where Peter Parker is bitten by a genetically engineered spider, the filmmakers used a real arachnid. Kutcher used a process he developed during the production of *Arachnophobia*, which he dubbed "the Spider Olympics." Here, he started with a large number of spiders and tested them for various capabilities—running, climbing walls, walking across water, and other behaviors demanded by the script. After whittling it down to just a handful of insects, he "filmed them and sent the footage to Spielberg and the rest," and they chose the spiders that they felt had screen tested the best. When it came to the distinctive visual look of the starring spider, Kutcher initially suggested they dress it in costume, but

they settled on employing Jens Schnabel to paint it, though Kutcher was keen to emphasize that they used paints that would not harm the insect and that he "built a device to hold the spider still while it was being painted without hurting it." The biting scene takes place during a field trip to a laboratory by Parker's school class where a scientist explains the many different kinds of spiders, using information provided by Kutcher during the script's development. The scientist then goes on to outline how the lab combined the traits of several different kinds of spiders to produce fifteen genetically enhanced "super-spiders," one of whom escapes and bites Parker, giving him his superpowers. This scene was shot in the rotunda of the Los Angeles Natural History Museum, and because they only had the location for two days, the entire crew worked a forty-eight-hour shift. This culminated in Kutcher warning Maguire of the risk of the real spider biting him, which Maguire accepted, before Kutcher climbed a ladder and got the spider to web down onto the actor's hand. Kutcher contrasted this with the approach taken during the production of *Ant-Man*, where no real-life ants were used and every ant seen on screen was produced via CGI.

47. Spyridon Michalakis, "Ant-Man and the Quantum Realm," *Quantum Frontiers* (blog), last accessed June 23, 2020, https://quantumfrontiers.com/2015/07/20/ant-man-and-the-quantum-realm/.

48. "Honest Reactions."

49. Michalakis, "Ant-Man and the Quantum Realm."

50. Darryn King, "The Science (and the Scientists) behind 'Ant-Man,'" *New York Times*, July 6, 2018, https://www.nytimes.com/2018/07/06/movies/antman-and-the-wasp-science.html.

51. "DVD commentary with Peyton Reed," *Ant-Man and the Wasp*, DVD, directed by Peyton Reed (Burbank, CA: Buena Vista Home Entertainment, 2018).

52. King, "The Science (and the Scientists) Behind 'Ant-Man.'"

53. "DVD commentary with Peyton Reed."

54. Joan Haran, Mwenya Chimba, Grace Reid, and Jenny Kitzinger, *Screening Women in SET: How Women in Science, Engineering and Technology are Represented in Films and on Television*, UK Resource Centre for Women in Science, Engineering and Technology (UKRC) and Cardiff University, March 2008, https://orca.cf.ac.uk/17535/1/report_3_haran.pdf.

55. "Commentary for *Black Panther* with Ryan Coogler and Hannah Beachler," *Black Panther*, DVD, directed by Ryan Coogler (Burbank, CA: Buena Vista Home Entertainment, 2018).

56. Mindy Weisberger, "The Amazing Tech in 'Black Panther' Is More Re-

alistic Than You Think," Live Science, April 17, 2018, www.livescience.com/62327-black-panther-tech-realism.html.

57. James Ferguson, email interview with Tricia Jenkins, June 6, 2020.

58. All quotes from Daniel Bodony are from his Skype interview with Tom Secker on June 26, 2020.

59. "Commentary for *Black Panther*."

60. "Commentary for *Black Panther*."

61. Robyn Spencer, "Black Feminist Meditations on the Women of Wakanda," in *Black Panther: Paradigm Shift or Not? A Collection of Reviews and Essays on a Blockbuster Film*, ed. Haki Madhubuti and Herb Boyd (Chicago: Third World Press, 2019), 32.

62. "Commentary for *Black Panther*."

63. Michira, "Images of Africa in the Western Media," Semantic Scholar, December 23, 2002, https://www.semanticscholar.org/paper/Images-of-Africa-in-the-Western-Media-Michira/db2a1578b44d45b6bc81e5d1f601ab5ae3f9fb14.

64. Zaheer Baber, *The Science of Empire: Scientific Knowledge, Civilization, and Colonial Rule in India* (Albany: SUNY Press, 1996), 10.

65. "Wakandan Technology Today: A CIA Scientist Explores the Possibilities," CIA (website), August 1, 2018, https://www.cia.gov/news-information/featured-story-archive/2018-featured-story-archive/wakandan-technology-today-a-cia-scientist-explores-the-possibilities.html.

66. Clifford Johnson, "The Hidden Superpower of Black Panther: Scientist Role Models," The Conversation, last accessed July 15, 2020, https://theconversation.com/the-hidden-superpower-of-black-panther-scientist-role-models-91042

67. Sidney Perkowitz, *Hollywood Science: Movies, Science and the End of the World* (New York: Columbia University Press, 2007), 217.

68. Perkowitz, 219.

69. Ayana Elizabeth Johnson, "The Shuri Effect: A Generation of Black Scientists?" *Scientific American*, February 22, 2018, https://blogs.scientificamerican.com/voices/the-shuri-effect-a-generation-of-black-scientists/.

70. Film revenue data sourced from BoxOfficeMojo.com.

Chapter Five. All New, but Not That Different?

1. Allan Austin and Patrick Hamilton, *All New, All Different? A History of Race and the American Superhero* (Austin: University of Texas Press, 2019), 15, 17.

2. Austin and Hamilton, 17.

3. Adilifu Nama, *Super Black: American Pop Culture and Black Superheroes* (Austin: University of Texas Press, 2011), 3.

4. Allan and Hamilton, *All New, All Different?*, 306, 308.

5. Jennifer Stuller, *Ink-Stained Amazons and Cinematic Warriors: Superwomen in Modern Mythology* (London: IB Tauris, 2010), 2, 4, 141.

6. Kaysee Baker and Arthur Raney, "Equally Super? Gender-Role Stereotyping of Superheroes in Children's Animated Programs," *Mass Communication and Society* 10, no. 1 (Winter 2007): 25–41.

7. Carolyn Cocca, "The Broke Back Test: A Quantitative and Qualitative Analysis of Portrayals of Women in Mainstream Superhero Comics: 1993–2013," *Journal of Graphic Novels and Comics* 5, no. 4 (2014): 411–428.

8. "Heroes," Marvel Cinematic Universe Wiki, last accessed August 24, 2020, https://marvelcinematicuniverse.fandom.com/wiki/Category:Heroes.

9. Carolyn Cocca, *Superwomen: Gender, Power and Representation* (New York: Bloomsbury, 2016).

10. Stuller, *Ink-Stained Amazons*, 2.

11. Cocca, *Superwomen*, 3.

12. Rebecca Wanzo, *The Content of Our Caricature: African American Comic Art and Political Belonging* (New York: New York University Press, 2020), 208, 214.

13. Tim Hanley, *Wonder Woman Unbound: The Curious History of the World's Most Famous Heroine* (Chicago: Chicago Review Press, 2014), x.

14. Jill Lepore, *The Secret History of Wonder Woman* (New York: Knopf, 2014); Hanley, *Wonder Woman Unbound*; Noah Berlatsky, *Wonder Woman: Bondage and Feminism in the Marston/Peter Comics, 1941–1948* (New Brunswick, NJ: Rutgers University Press, 2015); Jacob Held, ed., *Wonder Woman and Philosophy: The Amazonian Mystique* (Hoboken, NJ: John Wiley & Sons, 2017).

15. Andrea Zanin, "Wonder Woman: A Feminist Faux Pas?" in Held, *Wonder Woman and Philosophy*, 66.

16. Hanley, *Wonder Woman Unbound*, x.

17. Zanin, "Wonder Woman," 68.

18. Jean Bethke Elshtain, *Women and War* (Chicago: University of Chicago Press, 1998), 3.

19. Melanie Johnson-Moxley, "Bound to Face the Truth: The Ethics of Using Wonder Woman's Lasso," in Held, *Wonder Woman and Philosophy*, 92. This preference for nonviolence can be seen when Trevor crashes his plane off the coast of Themyscira. When the Amazonians rescue him, they do not torture him or threaten him with weapons to find out his identity. Instead, they em-

ploy the Lasso of Truth to interrogate him. The lasso—which likely originated in the comics from the fact that Marston helped invent the polygraph—does not cause pain unless the subject begins to lie or fight the compulsion to tell the truth. Johnson-Moxley writes that "the Amazon's method of cross-examination" has always been "the more merciful alternative to, say, Batman's violent and terrifying techniques." And in general, Wonder Woman "exercises compassion during the process," treating the individual's secrets with care, even from those who wish her harm.

20. Frances Early, "The Female Just Warriors Reimagined," in *Athena's Daughters: Television's New Women Warriors*, ed. Frances Early and Kathleen Kennedy (Syracuse, NY: Syracuse University Press, 2003), 57.

21. Kyle Killian, "How *Wonder Woman* Is, and Is Not, a Feminist Superheroine Movie," *Journal of Feminist Family Therapy* 31, no. 1 (2018): 1–3.

22. Robert Gerwarth and Erez Manela, "Introduction," in *Empires at War, 1911–1923*, ed. Erez Manela (Oxford: Oxford University Press, 2013), 3, 5.

23. Ben Quinn, "The Muslims Who Fought for Britain in the First World War," *Guardian*, August 2, 2014, https://www.theguardian.com/world/2014/aug/02/muslim-soldiers-first-world-war.

24. "Native Americans," United States World War I Centennial Commission, undated, https://www.worldwar1centennial.org/index.php/edu-home/edu-topics/588-americans-at-war/4994-native-americans.html; Olivia Waxman, "'We Became Warriors Again': Why World War I Was a Surprisingly Pivotal Moment for American Indian History," *Time*, November 23, 2018, https://time.com/5459439/american-indians-wwi/.

25. Patrick Watt, "Manpower, Myth and Memory: Analyzing Scotland's Military Contribution to the Great War," *Journal of Scottish Historical Studies* 39, no. 1 (2019): 100.

26. Nigel Steel, "Could Bloody Somme Ever Be Classed a Success?" *Telegraph*, July 2, 2014, https://www.telegraph.co.uk/history/world-war-one/inside-first-world-war/part-eleven/10928684/was-battle-somme-success.html.

27. Christopher Duffy, *Through German Eyes: The British and the Somme 1916* (London: Wiedenfeld & Nicolson, 2007), 93.

28. Sarah Everts, "A Brief History of Chemical War," Science History Institute, May 11, 2015, https://www.sciencehistory.org/distillations/a-brief-history-of-chemical-war.

29. Delia Harrington, "Wonder Woman, Violence, and the Machinery of War," Den of Geek, June 13, 2017, https://www.denofgeek.com/movies/wonder-woman-violence-and-the-machinery-of-war/.

30. Christopher Capozzola, "The United States Empire," in Manela, *Empires at War*, 235; Gerwarth and Manela, "Introduction," 14.

31. Wilson quoted in Sidney Lens, *The Forging of the American Empire: From the Revolution to Vietnam: A History of US Imperialism* (London: Pluto Books, 2003), 195.

32. Capozzola, "United States Empire," 235.

33. Joss Whedon, "Draft Script for Wonder Woman," August 7, 2006, 45, available at https://indiegroundfilms.files.wordpress.com/2014/01/wonder-woman-aug7-07-joss-whedon.pdf.

34. Whedon, 113–114.

35. Another aspect of Whedon's script that also offered a more subversive vision than made it into the final film was its portrait of Diana's sexuality. As Eileen Donaldson writes, in the comics, Themyscira is partially based on the Greek island of Lesbos, and Robert Kanigher, the writer who followed Marston, gave her the catchphrase "Suffering Sappho!"—"an overt reference to the lesbian poet of ancient Greece." Writers such as Phil Jimenez and Greg Rucka have also written a fairly queered Wonder Woman, yet her hints of lesbianism are completely erased in Jenkins's film. In Whedon's script, Steve and Diana never go to bed together and don't even kiss until the final scenes of the movie, which provokes Steve to comment, "Your whole life on an island with only women, and you can kiss like that?" to which Diana responds, "It's an interesting story." Steve continues, "It can't possibly be as good as the one I'm making up right now," to which Diana quips, "Are you sure about that?" This kind of pointed reference to Diana's queer identity is entirely absent from the final film, where Diana's romance with Steve follows a far more heteronormative pattern. See Eileen Donaldson, "Femininjustice: Female Justice as Monstrous in *Wonder Woman*: The Hiketeia," *Extrapolation* 60, no. 2 (2019): 167.

36. UK Ministry of Defence, "Joint Services Publication 579: Policy and Processes for Non-News Media Projects Part 1," July 2015, on file with the authors.

37. "Initial Application to Film or Photograph at an MOD Location," December 8, 2015, on file with the authors.

38. The sequel, *Wonder Woman 84*, was granted permission to film at the American air museum at RAF Duxford.

39. Josh Eels, "Ryan Coogler: Why I Needed to Make Black Panther," *Rolling Stone*, February 26, 2018, www.rollingstone.com/movies/movie-features/ryan-coogler-why-i-needed-to-make-black-panther-203737/.

40. David Greene, "Director Ryan Coogler Says 'Black Panther' Brought Him Closer to His Roots," *Morning Edition*, NPR, February 15, 2018, www

.npr.org/2018/02/15/585702642/director-ryan-coogler-says-black-panther-brought-him-closer-to-his-roots.

41. Racked, "Black Panther's Symbolic African Costumes," YouTube, February 9, 2018, www.youtube.com/watch?v=sL23-DBtqHg.

42. Rebecca Wanzo, "And All Our Past Decades Have Seen Revolutions: The Long Decolonization of Black Panther," Black Scholar, February 19, 2018, www.theblackscholar.org/author/hanks/page/2/.

43. Osman Faruqi, "Why Michael B. Jordan's Killmonger Is the Real Hero of 'Black Panther,'" Junkee, February 19, 2019, junkee.com/black-panther-killmonger-hero/147096.

44. Nicole Gantt, "A Powerful Black Panther and a Subtle White Shadow," in *Black Panther: Paradigm Shift or Not?*, ed. Haki Madhubuti and Herb Boyd (Chicago: Third World Press, 2019), 173.

45. Thabiti Lewis and Don Matthews, "Black Panther—We Need a Hero," in Madhubuti and Boyd, *Black Panther*, 166.

46. Emily Todd VanDerWerff, "With Great Power Comes Great Uncertainty: Marvel's Slowly Evolving Politics," Vox. February 26, 2018, https://www.vox.com/culture/2018/2/26/17029572/black-panther-marvel-politics.

47. Stephen Thrasher, "There Is Much to Celebrate—and Much to Question about Marvel's *Black Panther*," *Esquire*, February 20, 2018, www.esquire.com/entertainment/movies/a18241993/black-panther-review-politics-killmonger/.

48. Faruqi, "Why Michael B. Jordan's Killmonger."

49. Lynn Stuart Parramore, "Why Does a White CIA Agent Play the Hero to Killmonger's

Villain in 'Black Panther'?" NBC News, March 11, 2018, www.nbcnews.com/think/opinion/why-does-white-cia-agent-play-hero-killmonger-s-villain-ncna855401.

50. K. Tutashinda, "Wakanda Is a Beautiful Image but We Do Not Need a New Kingdom," in Madhubuti and Boyd, *Black Panther*, 136.

51. Phillip Agee, "Introduction," in *Dirty Work 2: The CIA in Africa*, ed. Ellen Ray, William Schaap, Karl Van Meter, and Louis Wolf (London: Zed Press, 1980), i.

52. René Lemarchand, "The CIA in Africa: How Central? How Intelligent?" in Ray et al., *Dirty Work 2*, 16.

53. Agee, "Introduction," ii.

54. Stephen Weissman, "An Extraordinary Rendition," *Intelligence and National Security* 25, no. 2 (2010): 201; Herbert Weiss, "Inside the CIA: Congo in the 1980s," *African Studies Review* 51, no. 2 (2008): 143–145. According to Weiss-

man and Weiss, Lumumba faced significant problems only a few days after the Congo achieved national sovereignty, as Congolese troops mutinied, and its wealthiest province, Katanga, declared its independence through secession with Belgian backing. In order to restore order, Lumumba asked the United States to send three thousand troops, and when they refused, he appealed to the UN, which created a peacekeeping force for him. When a host of European nations publicly supported Katanga's succession, however, Lumumba then turned to the Soviets, who eventually provided transport planes to fly troops into Katanga in order to maintain Congolese unity. According to Weissman, because Lumumba courted Soviet help, the Eisenhower administration hastily labeled him as an anti-Western communist agent and ordered covert action to "get rid of him" through assassination if necessary, even though "the extent to which his regime was dependent on communist advice or support was certainly exaggerated" (201).

55. Weissman, "Extraordinary Rendition," 203. Under Mobutu, Kasavubu retained his position, but Lumumba was ousted, replaced by Joseph Ileo, who had also received CIA financing during his past election runs. The CIA then began to discuss Lumumba's assassination with its new Congolese collaborators, telling Ileo that Lumumba was equally "dangerous in opposition as in office" and encouraged them to kill the ousted leader, even pledging arms for the mission.

56. Weissman, 214.

57. While Devlin knew of the transfer several days in advance, he did not share the information with US officials until three days later, effectively foreclosing the possibility that "the State Department, which would be expected to be informed of this central political information, would intervene to try and save Lumumba." Weissman, 214.

58. Weiss, "Inside the CIA," 145.

59. Victoria Brittain, "They Had to Die: Assassination against Liberation," *Race and Class* 48, no. 1 (2006): 66.

60. McSweeney, *Avengers Assemble*, 104.

61. Brittain, "They Had to Die: Assassination against Liberation," 105.

62. Charles Blow, "My Very Own Captain America," *New York Times*, July 29, 2011, https://www.nytimes.com/2011/07/30/opinion/blow-my-very-own-captain-america.html.

63. McSweeney, *Avengers Assemble*, 101.

64. Ewuare Osayande, "Would-be Wakanda: The Black Panther and the Paradox of the Congo," in Madhubuti and Boyd, *Black Panther*, 178.

65. See chapter 1 of Jenkins, *CIA in Hollywood*.

66. This newer, kinder image may also reflect the Trump era and its reversal of the Left's relationship with the CIA. As Lynn Stuart Parramore astutely writes, "Since the Ronald Reagan era, Republicans have typically viewed the CIA as the movie treats agent Ross: the ultimate good guy. By contrast, many Democrats have often been far more skeptical. In the Trump era, however, these positions have been essentially reversed. Conflicts between the president and the national security apparatus appear to have encouraged many Democrats' friendlier stance toward the agency. If there's a new stage in the rapprochement between Hollywood, American liberals, and the national security state, Agent Ross's leap from an inept comic book character to an adroit film persona may capture it." Parramore, "Why Does a White CIA Agent."

67. Tony Shaw and Tricia Jenkins, "From Zero to Hero: The CIA and Hollywood Today," *Cinema Journal* 56 (Winter 2017): 91–113.

68. "The Grill: 7 of Hollywood's Most Powerful Studio Executives Struggle to Find Theater-Worthy Films," YouTube, October 9, 2014, https://www.youtube.com/watch?v=jBi9NdsMYTY.

69. "Studio Executives Roundtable: Netflix, Warner Bros., Universal, Paramount, Disney, Amazon," YouTube, February 17, 2020, https://www.youtube.com/watch?v=BC6JHRb5Inc.

70. Cedric Clark, "Television and Social Controls: Some Observation of the Portrayal of Ethnic Minorities," *Television Quarterly* 8, no. 2 (1969): 21.

71. Wanzo, *Content of Our Caricature*, 211.

72. Gerry Canavan, "The Limits of Black Panther's Afro-futurism," Frieze, February 27, 2018, https://frieze.com/article/limits-black-panthers-afrofuturism.

Conclusion. The American Way, *The Boys*, and the Wrong Message?

1. Jeffrey Johnson, *Super-History: Comic Book Superheroes and American Society, 1938 to the Present* (Jefferson, NC: McFarland, 2012), 2.

2. Julian Chambliss, William Svitavsky, and Thomas Donaldson, "Introduction," in *Ages of Heroes, Eras of Men: Superheroes and the American Experience*, ed. Julian C. Chambliss, William Svitavsky, and Thomas Donaldson (Newcastle upon Tyne: Cambridge Scholars, 2013), 3.

3. Elisabeth Anker, *Orgies of Feeling: Melodrama and the Politics of Freedom* (Durham, NC: Duke University Press, 2014), 31.

4. Sonia Shechet Epstein, "The Science Advisor behind Netflix's *Away*," Sloan Science and Film, September 17, 2020, http://www.scienceandfilm.org/articles/3342/the-science-advisor-behind-netflixs-away.

5. NCAS Video, "The Science and Entertainment Exchange (Ann Merchant)," YouTube, March 30, 2012, https://www.youtube.com/watch?v=klk-j8svULw.

6. "Metacarta Secures Funding from In-Q-Tel," In-Q-Tel (website), October 16, 2002, https://www.iqt.org/news/metacarta-secures-funding-from-in-q-tel/; Kimberly Gill and Rob Painter, "ESRI, Pairing GIS with Cutting-Edge, Non-Geospatial Technologies for Richer Solutions," ESRI (website), last accessed July 7, 2020, https://proceedings.esri.com/library/userconf/proc05/abstracts/a2485.html; Jason Moll, "Tool Proves Value of NGA, In-Q-Tel Relationship," *National Geospatial Intelligence Agency's Pathfinder Magazine* 2, no. 1 (Spring 2013): 7.

7. Todd Gilchrist, "Co-Writers Markus & McFeely: *Winter Soldier* Will 'Punch You in the Face,'" CBR (website), March 6, 2014, https://www.cbr.com/co-writers-markus-mcfeely-winter-soldier-will-punch-you-in-the-face/.

8. Chambliss et al., "Introduction," 3.

9. Lee Miller and Wei Lu, "These Are the World's Healthiest Nations," Bloomberg, February 24, 2019, https://www.bloomberg.com/news/articles/2019-02-24/spain-tops-italy-as-world-s-healthiest-nation-while-u-s-slips.

10. Central Intelligence Agency, "The World Factbook: Life Expectancy at Birth," CIA (website), last accessed October 21, 2020, https://www.cia.gov/library/publications/the-world-factbook/rankorder/2102rank.html.

11. Central Intelligence Agency, "The World Factbook: Infant Mortality Rate," CIA (website), last accessed October 21, 2020, https://www.cia.gov/library/publications/the-world-factbook/rankorder/2091rank.html.

12. Environmental Performance Index, "Results Overview," Yale Center for Environmental Law and Policy, last accessed September 22, 2020, https://epi.yale.edu/epi-results/2020/component/epi.

13. Grant Suneson, "These Are the 25 Richest Nations in the World," *USA Today*, July 8, 2019, https://www.usatoday.com/story/money/2019/07/07/richest-countries-in-the-world/39630693/.

14. Abigail Hess, "The 10 Most Educated Countries in the World," CNBC, August 30, 2018, https://www.cnbc.com/2018/08/30/the-10-most-educated-countries-in-the-world.html.

15. Nan Tian et al., *Trends in World Military Expenditure, 2019*, Stockholm International Peace Research Institute, April 2020, https://www.sipri.org/sites/default/files/2020-04/fs_2020_04_milex_0_0.pdf.

16. Takacs, "Exceptional Soldiers," 97–98.

17. Mark Bowden, "Why Are We Obsessed with Superhero Movies?" *New York Times*, July 6, 2018, https://www.nytimes.com/2018/07/06/opinion/sunday/ant-man-wasp-movies-superheroes.html.

18. Ennis is known for being an anti-superhero comic book writer, whose versions of the Punisher and Judge Dredd are incompetent or dangerous. "I find most superhero stories completely meaningless," Ennis once explained. "So long as the industry is geared towards fulfilling audience demand—i.e., for the same brightly colored characters doing the same thing forever—you're never going to see any real growth. The stories can't end, so they'll never mean anything." This disdain for the superhero genre and desire to subvert it led Ennis to write a one-shot special in 1995 titled "Punisher Kills the Marvel Universe," where the Punisher kills every superhero and supervillain on earth, after which he went on to write *The Boys*. See Dave, "TV Review: *The Boys* Might be Amazon's Best Series to Date," Pop Culturalist, August 4, 2020, http://pop-culturalist.com/tv-review-the-boys-might-be-amazons-best-series-to-date/.

19. Amazon Prime Video, "*The Boys* Season 2 Cast at SDCC 2020—Full Panel," YouTube, July 24, 2020, https://www.youtube.com/watch?v=RGDGfJQMfP8.

20. Seth Abramovitch, "'We're Living in the Dumbest Dystopia': 'The Boys' Boss on His Superhero Hit," *Hollywood Reporter*, October 15, 2020, https://www.hollywoodreporter.com/live-feed/superheroes-are-inherently-maga-the-boys-boss-on-his-zeitgeisty-hit.

21. Nina Metz, "The Boys," *Chicago Tribune*, October 23, 2020, https://www.timeswv.com/news/marion_times/the-boys/article_4322ee70-1575-11eb-a8fc-3fcb6fc637e0.html.

22. Amazon Prime Video, "*The Boys* Season 2 Cast."

23. The Wrap, "Virtual Screening | THE BOYS presented by Amazon," YouTube, July 8, 2020, https://www.youtube.com/watch?v=4aDYM2OjMR4.

24. See, for instance, Adam Gabbatt, "Trump's Refusal to Condemn White Supremacy Fits Pattern of Extremist Rhetoric," *Guardian*, September 30, 2020, https://www.theguardian.com/us-news/2020/sep/30/trump-white-supremacy-extremist-rhetoric; John Haltiwanger, "Trump Is Increasingly Relying on White-Supremacist Ploys to Fire Up His Base as He Panics Over His Reelection Chances," *Business Insider*, June 23, 2020, https://www.businessinsider.com/trump-turning-to-white-supremacist-rhetoric-amid-panic-over-reelection-2020-6; Fabiola Cineas, "Donald Trump Is the Accelerant," Vox, October 9, 2020, https://www.vox.com/21506029/trump-violence-tweets-racist-hate-speech.

25. "'The Boys' Character Deep Dive: Cast Breaks Down the Seven, the Boys, and More," YouTube, August 17, 2020, https://www.youtube.com/watch?v=xyh6G8sAoyg.

26. Meghan Roos, "White Supremacists Killed More Americans than Muslim Extremists in Recent Years, Terrorism Report Shows," *Newsweek*, July 10, 2020, https://www.newsweek.com/white-supremacists-killed-more-americans-muslim-extremists-recent-years-terrorism-report-shows-1517096.

27. Betsy Woodruff Swan, "DHS Draft Document: White Supremacists Are Greatest Terror Threat," Politico, September 4, 2020, https://www.politico.com/news/2020/09/04/white-supremacists-terror-threat-dhs-409236.

28. Prime Rewind: Inside *The Boys*, "Inside the Diabolical First Season," Amazon, August 28, 2020, https://www.amazon.com/gp/video/detail/amzn1.dv.gti.82b9f5a4-f4d3-b2de-e776-bebaabd9b3b7?ref.

29. DesdeHollywood, "'THE BOYS' Eric Kripke: DC & Marvel Are Teaching the Wrong Lesson," YouTube, August 30, 2020, https://www.youtube.com/watch?v=lGeauvtXeYo.

30. Cooper Hood, "*The Boys* Is One of Amazon's Most-Watched Shows of 2019," Screen Rant, August 8, 2019, https://screenrant.com/boys-tv-show-amazon-most-watched-ever/.

31. Naratan Liu, "*The Boys* Showrunner Responds to Season 2 Review-Bombing," CBR (website), September 12, 2020, https://www.cbr.com/the-boys-showrunner-season-2-release-creative-choice/; Nellie Andreeva, "'The Boys' Spinoff Put on Fast-Track Development at Amazon Following Mothership's Record Season 2 Launch," Deadline, September 24, 2020, https://deadline.com/2020/09/the-boys-spinoff-fast-track-development-amazon-record-season-2-launch-ratings-1234584256/.

32. "*The Boys* Season 2: Showrunner Eric Kripke Reveals Tons of Cool NEW Info," YouTube, July 7, 2020, https://www.youtube.com/watch?v=q_dCPjPJXAA.

33. "Department of Defense Entertainment Media Weekly," March 15, 2019, on file with the authors.

SELECTED BIBLIOGRAPHY

This bibliography includes books, journal articles, and scholarly web articles referenced in the chapters. All websites, newspaper articles, archival documents, emails, and interviews appear in the notes only.

Agee, Phillip. "Introduction." In Ray et al., *Dirty Work 2*, i–ix.

Alford, Matthew. "The Political Impact of the Department of Defense on Hollywood Cinema." *Quarterly Review of Film and Video* 33, no. 4 (2016): 332–347.

———. *Reel Power: Hollywood Cinema and American Supremacy*. New York: Pluto Press, 2010.

Alford, Matthew, and Tom Secker. *National Security Cinema*. N.p.: Drum Roll Books, 2017.

Anker, Elisabeth. *Orgies of Feeling: Melodrama and the Politics of Freedom*. Durham, NC: Duke University Press, 2014.

Austin, Allan, and Patrick Hamilton. *All New, All Different? A History of Race and the American Superhero*. Austin: University of Texas Press, 2019.

Baber, Zaheer. *The Science of Empire: Scientific Knowledge, Civilization, and Colonial Rule in India*. Albany: SUNY Press, 1996.

Bainbridge, Jason. "You Were the World's First Superhero." In Chambliss et al., *Assembling the Marvel Cinematic Universe*, 150–167.

Baker, Kaysee, and Arthur Raney. "Equally Super?: Gender-Role Stereotyping of Superheroes in Children's Animated Programs." *Mass Communication and Society* 10, no. 1 (Winter 2007): 25–41.

Beckett, Jennifer. "Acting with Limited Oversight: S.H.I.E.L.D. and the Role of Intelligence and Intervention in the Marvel Cinematic Universe." In Chambliss et al., *Assembling the Marvel Cinematic Universe*, 203–217.

Berger, Arthur Asa. *Popular Culture Genres: Theories and Texts*. Thousand Oaks, CA: Sage, 1992.

Berlatsky, Noah. *Wonder Woman: Bondage and Feminism in the Marston/Peter Comics, 1941–1948*. New Brunswick, NJ: Rutgers University Press, 2015.

Bosma, Nathan, and Adam Barkman. "Iron Kant or Captain Kant." In Michaud and Watkins, *Iron Man vs. Captain America and Philosophy*, 145–154.

Brittain, Victoria. "They Had to Die: Assassination against Liberation." *Race and Class* 48, no. 1 (2006): 60–74.

Bruno, Peter. *Infinity Wars: Post 9/11 Superhero Films and American Empire*. Master's thesis, City University of New York, 2019.

Burke, Liam. "'A Bigger Universe': Marvel Studios and Transmedia Storytelling." In Chambliss et al., *Assembling the Marvel Cinematic Universe*, 32–51.

Burris, J. "Testimony Offered to the Research Subcommittee of the Committee on Science of the US House of Representatives Hearing on 'Undergraduate Science, Math & Engineering Education: What's Working?'" March 15, 2006. https://www.govinfo.gov/content/pkg/CHRG-109hhrg26481/html/CHRG-109hhrg26481.htm.

Capozzola, Christopher. "The United States Empire." In Manela, *Empires at War*, 235–253.

Chambliss, Julian, William Svitavsky, and Thomas Donaldson. "Introduction." In *Ages of Heroes, Eras of Men: Superheroes and the American Experience*, edited by Julian Chambliss, William Svitavsky, and Thomas Donaldson, 1–6. Newcastle upon Tyne: Cambridge Scholars, 2013.

Chambliss, Julian, William Svitavsky, and Daniel Fandino, eds. *Assembling the Marvel Cinematic Universe: Essays in the Social, Cultural and Geopolitical Domains.* Jefferson, NC: McFarland, 2018.

Chapman, James. *License to Thrill: A Cultural History of the James Bond Films.* New York: Columbia University Press, 1999.

Clark, Cedric. "Television and Social Controls: Some Observation of the Portrayal of Ethnic Minorities." *Television Quarterly* 8, no. 2 (1969): 18–22.

Cocca, Carolyn. "The Broke Back Test: A Quantitative and Qualitative Analysis of Portrayals of Women in Mainstream Superhero Comics: 1993–2013." *Journal of Graphic Novels and Comics* 5, no. 4 (2014): 411–428.

———. *Superwomen: Gender, Power and Representation.* New York: Bloomsbury, 2016.

Di Paolo, Marc. *War, Politics, and Superheroes: Ethics and Propaganda in Comics and Film.* Jefferson, NC: McFarland, 2011.

Donaldson, Eileen. "Femininjustice: Female Justice as Monstrous in Wonder Woman: The Hiketeia." *Extrapolation* 60, no. 2 (2019): 157–182.

Donovan, Josephine. *Feminist Theory: The Intellectual Traditions.* New York: Continuum, 2000.

Duffy, Christopher. *Through German Eyes: The British and the Somme 1916.* London: Wiedenfeld & Nicolson, 2007.

Early, Frances. "The Female Just Warrior Reimagined: From Boudicca to Buffy." In *Athena's Daughters: Television's New Women Warriors*, edited by Frances Early and Kathleen Kennedy, 55–65. Syracuse, NY: Syracuse University Press, 2003.

Eberwein, Robert. *The Hollywood War Film.* New York: Wiley-Blackwell, 2010.

Eisenhart, Margaret, and Elizabeth Finkel. *Women's Science: Learning and Succeeding from the Margins*. Chicago: University of Chicago Press, 1998.

Elshtain, Jean Bethke. *Women and War*. Chicago: University of Chicago Press, 1998.

Etzkowitz, Henry, Carol Kemelgor, Michael Neuschatz, and Brian Uzzi. "Athena Unbound: Barriers to Women in Academic Science and Engineering." *Science and Public Policy* 19, no. 3 (1992): 157–179.

Ewing, Jeffrey. "The Superhero Challenge to State Sovereignty." In Michaud and Watkins, *Iron Man vs. Captain America and Philosophy*, 197–208.

Flicker, Eva. "Between Brains and Breasts—Women Scientists in Fiction Film: On the Marginalization and Sexualization of Scientific Competence." *Public Understanding of Science* 12, no. 3 (2003): 307–318.

Fox, M. F. "Organizational Environments and Doctoral Degrees Awarded to Women in Science and Engineering Departments." *Women's Studies Quarterly* 28 (Spring/Summer 2000): 47–61.

Frank, Scott. "Reel Reality: Science Consultants in Hollywood." *Science as Culture* 12, no. 4 (June 2010): 427–469.

Frayling, Christopher. *Mad, Bad and Dangerous? The Scientist and the Cinema*. London: Reaktion Books, 2004.

Gangle, Rocco. "The Technological Subversion of Technology: Tony Stark, Heidegger, and the Subject of Resistance." In White, *Iron Man and Philosophy*, 25–37.

Gantt, Nicole Mitchell. "A Powerful Black Panther and a Subtle White Shadow." In Madhubuti and Boyd, *Black Panther*, 172–177.

Genter, Robert. "'With Great Power Comes Great Responsibility': Cold War Culture and the Birth of Marvel Comics." *Journal of Popular Culture* 40, no. 6 (2007): 953–978.

Gerwarth, Robert, and Erez Manela. "Introduction." In Manela, *Empires at War*, 1–16.

Grazier, Kevin, and Stephen Cass. *Hollyweird Science: The Next Generation, from Spaceships to Microchips*. New York: Springer Nature, 2017.

Gruenewald, Tim. "Superhero Films after 9/11: Mitigating Collateral Damage in the Marvel Cinematic Universe." In Laderman and Gruenewald, *Imperial Benevolence*, 141–167.

Hanley, Tim. *Wonder Woman Unbound: The Curious History of the World's Most Famous Heroine*. Chicago: Chicago Review Press, 2014.

Haran, Joan, Mwenya Chimba, Grace Reid, and Jenny Kitzinger. *Screening Women in SET: How Women in Science, Engineering and Technology Are Represented in Films and on Television*. UK Resource Centre for Women in Science, Engineering and Technology (UKRC) and Cardiff University, March 2008. https://orca.cf.ac.uk/17535/1/report_3_haran.pdf.

Harding, Sandra. *Whose Science? Whose Knowledge? Thinking from Women's Lives*. Ithaca, NY: Cornell University Press, 1991.

Held, Jacob, ed. *Wonder Woman and Philosophy: The Amazonian Mystique*. Hoboken, NJ: John Wiley & Sons, 2017.

Jenkins, Tricia. *The CIA in Hollywood: How the Agency Shapes Film and Television*. Austin: University of Texas Press, 2016.

———. "How the Central Intelligence Agency Works with Hollywood: An Interview with Paul Barry, the CIA's New Entertainment Industry Liaison." *Media Culture and Society* 31, no. 3 (2009): 489–495.

———. "Remembering the American Experience in Vietnam: A Look at the Film Industry's Relationship to the Department of Defense." *Journal of American Culture* 42, no. 2 (2019): 99–111.

Johnson, Jeffrey. *Super-History: Comic Book Superheroes and American Society, 1938 to the Present*. Jefferson, NC: McFarland, 2012.

Johnson-Moxley, Melanie. "Bound to Face the Truth: The Ethics of Using Wonder Woman's Lasso." In Held, *Wonder Woman and Philosophy*, 93–103.

Killian, Kyle. "How Wonder Woman Is, and Is Not, a Feminist Superheroine Movie." *Journal of Feminist Family Therapy* 31, no. 1 (2018): 1–3.

King, Geoff. *Spectacular Narratives: Hollywood in the Age of the Blockbuster*. London: IB Tauris, 2000.

Kirby, David. *Lab Coats in Hollywood: Science, Scientists and Cinema*. Cambridge, MA: MIT Press, 2011.

———. "Science and Technology in Film: Themes and Representations." In *Routledge Handbook of Public Communication of Science and Technology*, 2nd ed., edited by M. Bucchi and B. Trench, 97–112. New York: Routledge, 2014.

Laderman, Scott, and Tim Gruenewald, eds. *Imperial Benevolence: U.S. Foreign Policy and American Popular Culture since 9/11*. Los Angeles: University of California Press, 2018.

Lambright, Henry. *Why Mars: NASA and the Politics of Space Exploration*. Baltimore: Johns Hopkins University Press, 2014.

Lawrence, John Shelton, and Robert Jewett. *The Myth of the American Superhero*. Grand Rapids, MI: Wm. B. Eerdmans, 2002.

Lemarchand, Rene. "The CIA in Africa: How Central? How Intelligent?" In Ray et al., *Dirty Work 2*, 9–23.

Lens, Sidney. *The Forging of the American Empire: From the Revolution to Vietnam: A History of U.S. Imperialism*. London: Pluto Press, 2003.

Lepore, Jill. *The Secret History of Wonder Woman*. New York: Knopf, 2014.

Lewis, Thabiti, and Don Matthews. "Black Panther—We Need a Hero." In Madhubuti and Boyd, *Black Panther*, 166–168.

Losh, Susan Carol. "Stereotypes about Scientists over Time among US Adults: 1983 and 2001." *Public Understanding of Science* 19, no. 3 (2010): 372–382.

Loverd, Rick, Sara ElShafie, Ann Merchant, and C. Sachi Gerbin. "The Story of the Science and Entertainment Exchange, a Program of the National Academy of Sciences." *Integrative and Comparative Biology* 58, no. 6 (2018): 1304–1311.

Madhubuti, Haki, and Herb Boyd, eds. *Black Panther: Paradigm Shift or Not? A Collection of Reviews and Essays on a Blockbuster Film*. Chicago: Third World Press, 2019.

Maguire, Lori. "The American Military in *The Incredible Hulk* in the Vietnam War." In *The Ages of the Incredible Hulk: Essays on the Green Goliath in Changing Times*, edited by Joseph Darowski, 49–61. Jefferson, NC: McFarland, 2016.

Malloy, Daniel. "™ and © Stark Industries: Iron Man and Property Rights." In White, *Iron Man and Philosophy*, 115–128.

Manela, Erez, ed. *Empires at War, 1911–1923*. Oxford: Oxford University Press, 2013.

McCurdy, Howard. "Fiction and Imagination: How They Affect Public Administration." *Public Administration Review* 55, no. 6 (1995): 499–506.

McEniry, Matthew, Robert Moses Peaslee, and Robert Wiener. "Introduction." In *Marvel Comics into Film: Essays on Adaptations since the 1940s*, edited by Matthew McEniry, Robert Moses Peaslee, and Robert Wiener, 1–9. Jefferson, NC: McFarland, 2016.

McSweeney, Terence. *Avengers Assemble: Critical Perspectives on the Marvel Cinematic Universe*. New York: Wallflower Press, 2018.

Michaud, Nicolas, and Jessica Watkins, eds. *Iron Man vs. Captain America and Philosophy*. Chicago: Open Court Publishing, 2018.

Michira, James. "Images of Africa in the Western Media." Semantic Scholar, December 23, 2002. https://www.semanticscholar.org/paper/Images-of-Africa-in-the-Western-Media-Michira/db2a1578b44d45b6bc81e5d1f601ab5ae3f9fb14.

Mirrlees, Tanner. "The Economics, Geopolitics and Ideology of an Imperial Film Commodity." *Cineaction* 92 (2014): 4–11.

———. *Hearts and Mines: The U.S. Empire's Culture Industry*. Vancouver: UBC Press, 2016.

Moll, Jason. "Tool Proves Value of NGA, In-Q-Tel Relationship." *National Geospatial Intelligence Agency's Pathfinder Magazine* 2, no. 1 (Spring 2013): 3.

Nama, Adilifu. *Super Black: American Pop Culture and Black Superheroes*. Austin: University of Texas Press, 2011.

Nisbet, Matthew, Dietram Scheufele, James Shanahan, Patricia Moy, Dominique Brossard, and Bruce V. Lewenstein. "Knowledge, Reservations, or Promise? A Media Effects Model for Public Perceptions of Science and Technology." *Communication Research* 29, no. 5 (October 2002): 584–608.

Osayande, Ewuare. "Would-be Wakanda: The Black Panther and the Paradox of the Congo." In Madhubuti and Boyd, *Black Panther*, 178–182.

Partridge, Des. "Hardcore Hero." *Daily Telegraph* (Australia), May 1, 2008, 43.

Pautz, Michelle. "*Argo* and *Zero Dark Thirty*: Film, Government, and Audiences." *PS: Political Science and Politics* 48, no. 1 (2015): 120–128.

Pease, Donald. *The New American Exceptionalism*. Minneapolis: University of Minnesota Press, 2009.

Perkowitz, Sidney. *Hollywood Science: Movies, Science and the End of the World*. New York: Columbia University Press, 2007.

Pollard, Tom. *Hollywood 9/11: Superheroes, Supervillains, and Super Disasters*. New York: Paradigm, 2011.

Pumroy, Ryan. "Recruiting Soldiers of Steel: The Cross-Promotion of *Man of Steel* and the National Guard." *Journal of Popular Culture* 48, no. 4 (2015): 762–775.

Radford, Benjamin. "Superhero Science." *Skeptical Inquirer* 31, no. 4 (July/August 2007): 35–36.

Ray, Ellen, William Schaap, Karl Van Meter, and Louis Wolf, eds. *Dirty Work 2: The CIA in Africa*. London: Zed Press, 1980.

Robb, David. *Operation Hollywood: How the Pentagon Shapes and Censors the Movies*. Amherst, NY: Prometheus Books, 2004.

Schechter, Dan, Michael Ansara, and David Kolodney. "The CIA as an Equal Opportunity Employer." In Ray et al., *Dirty Work 2*, 49–69.

Schlund-Vials, Cathy. "Crisis of Memory: Memorializing 9/11 in the Comic Book Universe." *Modern Language Studies* 41, no. 1 (2011): 12–25.

Shaw, Tony, and Tricia Jenkins. "From Zero to Hero: The CIA and Hollywood Today." *Cinema Journal* 56 (Winter 2017): 91–113.

Smeulers, Alette, and Sander van Niekerk. "Abu Ghraib and the War on Terror: A Case against Donald Rumsfeld?" *Crime, Law and Social Change* 51, no. 3 (2009): 327–349.

Smith, Philip, and Michael Goodrum. "We Have Experienced a Tragedy Which Words Cannot Properly Describe: Representations of Trauma in Post-9/11 Superhero Comics." *Literature Compass* 8, no. 8 (2011): 487–498.

Sobchack, Vivian. "Sci-Why: On the Decline of a Film Genre in an Age of Technological Wizardry." *Science Fiction Studies* 41, no. 2 (2014): 284–300.

Spanakos, Anthony Peter. "Exceptional Recognition: The US Global Dilemma in *The Incredible Hulk*, *Iron Man*, and *Avatar*." In *The 21st Century Superhero: Essays on Gender, Genre and Globalization*, edited by Richard Gray II and Betty Kaklamanidou, 15–28. Jefferson, NC: McFarland, 2011.

Spencer, Robyn. "Black Feminist Meditations on the Women of Wakanda." In Madhubuti and Boyd, *Black Panther*, 30–33.

Stahl, Roger. *Militainment, Inc.: War, Media and Popular Culture*. New York: Routledge, 2009.

Stuller, Jennifer. *Ink-Stained Amazons and Cinematic Warriors: Superwomen in Modern Mythology*. London: IB Tauris, 2010.

Svitavsky, William. "Your Ancestors Called It Magic: Building Coherence in the MCU with Continuity in the Past." In Chambliss et al., *Assembling the Marvel Cinematic Universe*, 76–88.

Takacs, Stacy. "Exceptional Soldiers: Imagining the Privatized Military on U.S. Television." In Laderman and Gruenewald, *Imperial Benevolence*, 97–116.

Tasker, Yvonne. *The Hollywood Action Adventure Film*. New York: Wiley-Blackwell, 2015.

Turse, Nick. *The Complex: How the Military Invades Our Everyday Lives*. New York: Metropolitan Books, 2008.

Tutashinda, K. "Wakanda Is a Beautiful Image but We Do Not Need a Kingdom." In Madhubuti and Boyd, *Black Panther*, 135–141.

Wanzo, Rebecca. "And All Our Past Decades Have Seen Revolutions: The Long Decolonization of *Black Panther*." Black Scholar, February 19, 2018. www.theblackscholar.org/author/hanks/page/2/.

———. *The Content of Our Caricature: African American Comic Art and Political Belonging*. New York: New York University Press, 2020.

Watt, Patrick. "Manpower, Myth and Memory: Analyzing Scotland's Military Contribution to the Great War." *Journal of Scottish Historical Studies* 39, no. 1 (2019): 75–100.

Weiss, Herbert. "Inside the CIA: Congo in the 1980s." *African Studies Review* 51, no. 2 (2008): 143–145.

Weissman, Stephen. "An Extraordinary Rendition." *Intelligence and National Security* 25, no. 2 (2010): 198–222.Welch, David. "Introduction: Propaganda in Historical Perspective." In *Propaganda and Mass Persuasion: A Historical Encyclopedia, 1500 to the Present*, edited by Nicholas John Cull, David Holbrook Culbert, and David Welch, xv–xxii. Santa Barbara, CA: ABC- CLIO, 2002.

White, Mark, ed. *Iron Man and Philosophy*. Hoboken: John Wiley & Sons, 2010.

Woollacott, Janet, and Tony Bennett. *Bond and Beyond: The Political Career of a Popular Hero*. London: Macmillan, 1987.

Zanin, Andrea. "Wonder Woman: A Feminist Faux Pas?" In Held, *Wonder Woman and Philosophy*, 57–71.

INDEX